Entertaining

❧

Entertaining

by Martha Stewart

Text with Elizabeth Hawes

Photographs by Michael Skott and others

Design by Roger Black

Clarkson N. Potter, Inc./Publishers NEW YORK
DISTRIBUTED BY CROWN PUBLISHERS, INC.

Frontis: *A view of our restored nineteenth-century farmhouse in Westport, Connecticut.*

Published by Clarkson N. Potter, Inc., One Park Avenue, New York, New York
10016 and simultaneously in Canada by General Publishing Company Limited
Manufactured in Italy by Arnoldo Mondadori Editore, Verona.

Library of Congress Cataloging in Publication Data

Stewart, Martha.
Entertaining.
1. Entertaining.   I. Hawes, Elizabeth,
1940-   . II. Title.
TX731.S73   642   82-5401
AACR2

ISBN: 0-517-544199
10 9 8 7 6 5 4 3 2 1
FIRST EDITION

TO

ANDY,
my husband, for his encouragement, good nature, and support.

ALEXIS,
my daughter, for her patience.

MY FATHER,
for instilling in me a love for all things beautiful.

Contents

Acknowledgments

CREATING A BOOK AS LONG AND as complicated as *Entertaining* required an immense amount of energy and time. I wish to express my gratitude and heartfelt thanks to the many members of my family and to my friends who supported and encouraged me over a two-and-a-half-year period.

To Andy Stewart, my best friend, for his untiring help. I appreciate so much the long hours of photographing, cooking, and gardening that we did together for the book, and the planning, carpentry, painting, and homesteading that is the real basis for our lifestyle.

To Alexis, for her own special help and unique style.

Special thanks to my brother George for his exquisite craftsmanship and superb party management.

To my whole family, especially my mother, Martha Kostyra, and my sister Laura Herbert, for their cooking skills and ideas. To my mother-in-law, Ethel Stewart, and sister-in-law, Diane Love, whose personal styles have inspired me for years.

To Julia Child, who for twenty-one years has been my "companion" in the kitchen.

To Elizabeth "Betsy" Hawes, my longtime friend, who worked with me for one year on the text of *Entertaining* and whose judgment, advice, and beautiful way with the English language contributed so much to the entire book.

To Michael Skott, my dear friend, for his extraordinary photographs and his real creativity and patience.

To Roger Black, for his imaginative approach to the design of the book.

To the following present and former members of my kitchen staff who contributed to the events photographed in the book: Birdi Kins for her very special way with flowers, Sarah Gross for her crudités, Liz Wheeler for her fine cooking, Corey Tippin for his artistry, Guy Alexander for himself and our entire New York crew, Judy Van Derslice for a year of her energy, Dayle Zuckerman for her good humor, Dana Munro for her all-around help, Necy Fernandes for her efficiency and skill, and Jody Thompson for her ableness.

Thanks to Omar Honeyman, Jeff Severson, Bill Burdett, Ellen Byron, and Jeff Matz for the long hours at parties.

To Brooke Dojny and Dorian Leigh Parker and Charlotte Turgeon for their help in cooking and testing my recipes.

To my suppliers—especially Noel Ginzberg, Merc Mercurio, Max Frankel, all the Jaegers, and Allie McDonnell. And to the staff of Party Rental.

To Joann Barwick, Betty Boote, and the tireless *House Beautiful* staff, who gave me the opportunity to express my ideas in the pages of the magazine for three years.

To my writer friends—Jill Robinson, E. L. Doctorow, Erica Jong, and Anatole Broyard—whose dedication to their art inspired and encouraged me.

To Arnold Rosenberg, Barry O'Rourke, Frank Kolleogy, Richard Jeffrey, Joseph Kugielsky, Lilo Raymond, Ernst Beadle, and Susan Wood for their beautiful photographs and their kindness in allowing me to use their work.

To my dear, imaginative friends, Walter and Naiad Einsel.

To the really wonderful publishing family I have had the pleasure of working with—Alan Mirken for persuading me that I could fit this book into my life, Nat Wartels for his very real interest in the project, Jane West for her unflagging encouragement. To Carolyn Hart, my editor, for her patience, imaginative overview of the book, and long hours of work, and to Kathy Powell for her hard work and independent recipe testing. To Michael Fragnito, Carol Southern, Phyllis Fleiss, Nancy Kahan, and Susan Eilertsen for their support. To Deborah Waxberg and Joanna Nelson for their assistance with the layouts of the book, and to production editor Rosemary Baer. And special thanks to Rusty Porter and Teresa Nicholas for their contribution to the production of the book.

Of Kitchens and Learning

I GREW UP IN A LARGE family that *always* had guests. I loved the ease with which my mother added extra places, a big platter of vegetables, a special pie, flowers to the family table to create a special occasion. When I was in grade school I used to organize all the birthday parties in our neighborhood, just for the fun of arranging little dramas. And as I read all the classics, what remained most vivid in my memory were the banquet scenes in Sir Walter Scott, the Roman punch dinners in Edith Wharton novels, and the country weekends in Tolstoy's *Anna Karenina.* Entertaining al-

My kitchen filled with September produce and herbs from the garden. Part of my basket collection hangs from the rafters.

1

ways seemed natural to me, a matter of taking something very appealing to me—a favorite dish, a holiday, an activity—and making it bigger, to include others.

As places of learning, I remember three kitchens. The first was my mother's, of course, a large 1930s eat-in kitchen in suburban New Jersey. Because this was before the advent of frozen and fast food, the kitchen was the most important room in the house. It was a way station between the outside and the inside world, between garden and table. We had a large Victory garden, which soon grew to proportions that nearly preempted the grass. We had one McIntosh apple tree, one fig tree, and proliferating raspberry, strawberry, and blueberry patches. At Sunday dinner, my mother would present ten different vegetables and five fresh fruit desserts, the bounty of the moment. With six children, it all vanished as rapidly as the giant pot of oatmeal that was emptied each morning. Quantity was the rule. When my father took his skiff out into Barnegat Bay, he returned with not one but eighty fish; not two dozen but twelve dozen hard-shell crabs. So conditioned, I've never been afraid of quantity; on the contrary, I'm comfortable with profusion. My first "catered" party was a breakfast of heroic proportions for the Nutley High School football team.

My mother's parents had emigrated from Poland, and her cuisine adapted European family-style recipes to America. My early memories are bound up with mushroom soup and pierogi. Now when I make peach and plum pierogi or stuffed cabbage, the comfort of childhood comes back. My mother also drew upon the resources of my aunts and uncles, who were part of the food establishment, such as it was, in Jersey City in 1945. Uncle Joe (Woije Joe) was a butcher—I have his butcher block now—and his wife, Mary, made salads to complement the prime meats he sold. Another uncle, Woije Metzu, had an amazing delicatessen—the best Polish sausage I've ever tasted, handmade every morning by Aunt Katerin. My grandfather had a tavern, but also managed to purvey pickles, sausage, and sauerkraut on the side as part of a highwayman's lunch.

I spent summers in my maternal grandmother's kitchen near Buffalo. She had a real icebox, to which an iceman delivered blocks of ice, and a big black cast-iron coal stove, on which a canning pot always rested like a trophy. We often walked to a nearby orchard and picked golden-red Queen Anne cherries, and then hurried home to pit and preserve them.

The third kitchen belonged to Mr. and Mrs. Maus, the retired German bakers who lived next door. From their cellar, closed off from the outside by a rickety old wooden door, sweet, yeasty smells too good to be ignored wafted into our yard. The Mauses, happy, huge Bürgermeisters, dusted in flour, persisted in their profession as if they still had their bakery to fill every dawn. From the time I was four until I reached ten, when Mr. Maus died, I found excuses to visit them; I was welcomed as an apprentice and as a taster. With my brothers and sisters, I climbed up on a stool and sifted flour, helped stir, and sampled breads and cakes, plum and cherry kuchen, raspberry and apple strudels. As tangible proof of the strength of their art, and my memories, I retain Mrs. Maus's dough bowl, and a stash of recipes.

Recipes are like folktales, small parcels of culture. Think of what we learn about eighteenth-century entertaining from Martha Washington's famous cake recipe, obviously dating from her White House days, that began, "Take 400 eggs . . ." The history of cooking is in many ways like the history of language, or the history of folk music—a matter of borrowing, adapting, evolving. Until the turn of the last century, American ladies kept "receipt" books to hand on like dowries to their oldest daughters. They were called tempting things like *The Queen's Closet Opened.* I wish that tradition were still alive. The passing on of a recipe is as important to cooking art as the passing on of an idiom or story to the language.

After college, when I married Andy and went to

2

knowledge of cooking. At home, like all my contemporaries, I had Julia Child's *Mastering the Art of French Cooking* in hand, and worked my way through from cover to cover. Julia brought calm into the realm of haute cuisine and inspired confidence. I was determined to try everything. Looking back, I find it amusing to chart the course I steered: I began with pretentious items like duck Montmorency, tournedos Robert, crème caramel, and croquembouche with praline. Then, as I grew more confident, I turned to simpler peasant dishes, whose virtues

Legacies of my childhood. **Left:** *Mrs. Maus's dough-rising bowl.* **Below:** *Woije Joe's butcher block.*

Europe for the first time, I began my serious culinary education. On the street, in cafés and restaurants, we ate with enthusiasm, and with great innocence, for we had not planned our travels for the sake of meals. But in Italy and Germany, and particularly in France, the climate, the soil, the local markets, the saucepans, the stoves, even the way of arranging the food on the plate, of folding the napkins and setting the table, as well as the attitude of mind toward food, and the smells everywhere, all made food far more than a filling. I kept mental notes when I tasted a scone with real Devonshire cream, or the delicious vanilla ice cream served with heavy cream at Fortnum & Masons. In markets I asked, "What is this, and how do you cook it?" In restaurants when, toward the end of a meal, betoqued chefs paid their respects, awaiting compliments, I asked more questions and, to my great gratification, received gracious replies.

Back in New York, where I began working as a stockbroker, I had the opportunity for what A. J. Liebling once described as the requisites for writing well about food: a good appetite and an "apprenticeship as a feeder, when you have enough money to pay the check, but not enough to produce indifference to the size of the total." Meals in fine restaurants and conversations with some of the best New York chefs enhanced my

were in their flavor, not their showiness: boeuf bourguignon, pot au feu, and hearty soups. I was a working woman then and had to be organized—sauce base on Tuesday, dessert Wednesday, entertain eight on Thursday. I always had bones in the refrigerator and stocks frozen in ice cube trays.

I realize now that I had moved to the country long before we actually left West 101st Street. Our apartment living room was crowded with huge country trestle tables, our kitchen tangled with herb plants, and I was raising orchids in our bathtub. I read Mrs. Ely's *The Practical Flower Gardener* like a bible, wishing I too could

Above: *The perennial borders in full bloom.* Right: *The vegetable garden in August. Everything grows bigger than life.*

plant six varieties of cabbage and flowers in profusion. As a substitute, I planted an unrealistically large weekend garden in Massachusetts, where Andy and I were attempting to turn a one-room schoolhouse into a summer house. Then one day we took stock, read all the signs of our restlessness, and moved to a house in Connecticut.

We have built ourselves permanently into the country now, for we are dependent on what we have created, as it is on us—the house, the first barn, the second barn, the flower garden, vegetable gardens, orchard, the

4

chickens and turkeys and sheep. To give up one part would somehow upset the composite. Even if my cooking business didn't dictate a vegetable garden and eggs, and my table require flowers, the presence of it all—the Japanese peonies on the bush, the grapes on the vine, and the bees in their hive—pleases me.

My catering business began by chance. I had taught a cooking class for my daughter, Alexis, and her peers. Then, tentatively, I placed a single ad in the local papers offering my services as a caterer, only to find myself preparing blindly for a wedding for three hundred. The

Italian honeybees provide 80 pounds of honey for our kitchen.

menu was a novice's—extravagant, demanding and unprofitable: hors d'oeuvres, homemade pâtés, cold cucumber soup, salmon mousses, cold bass, chicken breast chaud-froid, and homemade breads. Down by Long Island Sound, on a sweltering August afternoon in an unsheltered beach club in Darien, I stood by the buffet table and watched the aspic melt off the oeufs en gelée, and the top tier of a basketweave cake slip starboard. I eliminated the oeufs and pushed the cake back in place. Nevertheless, it was a very good party, and I knew I was hooked. That first party was important, because I learned a lot of small things: that a tent in an atrium stifles any breeze; that fans can be rented; and that no one will know about your disasters if you don't tell him. In a larger sense, I learned how good spirits and optimism can carry the day.

At the same time, I organized a guild of local women to produce fresh foods for sale at the Market Basket in Westport, a small gourmet shop that also sold French saucisson, raisin pumpernickel loaves, and all the Fortnum & Mason products. And as my experience with food and entertaining grew, I began to contribute articles to magazines and then became a food editor. Suddenly food had a new national importance. Fashion magazines created lavish food and entertaining departments; all newspapers hired restaurant critics, who became public figures. Innovative French chefs became heroes. Men began to cook. And each year hundreds of cookbooks have appeared, extolling undiscovered and rediscovered cuisines, reminding us of the epicurean philosopher Brillat-Savarin's aphorism, "Tell me what you eatest, and I will tell you what thou art."

Opposite: *Flowers from the garden.*
Spring and summer blooms (clockwise from top left): *deep orange Oriental poppies bloom in late May and early June, 3½-foot Siberian irises bloom the entire month of June, imperial lilies bloom in July along with day lilies, bleeding hearts bloom all of May in the perennial border, delicate violas are smaller than pansies but hardy and everblooming, chive flowers bloom in profusion all of June.*

We planted giant sunflowers in the garden as food for the birds.

scured by the assortment of culinary objects I am displaying at the moment. A wood-burning stove stands between two windows which have a long view down upon the gardens in the foreground, Long Island Sound in the distance. Our cats inevitably curl up in an available basket near the stove. I have baskets everywhere, filled with fresh eggs—brown and white, and even blue, large and small, from an assortment of chickens—nuts, apples, or persimmons, or special produce bound for a party, or simply some vegetable or fruit of spectacular shape or color. In line with the counter of the kitchen, there is Woije Joe's butcher block, which I use to chop and to serve, and sometimes there is a wooden laundry rack nearby from which dangles drying pasta. On shelves are large jars of herbs and spices—I have to buy nutmeg, vanilla beans, and red, black, and white peppercorns in restaurant quantities; on rafters are dozens more baskets, drying herbs, drying flowers; and on three lofty racks are fifty-odd pots and pans. We put a dining table before the fireplace.

The kitchen is my favorite place to entertain for family and small groups of friends. Sometimes I'll stage a whole meal in the kitchen, and at other times I'll serve hors d'oeuvres there with drinks by the fire. In winter,

Two of our bronze turkeys, the mascots of Turkey Hill Farm.

My own kitchen in these times has grown almost wild with detail. I think it is very beautiful, because it is expressive. The other rooms in our farmhouse are ordered and formal, with few truly comfortable places to sit down—for, in fact, we don't sit down very much. I am outside in the garden, or in the kitchen working. Others might think the kitchen cluttered. It is far from streamlined, but it is very efficient, as it has to be when you cook for as many as two thousand in an area designed as a working-living space for three. Over the wide old fireplace, with a beehive oven, hangs a painting partly ob-

after a more formal meal in the dining room, I might urge everyone back into the kitchen for dessert and tea. The kitchen makes everyone feel comfortable and warm.

I am not alone in my feeling that home is not only the most natural but the most evocative place to entertain. Everyone now seems to be choosing a home setting over expensive restaurants; caterers are thriving because they accommodate and facilitate entertaining at home. In the decade I have been a professional caterer, there has been a culinary revolution. It has taught us to appreciate the aesthetics of food—the fresh, the simple, the home-

Feeding part of my flock of rare and unusual chickens.

Guard geese on parade.

made—and shown us the possibilities of many different tastes and styles. It has made food an adventure to be shared. It has also fostered a new style of entertaining that is informal, relaxed, and expressive, based not on intimidating prescriptions and pretensions, but on personality and personal effort. Whatever its shape and specifics, home is a very welcoming place. To entertain at home is both a relief and a rediscovery—of rooms and settings, of your favorite things, and particularly of your own taste and ideas. It is a time when people appreciate the individual effort, when a grandmother's recipe for noodle pudding or a platter of fresh garden vegetables will fare at least as well as a fantasy of spun-sugar dolphins.

I hope this book will give people ideas, just as other people, stories, experience, and food itself have given me ideas. It is not intended only for the culinary elite, who are working to refine their cuisine, but especially for all those people who regard cooking as "preparing meals," as drudgery or duty—and entertaining as an even greater worry. For them, I hope to show that there are many ways of entertaining and that each ultimately depends not on pomp or show or elaborate technique, but on thought, effort, and caring—much like friendship itself.

CHAPTER ONE

Entertaining with Style

MY INTRODUCTION TO grown-up entertaining came when I was in college, at a dinner party Andy's sister gave to celebrate our engagement. I remember roast chicken, corn on the cob, and chocolate cake, but more vividly, I remember white damask cloths, silver candlesticks, and a tiny crystal bell that was tinkled after each course and whenever I dropped my napkin. It is significant that when I last had dinner with Diane, who has a profound interest in the Orient, she served an Oriental dinner with chopsticks and had adorned the center of the table with stalks of Brussels sprouts and overgrown savoy cabbages.

Brightly colored ranunculas arranged in a pinkware bowl.
Basking in the late afternoon sun, they recall a Dutch still life.

The principle behind each dinner was the same: the desire to please someone in a personal way.

Entertaining is as simple as that. I think of it as one friend treating other friends. Sometimes entertaining is based on desire—for celebration, the cultivation of a new friendship, or just good times; at others, on need—a social or professional obligation, a mood that calls for company. The specifics vary—a neighborly cup of tea, a gala buffet, an impromptu picnic—but each is an intimate, important part of the whole process of socialization.

In the last several decades, home entertaining in America has evolved dramatically from a matter of rules and regimens into a very personal, freewheeling affair. There are no longer rigorous prescriptions for 6:30 dinners and 4:30 weddings, matching napkins, floral centerpieces, and canvasback duck entrees, upon which one's social status hangs, for the growing body of experience in America—social as well as culinary—has fostered a new openness and respect for diversity. When the Emily Post etiquette book was rewritten in 1965, it asserted that a strict code of social behavior was as obsolete as the old social pyramid. I still shudder with a sympathetic case of nerves when I read the pompous little book of entertainment advice written in 1888 by Ward McAllister, Mrs. Astor's famous adviser, or see in Edith Wharton's fiction the severe and detailed instructions for the handling of social habits and rituals—the gardenia in the lapel, the proper time for after-dinner calls, and the proper drinks to serve the guests. But there is no such cause for anxiety today, for there is no longer one proper behavior, or one taste (to be offended), but many to celebrate.

Entertaining is, therefore, an opportunity to be individualistic, to express your own ideas about what constitutes a good party. For one hostess, it might be a small and elegant dinner, with poached salmon; for others, a large and boisterous pasta buffet, make-your-own sandwiches and an old movie, omelettes on the patio, or tempura in the kitchen. There are as many good formulas as

An open doorway invites us into the formal parlor where a table is set with silver and old English china for afternoon tea.

there are personalities. And invariably it is the evidence of a unique personality at work that makes an event special. Sometimes this resides in a detail—a bucket of wild flowers at the door or a child's ceramics on the dinner table; sometimes in a tactical decision—to eat in the kitchen or to change the seating arrangement between courses; or a menu choice—Cincinnati chili or wild boar. Over the years, the hostesses I have most admired, who have proved the most successful, have carefully assessed their energies, abilities, and interests, and operated according to a strong sense of what they liked and what they did well: my sister-in-law, who has incorporated many Oriental ways into her parties; the woman who was nostalgic about the thirties, loved to dance, and so organized a *soirée dansante* with desserts; the man who hated to cook but had a passion for good champagne and served only that with caviar; the energetic young vegetarian couple who prepared an economical yet spectacular outdoor salad buffet for their wedding.

And there are the many good hostesses who choose to use the services of a caterer for certain occasions. With the abundance of caterers and the diversity of their tastes and talents, this decision can take many forms—from hors d'oeuvres or crêpes to a large-scale production. Engaging a caterer will lighten your responsibilities when time is short, provide skill in an area where you have none, or simply introduce you to an exotic cuisine. But it should not mean you surrender either your individuality or your taste. To the contrary, you must make your own ideas and style patently clear, or you may end up with a party that, however fashionable or smooth, has nothing to do with you. Choose a caterer carefully (word of mouth is far more reliable than the Yellow Pages), ask him the same questions you ask yourself, learn from him, use his ideas and skills, but fashion them into an ensemble that is distinctly your own.

❧

Making Guests Comfortable

*T*HERE IS MORE TO CREATing a memorable event than articulating your own personal style, however. These days, with all the emphasis on imaginative food, there is a tendency for any hostess to think that her responsibilities are discharged with the effort of concocting beautiful platters and conjuring up a lively list of guests. Entertaining well, however, demands more than presenting a lovely situation. Entertaining, by its nature, is an expansive gesture, and demands an expansive state of mind in charge.

I'll always remember a certain picnic in D. H. Lawrence's novel *Women in Love,* because it had that magical feeling that one always hopes for in any party, large or small, formal or informal. Lawrence's characters stumble upon a quiet meadow, spread out a lacy coverlet, and share a simple meal of chicken, bread, and fresh figs. Somehow, because the company is warm and the trees are evocative, and the figs indescribably plump, the small gathering becomes the kind of extraordinary, spontaneous, once-in-a-lifetime event that ultimately is the most gratifying to every host and guest. Some events seem fortuitous, like Lawrence's picnic, without any planning or foresight. I recall one evening when a guest impulsively sat down at the piano and played a spectacular medley of 1950s ballads—"Wake Up, Little Susie" and "Heartbreak Hotel"—which we all sang with nostalgic passion; another when two Italian guests brought a whole crowd to life with funny and moving childhood tales; another when guests at a formal dinner filled up their Baccarat goblets with water to different levels and attempted, like children, to make music. These interesting developments, which eventually made the evenings, were unpredictable, and yet they had something to do with the way a hostess had organized each gathering, with sensitivity to the guest list, with an eye toward a convivial situation. She had, in each case, made everyone comfortable enough to be his own natural, impulsive, expressive, social self. Many occasions, however beautifully orchestrated, don't have that ease and end up, like the guests, polite, proper, polished, but dull.

One of the most important moments on which to expend extra effort is the beginning of a party, often an awkward time, when guests feel tentative and insecure. This is particularly true at a large buffet or cocktail party, when you will find guests fixing their eyes on the door in anticipation of other guests, or maybe an early escape. At this moment, some hostesses give a house tour; others might take a guest aside to show him a new book or record. It is a time for a gesture to make that person feel he is in a home and not a restaurant. I usually bring early arrivals into the kitchen with me, where I am often still chopping, arranging, or just meditating on what is to come. I give them a drink, and depending on their interests, I might ask them to lend a hand with the salad or the coffee grinding. The kitchen is a warm, easy place, and it breaks any ice. As other guests arrive, the kitchen expands, and when it is full, we adjourn to the parlor.

During a party, it is important not to disappear for long periods of time. It is permissible to take time to toss a salad, glaze an apple tart, or sauté veal scallopine, but if a menu demands more than 15 minutes of last-minute preparation, it is the wrong menu, for presumably you are not a restaurant chef, but a friend whom guests expect to see. Likewise, I think the worst thing a hostess can do is to begin to clean up the kitchen while the guests are still present. If you are compulsive about clean surfaces, hire someone to assist; or do as an inventive friend of mine has done: install big drawers lined with plastic tubs in your kitchen, to keep the post-dinner disorder out of sight. The clatter of dishes and the rush of dishwater are

as dramatic a sign of "the end" as chairs being upended on a table in a restaurant. It also makes guests feel obligated to help. I had to learn this lesson the hard way: when I first started entertaining, I inevitably invited too many guests and attempted dishes that were too elaborate, necessitating long periods of time in the kitchen. I would rejoin the company only to find that they had made do without me and barely acknowledged my return. The magic was gone; and I was angry with them and angry with myself. I quickly learned to be a participating hostess rather than a reclusive cook.

Music can help establish and sustain an easy mood. Before even a small dinner party, I automatically sort out what I will put on the stereo—Mozart quartets, classical guitar, or, if I think we may need a point of interest to enliven the gathering, a Cole Porter album, or an old Simon and Garfunkel album. Other people, in other moods, might choose Bach, rock, jazz, or blues. In the case of a party with a theme, like some of the ethnic dinners in Chapter Six, music becomes more important and should be given careful consideration. The fantasy of a Hawaiian luau, for example, becomes more fun when you add the strains of island music, or the sounds of a tropical rain forest. (There *are* such recordings, full of birdcalls and sudden tempests.) The Italian party suggests popular Italian ballads or opera; the Russian, the balalaika or a melancholy guitar.

As for conversation, a hostess cannot guarantee its flow single-handedly, but she can choose guests with both compatible and conflicting interests, to support at least gentle controversy, which is more lively than unspoken accord. A roomful of psychiatrists, or nuclear physicists, or veterinarians are bound to talk shop. On the other hand, a roomful of total strangers may result in self-conscious silence. Unless you are prepared to be a tireless catalyst of good conversation, it is best to avoid either situation, or add at least one reliable extrovert to

Left: *Iced tea and summer fruits—simple refreshments by the pool.*

Tulips, lilies, freisias, and ranunculas.

the group. It is fun to make up a guest list, to act on social hunches, and play matchmaker. When you meet someone interesting at a party, it is a natural reaction to think of all the other people who would like to meet him too. Sometimes I do this years in advance—putting people together in my mind. Then one day the moment arrives to act on these instincts.

Any form of entertaining involves expanding a private world to include others. It calls for an extrovert's heart and an introvert's soul. It is essential that you consider guests' inclinations and interests in the planning, but it is equally important that you follow your own instincts. Entertaining, like cooking, is a little selfish, because it really involves pleasing yourself, with a guest list that will coalesce into your idea of harmony, with a menu orchestrated to your home and taste and budget, with decorations subject to your own eye. Given these considerations, it has to be pleasureful. This does not mean you will not be subject to nervousness. Nervousness is as natural as stage fright, because a hostess has a lot on her mind—responsibilities, details, hopes and fears. But nervousness also generates energy, and can be directed toward making everything perfect. Sometimes in the awkward moments before a party begins, when authorities say you should be relaxed and enjoying a drink and I am not, I remind myself that I, too, am going to a fine dinner, designed specifically by me, in the company of good friends, selected specifically by me. Then I head upstairs to dress for such a grand occasion.

Creating an Ambience

MOST PEOPLE APPROACH the idea of entertaining with a specific party in their head. "Let's have some people to dinner," or "We owe so many friends, we should have a big cocktail party at Christmas," or "Frederick's birthday is next month—it would be fun to do something unusual for it." Then, when the specifics of who and when come into play, one form of entertaining may evolve into another: an interesting guest list too large for a sit-down dinner becomes a buffet or substantial cocktail party; a cocktail party is transformed into a dessert party; a dinner buffet gives way to an omelette brunch. The last question—"How do I do this party?"—is the crucial one. It involves making decisions about location, decoration, and table that, however pragmatic, must also be aesthetic, because ultimately they add up to style.

Sometimes when I wander through my own home, or a client's home, looking for the appropriate setting for a party, peering into cupboards for interesting accessories, I feel like a stage director looking for the right set and props to bring his play to life. Parties *are* productions, not unlike theatrical productions. Some have lavish sets and big casts, like Broadway. Others use makeshift spaces and exotic decor. Each has a style, a season, and a raison d'être.

I wanted to write this book before I had a professional kitchen so that I could illustrate honestly the many different kinds of parties that, with thought and planning can be accomplished in an everyday space. As a general rule, a home should not have to be rearranged, redecorated, or refurbished for entertaining, because it is already expressive and interesting, simply by force of the people who live there. But it is not always easy to articulate how certain rooms might be made receptive to different forms of entertainment. Few people have baronial dining rooms, ballrooms, or galleries any more. Yet we do have halls, kitchens, family rooms, and porches with potential. Finding an appropriate place for a party, or creating it, calls for looking at familiar spaces with a fresh eye.

We are all predisposed to seeing our rooms as they have been shaped by comfort and convenience—the hall as a reception area, a certain closet as a place to store linens, a garage as a garage. Yet a wide center hall might be the perfect place to set up a long table for a large dinner party; the linen closet might make a handsome bar; and the basement or garage, cleared out and hung with quilts or calico, could be a fine place to have a country square dance some summer night. I have very cramped spaces in my house, but I have found that I can tuck four or five rented 24-inch tables in a number of spaces—in the hall, the library, or the parlor, or even in all of these rooms—and thus accommodate up to twenty extra people for a sit-down meal. Draped with a pretty cloth and set with a candle, they make an intimate, charming scene. I know a woman who transformed a screen porch into the perfect place for a large and lively winter buffet by lining the outside with plastic and the inside with heavy drapes, and adding a space heater and masses of fresh flowers. By being determined and inventive, she found a way to rise above the season, to save wear and tear on her house, and to entertain with style. Professionally, I have *had* to be inventive with space, particularly in New York City, where the dimensions of home have shrunk so dramatically. I have often used a broom or coat closet as a bar, or, lacking that resource, simply arranged glasses and bottles on a butler's tray or an end table. Carefully arranged, these setups can be just as attractive and efficient as an

An open porch with a view of Long Island Sound is a breathtaking backdrop for a garden-fresh Georgia peach tart.

staircase—can be equally effective. In assessing your possibilities, look at a room for more than its volume. Keep in mind a balance between charm and utility. Think of the corners of your home that you find inviting or interesting, or simply comfortable. A fireplace, a wide sweep of windows, or statuary provides a focus around which a crowd could congregate. If you have an orchard in blossom or a babbling brook, use it. Set a table before a spectacular view, or in the midst of a beautiful garden. Last summer, a long stand of mammoth sunflowers in my garden inadvertently became the backdrop for a party, because guests were drawn to it and then stayed there. I would replant them now for that purpose alone.

A few occasions do demand serious reorganization—a wedding, a dance, a dinner of very large proportions. In the case of the first, professionals such as the tent or dance-floor rental people can supply valuable advice on how best to accommodate the necessary additions into your home. For a dance, or a very large dinner, you also might consider clearing out at least a portion of your home to provide a bare stage to which you can add necessary rentals. Moving companies can even be hired to keep furniture in their vans overnight if you lack a garage or loft for temporary storage. Or if you happen to have very few furnishings and a large space, seize the opportunity to entertain expansively. The best house for parties that I know belongs to friends who have only a half dozen pieces of furniture in a cavernous expanse. Once a year, with only a minimum of effort, they host an enormous, fabulously successful musical party.

Entertaining provides a good excuse to put things in order (polish silver, wash forgotten dishes, wax floors, paint a flaking windowsill) and, sometimes, to be more fanciful or dramatic with details than usual. It is the moment to indulge in a whole bank of flowering plants to line the hall, or to organize a collection of antique clothes on a conspicuous coatrack, or to try the dining-room table at an odd angle. Such decorative innovations add in-

elaborate service bar. I have used a bedroom for dining, leaving the bed in place, adding a table and chairs, and using linens that complemented the existing decor, just as kings and queens of old did in their state bedrooms and Americans did in the eighteenth century.

Changing the use of rooms is fun for both the host and the guests, for it breaks tired habits. A formal dinner in a candlelit basement, or cocktails in a Victorian bedroom or a greenhouse, can have special moment and drama. A simpler decision—to center drinks around a spiral

terest to the setting, supply potential material for conversation, and heighten the whole tone of an event. Recently, before a small dinner party, a friend of mine was inspired to wash every window in his very glassy apartment. He reported that his wife thought him compulsive, but their guests had been drawn immediately to his handiwork, and had spent the evening gazing out at the city, enchanted, exclaiming like tourists.

Some parties invite theatrical decoration. It is fun at a birthday party to fill a room with helium balloons or to enlarge childhood snapshots to poster size and mount them on walls. (Balloons are also nice at garden parties, formal dances, and dessert galas.) It is evocative at a theme party like a Hawaiian luau to transform the room into a tropical garden (borrowing or renting large plants and purchasing a few exotic succulents). And sometimes, on an impulse no more substantial than mood, you may be inspired to change the lighting—to spots for a sophisticated dinner, to candles for Christmas, to kerosene lanterns for a barbecue. Even if you are not interested in special effects, it is essential to see that a room is properly lit—neither dingy nor harsh. And if you have created a

*A **striped quilt** is set for a sunny summer picnic of fresh fruit, breads, wine, and cookies.*

spectacular centerpiece or hors d'oeuvres platter, you want everyone to see it. Last year in the garden of the Cooper-Hewitt Museum in New York, my fantastic cocktail table literally disappeared from view as night fell and we realized that the museum did not have any kind of artificial illumination outside. Candles narrowly saved the evening.

As I review parties that I have organized, I think of other decorative decisions that influenced the mood and character of a gathering and were almost as responsible as the substance of the menu or the quality of the guest list for the success of the party. At a lavish dessert affair, it was a last-minute decision to pile an outlandish number of giant strawberries on an oversized silver platter to create a centerpiece. This was not only festive—and surprising in the month of January—but it was also animating, for guests plucked away at it like mischievous children. At a party for an advertising firm, it was the hostess's idea to incorporate the firm's products—pet chows, soaps, and digestive aids—into an amusing decorative scheme.

🍃

Setting the Table

Many years ago, I learned from experience that a centerpiece can be more than a garnish or token decoration. I had invited some friends from Japan to dinner and I was concerned that the meal be thoughtful and interesting to them. I prepared poached bass in a light champagne sauce, a delicate salad, and warm lemon soufflé tarts. For the table itself, I went out to the garden for inspiration. I returned with a huge flowering kale from the vegetable patch, for with its great bowls of curly leaves and purple and green hues, it was a spectacular sight in itself. It wasn't an entirely unconscious decision, because the seeds were from Japan and therefore the plant represented a sort of bond between nations. What I didn't know until conversation

unraveled around the centerpiece was that the flowering kale is the symbol of the New Year in Japan, and thus provided a token of affection and good wishes.

The table can establish or augment a mood, for it is in fact a stage set and should be so considered. A table is an empty space, and filling it is a gesture of thoughtfulness. The person who probably inspired me the most to look carefully at everything as a potential table decoration is a Japanese sculptor named Sofu, who has published a book of design in his own country. He looks to nature for odd shapes and unexpected combinations of objects, and his resulting compositions are startling in

A ruffled pillow sham is a charming table cover for breakfast.

their beauty. He will take a brown pomegranate, an orange pomegranate, a gnarled branch, and a bird's nest and assemble them into something both natural and original. Since studying his book, I have found a convoluted brown tree fungus in which I fix a delicate branch or a bloom, and I have taken to displaying savoy cabbages, or the stems of ruby Swiss chard. It is important to me to have something around to attract attention, and sometimes this is accomplished by simply altering the expected proportions of a common arrangement—filling a giant basket with gypsophila, or setting one tree peony

Old garden furniture and Fiestaware set out for lunch in front of the pumpkin patch.

in a central bowl or one tulip before each place. I change my ideas according to what I have seen, my garden, a museum show, a book. It is easy to scan art books for ideas, and to train yourself to see the inherent aesthetics of a duck decoy or a bunch of wild berries. A strip of sod planted with a few well-chosen flowers or herbs makes an evocative centerpiece, as does a beautiful log surrounded by small bottles holding flowers. Think first of what you consider interesting, and draw readily upon collections you have amassed—old bottles, toys, dolls. Another source for decoration is food itself, which, beyond its col-

or, texture, and shape, has the virtue of being potentially edible: four pears, a pyramid of oranges or lemons, a still life of potatoes, a single huge Bermuda onion. I always polish fruit until it gleams and picks up light. As a guiding principle, simplicity should rule. Avoid Styrofoam bases and elaborate collages assembled with pins and needles, for inevitably they are fussy and unnatural.

One of the easiest ways to change the look of a table is to change linens. By linens I don't necessarily mean French lace or Irish damask, for there is a wealth of less costly substitutes that are at least as appropriate. I have a friend, for example, who has for years collected odd lots of batik, and when an occasion arises, she simply layers them on her table, as the spirit strikes her, and puts a fabulous brass candlestick in the center. Each invention can make a huge difference in the tone of an event. I don't use tablecloths very much, and when I do I avoid the wrinkleproof synthetics, for I find them either ordinary or scratchy. Generally, there are more interesting choices—quilts, rugs, pieces of colorful yard goods, or, for a large outdoor buffet, a layer of straw on the table. I haunt tag sales and have collected a stash of old linen towels, which can function as man-sized napkins or place mats; rag rugs and pieces of lace, embroideries, and old cotton prints.

With a simple table, the placement of napkins can add a decorative flourish. Try not to be contrived, but for a special occasion, a napkin folded into a fan shape and tucked into a goblet provides an elegant frill. I prefer the fan or a loose knot to the trickier napkin maneuvers, which I leave to Chinese restaurants. And when a napkin is very large, or ornate, I put it right on the plate; when someone has a collection of interesting napkin rings, I adapt the table design to make a point of them.

For the opening night party of the Roy Lichtenstein exhibit at the Whitney Museum, I airbrushed used rent-

Pansies surround a glistening crème caramel.

al tablecloths with decorative motifs lifted directly from his paintings, including fresh globs of paint. (To make a further point, I decorated the table with a sneaker, goldfish in glass beakers, and a giant silver tray holding lemons, apples, and bananas.) These days, almost anything goes, provided it pleases you.

I also love collecting dishes and think it is fun to eat off a different set of plates once in a while. At Sunday breakfast, we might eat off a childhood legacy of Bunnykins bowls; some evenings, I pull down enough qualifying dishes to establish a Chinese theme. I don't possess anything particularly valuable, but I have glasses of many hues, a few special cobalt, amethyst, and teal goblets, and an odd enough assortment of side dishes to make interesting, suggestive tables. As a base, however, I have plain plates of neutral colors—white, cream, black drabware—upon which food stands on its own merits.

Table dressings have become as modish and as faddish as clothes. With all the attention food and food presentation are given in newspapers, magazines, department stores, and boutiques these days, there is an astounding outpouring of gimmicky new tableware, most of it so contrived and specialized that it has no hope of a long life. It may be tempting, when you admire a spread in *Gourmet* magazine, to rush out and buy for yourself the featured set of cheese plates with gilded cows, or pink-frosted goblets, yet in a month's time that hot item will have been replaced by another, and your wonderful acquisition will be relegated to the closet, to keep company with other misbegotten indulgences. Keep in mind that a table should be harmonious, and buy things that go with your home, that have age or inherent charm or utility, not cachet.

When I think of specific tables I like, they demonstrate this lesson, each in its own style. Perhaps the most perfect Americana table is set by Mary Emmerling, who since writing her book (*American Country,* 1980) has become the spokesperson for the American Country style.

Above: *Our library set for an intimate family Christmas Eve dinner*. Right: *Thanksgiving with an Americana accent*.

She begins with pieces of the red woolen cloth she collects for mats, or, alternately, a rag runner as a cloth, and sets out a modern set of redware or slipware dishes, and then adds masses of fresh flowers. Patty Gagarin, a friend who owns an antiques store in Fairfield, Connecticut, which spills over into her house, uses very fine old china that must have come out of the holds of antique sailing ships, in combination with country elements—a rustic table swathed with red-and-white-checked fabric and pewter. Another near neighbor has a formal classic

22

style—big starchy handmade napkins, glistening old world crystal, and a different set of antique dishes for each course, laid out on a bare table. Even with the appearance of finger bowls, her table doesn't become forbidding or stuffy, for it is serene and comfortable. Such beauty does not necessarily depend on the rarity of the china. My sister Laura sets an equally memorable table with pink or blue Depression glass, which she keeps sparkling. (Her refrigerator is a sight to behold, with everything, even the sour cream, stored in period glass refrigerator jars.) Diane Love sets an aesthete's table: a strong centerpiece—a massive bowl or a pair of large carved wooden fishes—Japanese stoneware dishes, chopsticks, and plain napkins. An all-glass table, an array of handmade pottery, a mixed lot of blue-and-white dishes, a series of two or three round tables all covered with orange moiré but set with a mix of dishes and a different flowering plant—each has an aesthetic unity and interest.

Making Food Look Beautiful

ALL THIS IS OF COURSE prologue. The food is the heart of the matter. By itself, a plate of food can be rendered very beautiful, which is flat-tering to the receiver. One of the dictums of La Nouvelle Cuisine is to use the freshest ingredients possible, with an eye not only to taste but to texture and color, for guests are as affected by the food they see as strongly as by the food they eat. The senses collaborate in the appreciation of food, and a well-composed plate is, for a moment, as satisfying as a Cézanne still life.

Think of how the colors of your food might contrast with or complement your dishes; think, too, of how the colors work together on their own. Sometimes the size of ingredients makes a statement. Carrots left whole and then aligned in a graceful diagonal on a plate have a different, interesting look. A stew appears dramatically hearty if you choose large mushrooms and whole vegetables (baby carrots, new potatoes) and cut the meat into two-inch cubes. A chicken salad composed of big chunks of white meat makes an extravagant statement, while the same ingredients finely julienned make a delicate one. A sweet spring lamb is more appropriately carved into several thin slices than one hefty slab. In assembling a plate, respect the integrity and the nature of each element: don't be haphazard, don't crowd, for the results are worth the extra few moments of time.

Two presentations of elegant yet simple foods: whole braised vegetables (left), and french fried Cornish hens in potato baskets.

Organization

THE MOST IMPORTANT
thing I have learned from my time in the kitchen is the importance of organization. I didn't used to be particularly well organized, and I was never a list-maker. And so, on many different occasions, I paid for my nonchalance. I forgot the cocktail napkins for a chic late-night party in a remote area of Connecticut, where no stores were open past six o'clock, and saved myself only by cutting up paper towels into rough squares. I failed to check out refrigerator space and ended up storing my salmon mousses in a snowbank. I agreed to make sautéed squab before discovering that I would be working on countertop Corning burners that don't get very hot, and I boiled pasta in the oven of an old stove after the electric burners of the stove died before my eyes. All these and many other unexpected lessons taught me to plan in advance, to check out equipment, and to commit everything to lists. Such strategy, I now know, moderates the anxiety and pressure that come with cooking for three, thirty, three hundred, or three thousand, and eases that dreadful last-minute harried state of mind. Making lists is exerting a form of control over an event; having as much of a meal as

possible executed in advance makes the actual happening seem easy.

When a client calls me, I have an informal list of questions that must be asked, to help him organize the event, and to help me define its character. These are items about which you can ask yourself, committing the salient facts to paper:

1. THE DATE, ESPECIALLY THE SEASON
2. THE NUMBER OF GUESTS
3. THE LOCATION:
   INDOORS OR OUTDOORS
   AT HOME OR IN RENTED SPACE
4. THE REASON FOR THE PARTY,
   TYPE, AND TIME:
   BREAKFAST/BRUNCH/LUNCH/COCKTAILS/
   DINNER/DESSERT/LATE SUPPER
5. BUDGET
6. MUSIC OR ENTERTAINMENT

Determining your requirements calls for a realistic appraisal of your resources—your space, equipment, budget—as well as your time and your ideas. Each decision at least partly depends on other decisions—the hour on the number of guests, the number of guests on the location, the location on the season, etc. But ultimately, each decision rests on your ideas about the sort of affair that suits and expresses your style, your mood, and your circumstances. At a certain moment in time, it might be

Above: *Small 24-inch tables set for 4 provide additional seating in small rooms and narrow hallways. Antique linens and unmatched plates make each table different and the total effect interesting.*

Left: *A formal setting for tea in our stenciled parlor.*

a rock 'n' roll dessert party; at another, a small sit-down dinner. In the city, it might be cocktails with Oriental hors d'oeuvres; in the country, a soup party.

In making preliminary decisions, it is useful to consider the basic responsibilities of the different forms of entertaining. Remember, as a general rule, that it is better to think big at first, and then simplify later. The reverse, trying to make a small affair grandiose, poses problems when arrangements have been made and time is limited.

The Date: You should plan as far in advance as possible, knowing that invitations can be sent out three to four weeks in advance for formal affairs, earlier for a very important event. You can anticipate the approach of certain occasions—a graduation, bar mitzvah, 50th wedding anniversary—and in these cases plan as much as six months in advance. For informal dinner parties, calling by telephone several weeks in advance is sufficient.

I think it is extravagant to spend money for printed invitations unless the occasion is formal, or mock-formal like a *soirée dansante*. Hand-written invitations can be very beautiful and are always personal. I remember one done in mixed-up Spanish for a Mexican party, and a child's creation for his birthday party, executed with rubber stamps. Both were amusing and made me want to attend. If you are sending invitations, be sure to include an R.S.V.P. Not knowing how to calculate quantities for an event is a sure cause of nervousness. I don't hesitate to call people for responses, because I need to know, and as I am not embarrassed, they are not either.

The Guest List: The guest list is a personal matter, an idiosyncratic mix of the people you think will make an interesting ensemble. It may be simply a group of people you like; it may be family, club members, or professionals you need to entertain. In any situation, you must be strict about the size that fits your space and coordinate that size with the location and type of event.

The Location: Think of receptive spaces in your home and calculate how many people will fit comfortably. If your guests will be standing, as at a cocktail party, the average-sized room can generally accommodate thirty people, a three-room expanse (living room, dining room, family room or kitchen) about sixty. For any form of buffet (omelettes or desserts, as well as dinner), you must consider seating possibilities—which could be floor cushions or quilts spread on a lawn—and equipment as well as elbow room. You must evaluate the specifics of your accommodations like a critic, coldly appraising a small oven, a cranky well, or a single bathroom as well as room size, for it is better to have several small parties than one ungainly bash. Take heed of my friend who persists in having a springtime open house for two hundred, which always climaxes with her small well running dry. Rooms fill with dirty dishes, guests grow

Three different settings of commonly available rental items. An unusual tray, a specially folded napkin, or a single flower blossom lends individuality to otherwise standard table fare.

parched, and the desperate forays to the neighbors begin. Blissfully lighthearted, she dismisses this handicap, but her friends now think of the event as the annual "well party," and hope for a rented water truck.

If in the end you find your space limiting but you are determined to have a large party, consider renting a place. Investigate your area for historic houses, vacant mansions, barns, warehouses. Many communities lease landmarks, barges, and subway stations; even better, and probably less expensive, find an interesting location on your own—a loft, a greenhouse, a beach house, a school gymnasium, a museum gallery, a historical society, a women's club, a firehouse, an automobile showroom.

The Reason, Type, and Time: It may be a social debt, a business obligation, a birthday, anniversary, visiting dignitary, Christmas, the Superbowl, or simply the sociability that comes with good spirits that prompts a party. Whatever the reason, the possibilities are far vaster than breakfast, lunch, and dinner. These meals, executed in sit-down fashion, are the prototypes, the classics. Then there are the hybrids—the brunches, cocktail buffets, kitchen parties, dessert parties, and omelettes at midnight. In addition to the date, size, location, and budget, your equipment should help you define your choice:

For a cocktail party, the least expensive and most versatile of parties, all you need are: glasses, trays, cocktail napkins, bar equipment, bar table, tablecloth.

For a sit-down meal, you must have (or rent) dishes, flatware, glassware appropriate to the type of meal and the number of courses, linens, sufficient seating, serving pieces (mix and match; borrow or rent to fill in).

A buffet is almost as versatile a possibility as a cocktail party, for it can be a country breakfast or a Chinese feast, small, medium, or large. You must consider as basic provisions: the buffet table, linens, dishes for main course and desserts, serving dishes, and cutlery.

Budget: In fixing a budget, think first of drinks, because liquor or good wine can be the major expense. But don't feel you have to be as well stocked as a restaurant. Fine wine and mineral waters are as acceptable these days as an open bar for cocktails.

Staying within a budget demands a cool head in these days of inflated food prices. You need not sacrifice quality, but you may have to be innovative—substituting an omelette party, or a Mexican dinner, for fillet of beef or poached salmon.

The basic categories of expense to estimate initially are: liquor, food, rentals, service, music or entertainment, and flowers or decorations.

Music and Entertainment: Music is, to my mind, an essential element in any party, but the form it takes depends on your budget and style. Generally, it is background support, to create and sustain a comfortable and appropriate mood, supplied by records or tapes. For the larger, more theatrical parties, live music should be considered. A single strolling guitarist, accordionist, or flutist can add a very special quality to an outdoor omelette brunch or a late-night dessert party. A string quartet, a rock band, a pair of fiddlers, Renaissance balladeers—there are many different possibilities depending on the sort of production you favor, and, of course, on your budget. If you wish to provide music for dancing, the choices range from a rented jukebox or hired disk jockey through young neighborhood rock groups to an established and expensive swing band like Lester Lanin, Mike Carney, or Bill Lombardo (nephew of Guy). Music schools and high school and university job bureaus are potential sources of good musicians who might enjoy playing for the experience, the exposure, and a reasonable fee. In New York, I turn regularly to Juilliard, the New York School of Music, and the High School of Performing Arts, and I have discovered a cadre of young virtuosos, eager to perform, happy to don formal attire or even a troubadour's dress for a night.

Once the framework of time, place, and style is established, I turn to the specifics of the menu, taking cues first from the season. Spring, for example, conjures up lamb, suckling pig, peas, chives, strawberries, asparagus. Alice B. Toklas used to celebrate spring by offering a huge platter of asparagus, accompanied only by a bowl of cream whipped and flavored with salt. Among the most memorable dishes in my life have been a plate of fresh-picked tiny green beans, one July evening in England, and a bowl of sautéed wild mushrooms in cream, in France. Both hosts knew that at that particular moment, they were offering the greatest and simplest treat possible. In planning your menu, think too of your favorite things, dishes you make well, dishes you have wanted to try. Sometimes I even ask close friends beforehand what they feel like eating. But also allow for substitutions, in case an ingredient is unavailable. Shopping the stores ahead of time to compare quality and check availability is wise. Grocers are helpful allies, and can often find out in advance if a certain meat or vegetable will be in the markets.

A menu is not the formula it once was, for people are too interested in food to be dogmatic. The feeling of our time is for taste and simplicity—for cooking in which ingredients taste of what they are. Certain rules about variety and contrast always apply. A menu consisting of quiche, duck in pastry, and apple tart; or vichyssoise, sole in cream sauce, and chocolate mousse is obviously one-sided. And a plate of mashed potatoes, cauliflower, and scallops is ugly. But otherwise, a menu is a personal invitation. I like a sit-down meal to have three courses, because I find a first course gracious, whether as simple as a slice of melon with or without prosciutto, or as elaborate as a salade composée. But that is no more hard-and-fast than whether to serve salad before, with, or after the entree.

After I decide on a menu, I estimate what service assistance will be necessary for a smooth operation. For a small dinner party, one person in the kitchen to rinse plates, stack dishes, and make coffee is useful but nonessential help; for a party for twelve, an imperative. Likewise, one bartender is a refinement for a small cocktail party, a necessity for a large one. As a rule of thumb, I count one experienced or two novice bartenders for each forty or fifty guests. Hiring additional help is subject to your budget and your own sense of organization.

My own roster of bartenders and waitresses is drawn mostly from a rich supply of unemployed or semiemployed young actors and writers who are interested in meeting people, in activity, in potential "material." I began with a few New York contacts, who, by word of mouth—an underground network of friends—quickly expanded to a full corps. Generally, I avoid professional service, complete with tricot uniforms, for I've found the obvious advantages of experience are often negated by demeanor. I look for someone who is neat and pleasant-looking, outgoing, and has some interest in serving or preparing food—not necessarily cooking, but arranging platters or garnishing trays. These requisites are becoming easier and easier to find as the nation's interest in food expands.

Young actors are only one source of help. Consider first perhaps a daughter and her friends, a college-age son and friends, or local teenagers. (Party work is desirable because it is interesting socially.) Investigate the services-offered columns in local papers, and employment bureaus at high schools and colleges. Interview, discuss duties and dress in advance and in full, and make timetables and checklists for on-the-spot reference. Confusion over small details like dress or access to kitchen cupboards can mean the downfall of a nice relationship. Our usual uniform for more formal events is black tie and tuxedo for men, and black skirt and white lacy blouse with black neck bow for women. If needed, I provide aprons, often similar but rarely matched. For informal events, I take a dress cue from the general theme of a party—peasant, farmhand, Italian, Victorian, or maritime apparel—but let my staff have fun. They have never been outrageous, but always entertaining and inventive. For a 1950s party, it is slick hair and white T-shirts for the bartenders. For a bat mitzvah staged as a kibbutz party in a Boy Scout camp in the woods, I asked for Israeli garb. When I drove up, I was greeted by a totally convincing legion of khaki jumpsuits, dark sunglasses, berets, and knee-high boots.

A last word of advice: paying by the hour is simplest and fairest, and gratuities are thoughtful gestures that will guarantee enthusiastic return engagements.

On a small scale or a large scale the rewards of entertaining are many. Think of the pleasure of treating yourself to a favorite meal; multiply this by a guest list and you begin to calculate the pleasures of entertaining.

Large parties require additional help: bartenders, busboys, and waitresses. Here is some of my staff dressed and ready for service (left to right): Rena Niculescu, Carolyn Kennedy, Jorie McKinnon, Ellen Byron, (Martha), Birdi Kins, Dayle Zuckerman, Catherine Tambini, Dana Munro.

CHAPTER TWO

Cocktails and Hors d'Oeuvres

THE COCKTAIL PARTY IS probably America's greatest contribution to the world of entertaining. As an event, it became popular after Prohibition, presumably because drinkers needed a little buffer to counterbalance their intake of alcohol, much as, centuries before, Burgundian wine tasters struck upon the gougère, that delicate little cheese puff, as the proper ballast to quantities of wine. Indeed, the cocktail party is curiously and distinctively American; it suits the national informality, ingenuity, and love of snacks. To please American guests, some hosts in foreign countries will stage well-intentioned but awkward approximations of a cocktail party. Last year in Japan, we were served American drinks and a great mound of salami and other sausages that our proud hosts had purchased at an international delicatessen. In Italy, I've been served an odd assortment of tinned English cheeses, American potato chips, and Italian antipasto—which was the right idea, but not exactly finger food. The French, who on the other hand don't snack at all, restrict themselves to drinks—"un Scotch"—because they don't want to spoil dinner. At home, when I'm giving a small dinner party, I generally adhere to the French principle, because when I've spent several hours cooking up a fabulous dinner, I don't

Antique cut-glass saucer glasses can make champagne look even more elegant than modern flutes.

3 1

want to diminish appetites or upstage dinner.

A cocktail party is a very adaptable form of entertaining. It can be a small gathering—six or eight friends enjoying an hour together before a concert or theater—or a large extenuated bash. It can consist of drinks and a few interesting hors d'oeuvres, or it can be more or less a dinner substitute, more when the fare is substantial and includes something sweet as a finale, less when it is a series of little tastes. It can be as simple or elaborate as suits you, and it can all be prepared in advance for relatively little expense.

To a certain extent, the appointed hours of a cocktail party determine its nature. If your invitation specifies 6:00 to 8:00 P.M., that signals that you are offering a prelude to dinner or another event; if it reads 6:00 to 9:00 P.M., or 7:00 to 9:00 P.M., or simply 7:00 P.M. (which to me indicates it will last as long as people are having fun), a guest might reasonably expect something substantial enough to pass as a meal. Unless there is a particular reason for an earlier hour—like a professional reception—a cocktail party is best planned to begin comfortably after working hours, or not before 6:00 except, of course, on weekends.

Giving a cocktail party offers an opportunity to create a very special social scene. A hostess can bring together any number of odd and interesting friends, for any number of reasons, with only the idea of a lively composite in her mind. While it is never a good idea to invite ex-wives, ex-husbands, or archenemies, there is considerably less need to be careful with a cocktail party, for the time is short, and the guests are numerous and mobile. It is a time to include a new neighbor, an eccentric uncle, the carpenter, or the dentist without any risk of compatibility problems. Contrasts are good and diversity is energizing, for the object of a cocktail party is to create a comfortable situation, with drinks to relax and food to fortify, in which people mix. Because guests don't expect to sit down, it is more congenial to have a full rather than a sparsely populated room. Generally speaking, the average-sized room will accommodate about thirty people, a three-room spread (living room, dining room, family room or hall) between fifty and sixty. There is no obligation to invite the maximum number on all occasions, but unless a party has a specific purpose (like a pretheater gathering), or a specifically defined guest list, a good guiding principle is to have more people rather than fewer. It is also wise to invite more people than you have seats, for once everyone sits down, an essential movement and fluidity is lost. Twelve or thirteen people for cocktails is often an awkward assembly for just that reason.

One of the great advantages of a cocktail party is that its mechanics are simple. You don't have to worry about seating arrangements, about renting or rearranging furniture. You have only to make provisions for coats, in a bedroom or on a rented coatrack. You don't have to worry about cooking, for most of the food can be prepared in advance. During the course of a party, you have only to pop things in the oven, replenish platters, and from time to time clear away empty glasses and unsightly ashtrays. One or two hired helpers can eliminate even those duties, and free you to circulate and socialize as freely as a guest. Remember, however, that you, as hostess, are the social agent who brought this gathering together, and possibly the only common bond between different groups of people. Consequently, you have the resources and the responsibility to make meaningful introductions, to help the shy and self-conscious, and to initiate conversation when needed.

The Bar

*T*HE BASIC QUESTIONS OF quantity and kind can be answered quite matter-of-factly. The chart of alcohol equivalents opposite has been

The Ideal Home Bar

LIQUOR

BOURBON 1 LITER
GIN 1 LITER
VODKA 2 LITERS
  (1 LITER IN
    THE FREEZER)
SCOTCH 2 LITERS
BLENDED WHISKEY 1 LITER
LIGHT RUM 1 LITER
DARK RUM 1 FIFTH
DRY SHERRY 1 FIFTH
CREAM SHERRY 1 FIFTH
DRY VERMOUTH 1 FIFTH
SWEET VERMOUTH 1 FIFTH
CASSIS OR
  FRAMBOISE 1 FIFTH
LILLET 1 FIFTH
DUBONNET 1 LITER
PORT 1 FIFTH
COGNAC 1 FIFTH
TEQUILA 1 FIFTH
COINTREAU 1 FIFTH
GRAND MARNIER 1 FIFTH
AMARETTO 1 FIFTH
COFFEE LIQUEUR 1 FIFTH
  (KAHULA, BAILEY'S IRISH)

BEER

LIGHT SIX PACK
DARK SIX PACK
IMPORTED SIX PACK

BASIC BAR EQUIPMENT

ICE (FIGURE ¾ TO 1 POUND
  PER PERSON)
ICE BUCKET
LEMONS, LIMES, ORANGES
GREEN OLIVES
COCKTAIL ONIONS
LEMON ZESTER
SHARP KNIFE
GOOD CORKSCREW
PITCHER
JIGGER MEASURES
BLENDER (OPTIONAL)
COCKTAIL NAPKINS

MIXERS

PERRIER
CLUB SODA
TONIC
GINGER ALE
COLA
DIET COLA
TOMATO JUICE
ORANGE JUICE

WINES

BLANC DE BLANCS
  SIX 1½-LITER BOTTLES
RED WINE THREE
  1½-LITER BOTTLES

ALCOHOL EQUIVALENTS

ONE LITER ALCOHOL = 33.8 OUNCES = TWENTY-TWO 1½-OUNCE DRINKS
ONE 750-MILLIMETER BOTTLE WINE = SIX 4-OUNCE GLASSES
ONE 1½-LITER BOTTLE WINE = TWELVE 4-OUNCE GLASSES
ONE BOTTLE CHAMPAGNE = SIX FLUTE OR SEVEN SAUCER GLASSES
ONE CASE CHAMPAGNE = SEVENTY-TWO DRINKS

corroborated by my friend Noel Ginzberg, a liquor merchant. Always assess your crowd, however; if it includes very heavy drinkers, or teetotalers, adjust accordingly, remembering it is always safer to err on the side of excess, since unopened liquor can usually be returned. Add any unusual liquor you think appropriate—Wild Turkey for a Georgia friend, beer if you are expecting young people.

There is more to serving drinks well than providing appropriate brands in sufficient amounts, however. Drinks will be more interesting and more fun—an entertainment in themselves—if on occasion you add something unexpected to your bar: an old Scotch, a bottle of *beaujolais nouveau* at harvest time, a homemade batch of margaritas or hot toddies. This not only shows extra effort, but gives a gathering more personality; it says, in effect, that you have something special to share. Therefore, if you fancy a new liquor, or a particular taste—iced vodka, French cider, champagne—don't hesitate to make an event of it, serving it as the main offering, perhaps in unusual glasses, with just your everyday liquor closet as backup. If you make a special drink, feature it on occasion.

Drinks deserve as much thoughtful attention to aesthetics as food does, for the look of a bar and the presentation of a drink set a tone for an event. For small gatherings, if you do not have a home bar from which you serve, set up your supplies attractively on a sideboard, end table, tray, or kitchen counter. If you have unusual bottles or beautiful decanters, use them; add a single rose to an empty decanter. For larger parties, up to thirty people, you will need help with bar service. The most elegant operation is to set up a basic bar in a peripheral area of your home like a pantry or hall, and have someone taking drink orders and serving them from a tray. But you can also set up a centrally located service bar, manned either by a bartender or by the guests themselves. For more than thirty guests, you must also organize such a bar, unless you have a very large staff to pass drinks. Service bars must be streamlined and very carefully arranged. Choose a convenient uncongested area in which guests can circulate comfortably. Use a six- or eight-foot table, covered with a decorative cloth, as a base. Stress simplicity in your setup, for a party bar must work efficiently. Bottles and glasses have a gleaming look anyway, which can be attractive in a High Tech sort of way if they are neat, straightforward, and functional.

Glasses are an important consideration, for they are a large part of the decor, particularly at a cocktail party. Experiment with glasses, for the highball glass and the wine goblet are just the basics. One friend serves neat drinks in old jiggers; another uses a collection of small earthenware cups, without handles. I often use some ornate heirloom cut-glass goblets for white wine aperitifs, and I serve limeade or iced tea in tall green goblets. Somehow everything tastes even better when so dignified. If you are renting glasses, it may take more time and a survey of several rental agencies to find elegant or unusual glasses, but it is worth the time. Whatever your choice, make sure that it is sparkling clean.

Garnishes, too, offer a way to individualize a drink. I think it is important to have lemon peel and olives and the other appropriate addenda on hand for classic highballs. But sometimes I make a long spiraling curl with a zester in place of the usual insignificant twist; other

Rental glasses come in an amazing variety of sizes and shapes. Top, from left to right: *champagne flute, 8-ounce white wine, 10-ounce all-purpose glass, 14-ounce bubble glass, 10½-ounce crystal wine glass, 10-ounce executive, 8-ounce old-fashioned, 3½-ounce champagne, 10-ounce highball, 2-ounce cordial, 12-ounce Pilsner, 14-ounce Hoffman House, 8-ounce water glass, 8-ounce stemmed old-fashioned, 6-ounce Dutch flute, 4-ounce wine, 9½-ounce Vendage, 8-ounce all-purpose wine.*

Center: *Same glasses filled with a colorful variety of drinks.*

Bottom: *A sampling of my collection of old and colored glasses.*

times, I add big chunks of lemon or lime to a drink instead of slivers, or a slice of orange to a spritzer.

Hors d'Oeuvres

As FOR FOOD, ONE CAN BE much more creative with a cocktail party than with a dinner, because guests tend to be more adventuresome with one biteful than with a whole plateful of something new. It is a time when you can be original, exotic, and innovative with very little risk. Hors d'oeuvres also lend themselves to many different variations. For example, one of my favorite hors d'oeuvres used to be a small portion of crabmeat on a cucumber round (sliced neither so thin that it would bend nor so thick that it was cumbersome); when crabmeat became expensive, I substituted a spoonful of chicken salad with pecans, and lately I have been using taramasalata, made with codfish roe, or a very simple mousse of smoked trout whipped with cream and horseradish. Snow peas began for me as a crudité; then one day I split them open and filled them with minted cream cheese, which subsequently gave way to stronger cheese like Boursin or St. André. I used the pea pods that fell apart to wrap around cooked shrimp. With miniature quiches, I experimented first with fillings (leek, endive, tomato), then with the crust (I tried puff pastry), and then I eliminated the crust altogether and made little custards or frittatas. I wrapped prosciutto around melon in the classic manner, then figs, papaya, and asparagus. One idea quickly turned into many.

How much and how many is one of the thorniest problems that comes with a cocktail party, particularly a large one. One doesn't want a refrigerator full of tiny leftover perishables, nor does one want to see guests gazing longingly at a platter emptied of everything but a sprig of parsley. It is, of course, far safer to err on the side of generosity. But it is also possible to be quite precise with quantity in making advance calculations. In general, for a two-hour cocktail party I plan eight different hors d'oeuvres, with three of each kind per guest. If the hors d'oeuvres are hearty, I revise that figure to two per person. If they are shrimp, or caviar, I further augment the portion per person, because such expensive treats bring out everyone's gastronomic zeal. Overall, I've observed that people will eat more when there is more variety. As the length of a cocktail party grows, it is wise then to increase both the amount and diversity of the offering.

All the hors d'oeuvres in this book are bite-size, because I think that the small scale is the beauty of this form of food. Individual hors d'oeuvres are also neat, obviating the need for plates, and practical. A pot of pâté or a mound of steak tartare fares well in small, manageable groups or a buffet line, but becomes very messy with a large mobile group. Pâté prearranged in celery stalks or on apple slices, however, or tartare in cherry tomatoes retains its fresh look. Some of my hors d'oeuvres are quite substantial; others are mere wisps of taste. Part of the knack of creating a satisfying selection is creating a balanced menu, in which there is a certain play between the substantial and the frilly, between, say, carpaccio on French bread and Roquefort grapes.

The beauty of any hors d'oeuvre ultimately resides in its freshness. Any offering—tiny pastry made and frozen a month before; a smoked trout purchased several

Ideas for individual hors d'oeuvres. From left to right, top to bottom: *chili in corn cups, dill crêpes with red caviar, seviche of scallops with cherry tomatoes, Roquefort grapes, stuffed snow peas, pâte à choux filled with curried chicken, biscuits with country ham, smoked salmon on dark pumpernickel, chicken salad on cucumber rounds, melon and prosciutto, almond-stuffed dates with bacon, puff-pastry straws, ginger muffins with cream cheese and kumquats, pâté on apple slices, baked new potatoes with sour cream and caviar, stuffed grape leaves, cherry tomatoes stuffed with steak tartare, potato pancakes, smoked turkey on corn muffins, carpaccio on French bread, poppy-seed puffs, chicken saté, fig and prosciutto, blini with sour cream and caviar.* ►

days before; snow peas blanched in the morning and stuffed thereafter—must look and taste as though it has just been made. This doesn't involve tricks or artifice, but knowing how to treat and store different ingredients, knowing that each food has a different sort of metabolism; that while carrots should remain moist, asparagus and beans will wilt under the same conditions, that smoked trout should be carefully wrapped in plastic, but carpaccio will fade if so treated.

The arrangement of hors d'oeuvre trays can further enhance the aura of freshness. Think of a platter as a background rather than merely a container; certain materials display certain foods more eloquently than others. Deviled eggs look awkward on a brass or copper tray, but wonderful on glass, for example. Big flat basket trays are more appealing when they are not overloaded, for the woven texture, peering through rows of hors d'oeuvres, is interesting. Often I cover the bottom of a tray with a layer of moss or glossy banana, palm, lemon, or grape leaves, purchased in bunches from a florist; the greens counterpoint the color and texture of different hors d'oeuvres and keep them fresh-looking.

Generally, I don't mix different hors d'oeuvres on a tray because I like the look of profusion in one-of-a-kind, and I also find that the decision that confronts a guest when passed a platter of eight possibilities inevitably stops conversation cold. I also use only natural wood toothpicks and only when absolutely essential—for things too hot or too messy for fingers; for construction purposes: affixing shrimp to a cabbage to create a sort of porcupine ball; and for combinations that will not hold together naturally. Many hors d'oeuvres regularly served with toothpicks do not actually need them—prosciutto, for example, adheres very nicely by itself to melon, and you do not wind up with a sea of used toothpicks on a tray.

It is important to think of how your tray will look after you have served even half its contents. Although they have a fine, pristine, classic look, especially on a silver tray, doilies absorb grease and moisture, and in no time become a discouraging sight. They should be used with nonbuttery foods, and changed frequently. A less fragile bedding for the same effect might be a starchy white cloth napkin. In the case of blini or toast triangles, it will also serve as an insulator. For the crowning touches, be fanciful, but be simple: a deep red peony on a tray of blini with red caviar or a purple chive flower planted in a bowl of green mayonnaise can transform a humdrum lineup into a visual feast.

The following menus include recipes that are the accumulated wealth of six years in the catering business. I love to create hors d'oeuvres and in recent years have offered bonuses to my cooks for coming up with recipes for new, usable hors d'oeuvres. This system has proved fun, and out of it have emerged taramasalata on cucumber, whitefish mousse in cherry tomatoes, almond-stuffed dates wrapped in bacon—and many, many more.

Almost all of the basic ingredients herein are quite commonplace; the exceptions can be found in specialty food shops or gourmet departments. For any cocktail party, the following are important tools of the trade and special equipment that will make light work of delicate operations:

VERY SHARP STAINLESS STEEL KNIVES, AND SHARPENERS	ELECTRIC HAND MIXER	ROUND, NATURAL TOOTHPICKS
VERY SHARP LIGHTWEIGHT JAPANESE CLEAVER	PASTRY BRUSH	ASSORTMENT OF TINY QUICHE PANS
	PEPPER MILL	
	COOKING SPATULAS OF VARIOUS SIZES	PASTRY BAG WITH AN ASSORTMENT OF TIPS, INCLUDING SMALL STAR TIP AND LARGE STAR TIP
LARGE PORTABLE BREAD BOARD	WIRE WHISKS	
SHARP VEGETABLE PEELERS	MELON BALLER	
	APPLE CORER	
SMALL, FLAT HAND GRATER	LEMON ZESTER	
	SMALL SPREADING SPATULAS	
FOOD PROCESSOR OR BLENDER	BAMBOO SKEWERS OF DIFFERENT SIZES	FLAT METAL TRAYS FOR STORING HORS D'OEUVRES IN REFRIGERATOR
GARLIC PRESS		

Oriental dishes in blue and white create the appropriate feeling for this small cocktail party.

Cocktails for Eight to Twelve: Oriental

A SMALL GATHERING OF FRIENDS for cocktails is a gracious prologue to the theater, a concert, a large charity dinner, or just a late dinner in a restaurant. The food, which can be prepared in advance and served from the coffee table, is not meant to be substantial, merely an interesting snack to ward off hunger pangs. This menu is simple, light, and varied; it includes several Chinese dishes, which give the whole an exotic cast.

❧ MENU ❧

Tea Eggs

Ginger Shrimp Toasts   Chinese Pearl Balls

Cherry Tomatoes Stuffed with Sour Cream and Red Caviar

Shrimp Vinaigrette Wrapped in Snow Peas

Steak Tartare with Pumpernickel Triangles

Mixed Drinks, Wine, Iced Vodka

Tea Eggs
8 TO 16 PIECES

These look like rare, marbleized gems. Smoky and flavorful, they are centuries old in culinary tradition.

4 eggs
1 tablespoon sesame salt
2 tablespoons dark soy sauce
1 whole star anise
3 teaspoons smoky tea (Earl Grey, Hu Kwa)
  Sesame salt

Boil eggs for 20 minutes over low flame. Cool in water. When cool, drain eggs and tap the shells all over with the back of a spoon until the shell is completely crackled.

Return eggs to pan, cover with cold water, salt, soy, anise, and tea. Bring to a boil, reduce heat and simmer very slowly for 2 to 3 hours. Turn off flame and leave eggs in liquid for 8 hours.

Tea eggs are then drained and left in their shells until ready to use. Keep well wrapped in the refrigerator (up to 1 week).

To serve: Carefully peel the eggs. White of eggs will be marbled with dark lines. Cut into halves or quarters. Serve with sesame salt.

Ginger Shrimp Toasts
30 HORS D'OEUVRES

These can be prepared ahead and reheated during the party.

1 pound shrimp, peeled and deveined
1 medium onion
1 quarter-size piece of fresh ginger
  Salt and pepper to taste
2 egg whites
30 strips (1 × 3 inches) day-old good-quality white bread
½ cup fine dry bread crumbs

  Vegetable oil for frying

GARNISH
  Fresh parsley

In the food processor or blender, blend together the shrimp, onion, ginger, and salt and pepper. With the motor running, drop the egg whites through the feed tube and process until the mixture is well combined.

Below: *Tea eggs.*

Spread shrimp mixture onto the strips of bread and coat the mixture with bread crumbs. Chill until ready to cook.

Heat oil in a large skillet; when hot, fry toast on both sides until golden brown. Drain on paper towel and serve garnished with fresh parsley.

Chinese Pearl Balls

APPROXIMATELY 36 PIECES

These crunchy, bite-size pork balls can be made ahead and steamed in the kitchen as guests arrive.

- ¾ cup sweet or glutinous rice
- 6 dried Chinese mushrooms
- 1 pound lean pork, finely ground
- 1 egg, lightly beaten
- 1 tablespoon soy sauce
- ½ teaspoon sugar
- 1½ teaspoons salt
- 1½ teaspoons finely minced ginger root
- 8 water chestnuts, finely chopped, fresh if possible
- 1 scallion, finely chopped

Soak the rice in water to cover for 4 hours. Drain and pat dry. Soak the mushrooms in ½ cup warm water for 1 hour. Drain and discard the tough stems. Chop the caps finely.

Mix together all the ingredients, except the rice, until well blended. Your hands are best for this job. Form balls 1 inch in diameter.

Spread the rice on a baking sheet. One at a time, roll the pearl balls in it, coating completely. Set the balls on a baking sheet lined with waxed paper. Refrigerate. The balls can be frozen at this point.

To steam pearl balls, put steamer in a pan or wok and add water so that it comes to within 1 inch of steamer bottom. Put balls on steamer racks. Bring to boil. Cover and steam for 30 minutes. Serve hot.

Cherry Tomatoes Stuffed with Sour Cream and Red Caviar

APPROXIMATELY 24 HORS D'OEUVRES

Hollowed-out cherry tomatoes make appealing containers for savory fillings. Try whitefish mousse, finely chopped egg salad, or curried rice salad as an alternate stuffing.

- 1 pint ripe cherry tomatoes
- ½ cup sour cream
- 1 ounce red salmon caviar
  Small bunch fresh dill

Cut off stem end of cherry tomatoes and hollow out the seeds with a small melon ball scoop. Turn upside down on a rack or piece of paper towel to drain.

An hour before serving, using a pastry tube or a small spoon, fill tomatoes with sour cream and top with a few grains of caviar. Garnish with a tiny sprig of dill. Put the tomatoes on a platter with a thick bed of dill or parsley to keep them from rolling.

Above: *Ginger shrimp toasts.*

Left: *Chinese pearl balls*

Shrimp Vinaigrette
Wrapped in Snow Peas

APPROXIMATELY 30 HORS D'OEUVRES

A colorful hors d'oeuvre served on a cabbage. The recipe can be doubled or tripled for large occasions.

- 1 bay leaf
- 1 pound large shrimp (28 to 30), peeled and deveined
- 15 to 20 snow peas
- 1 small green cabbage

VINAIGRETTE

- ½ cup olive oil
- 3 tablespoons white wine vinegar
- 3 tablespoons Dijon mustard
- 1 tablespoon chopped shallots
- 1 teaspoon finely minced ginger
- 1 clove garlic, finely minced
- 1 tablespoon chopped dill
  Pinch sugar
  Salt and pepper to taste

Add bay leaf to a large pot of water and bring to a rapid boil. Add shrimp and cook, stirring constantly, until just done (2 to 3 minutes). Be sure not to overcook. Drain shrimp, immerse in very cold water to cool, and drain again. Put in glass or steel bowl.

Mix vinaigrette ingredients in a covered jar. Shake well and pour over shrimp. Coat well, cover bowl, and refrigerate for 1 to 2 days, tossing every 12 hours.

String the peas and blanch in boiling water for 30 seconds. Drain and immerse in iced water. Drain again. Split the pods lengthwise so that you have 30 to 40 separate halves.

Cut a thin slice off the bottom of the cabbage so that it will stand upright. Wrap a pea pod around each shrimp and fasten by piercing with a round natural wood toothpick. Then stick each shrimp into the cabbage. Serve cold or at room temperature.

VARIATION: In place of snow peas, wrap each shrimp with a paper-thin piece of prosciutto.

Steak Tartare with
Pumpernickel Triangles

50 HORS D'OEUVRES

- ½ pound top sirloin, freshly ground
- 1 clove garlic, pressed or crushed
- ¼ cup tiny capers
- 2 tablespoons finely chopped parsley
- 1 egg yolk
- 1 scallion
  Salt and freshly ground black pepper
  Dash Tabasco
  Lemon juice

- 1 1-pound loaf pumpernickel bread, thinly sliced
  Unsalted butter

Mix the meat, garlic, capers, parsley, egg yolk, and scallion until blended. Season to taste with salt and pepper, Tabasco, and lemon juice.

Pack into a glass bowl or earthenware crock and serve on a platter with triangles cut from pumpernickel slices and spread with sweet butter.

NOTE: I generally purchase extra-lean top sirloin from my butcher the day of the party. I ask that it be finely ground and wrapped in brown butcher's paper, which helps keep the meat red. You can grind your own meat in a food processor but the texture is superior if ground in a meat grinder.

Shrimp vinaigrette is delicious by itself, or wrapped with colorful snow peas.

Cocktails for Twenty-five: Many Tastes

THIS IS THE PROTOTYPICAL cocktail party, large enough to be lively, small enough to be comfortable and fluid in several rooms. The hors d'oeuvres are inventive but not difficult to make, and with proper organization, the party should come off with ease.

The menu includes some of the most often-requested hors d'oeuvres in my repertoire, including tiny individual quiches, roquefort grapes, and stuffed snow peas.

❧ MENU ❧

Snow Peas with St. André

Miniature Leek and Smoked Salmon Quiches

Carpaccio on French Bread   Pâté on Apple Slices

Blini with Red Caviar and Sour Cream

Almond-Stuffed Dates with Bacon

Roquefort Grapes   Endive with Herb Cheese

White Wine Bar

A silk rag rug provides a colorful background for the assortment of hors d'oeuvres at this cocktail party.

43

Miniature Leek and Smoked Salmon Quiches
30 TO 35 QUICHES

Tiny quiches are everybody's favorite hors d'oeuvre. The combination of smoked salmon and gently sautéed leek is wonderful. Tiny quiches are baked in small (2- to 3-inch) individual tartlet pans of various shapes.

1 **Perfect Plain Tart and Tartlet Crust (page 236)**

FILLING
2 large leeks
2 tablespoons butter
¼ pound smoked salmon, sliced thin

CUSTARD
3 large eggs
1½ cups light cream or half-and-half, or ¾ cup each milk and heavy cream
½ teaspoon salt
Freshly ground black pepper

Prepare the crust and line the tartlet pans according to master recipe.

Cut off all but 1 inch of the greens from the leeks. Wash them very well to remove any sand and cut the leeks crosswise into thin pieces. Sauté very gently in butter for 10 to 15 minutes, or until soft.

Cut the salmon into small squares. Beat the eggs until blended. Add the cream and season to taste. Preheat the oven to 375°.

Put a teaspoon of sautéed leeks in each tartlet and top with a piece of smoked salmon. Spoon in enough of the custard to almost fill each shell. Put individual tins on a baking sheet and bake 20 to 30 minutes, or until golden brown. Let stand 10 minutes before serving, or serve lukewarm.
N O T E : Miniature quiches can be made in advance, baked, cooled, and frozen right in the pans. Reheat in a 375° oven for 10 minutes.

Carpaccio on French Bread
APPROXIMATELY 70 PIECES

SPECIAL HERB BUTTER
½ pound (2 sticks) unsalted butter, softened
3 tablespoons chopped parsley
1 clove garlic, pressed
4 shallots, minced
1 teaspoon minced tarragon or ¼ teaspoon dried tarragon
1 teaspoon lemon juice
Pinch white pepper

SAUCE
¼ cup white vinegar
12 cornichons (tiny sour French gherkins)
2 cups chopped parsley
2 cloves garlic
3 anchovy fillets
½ cup capers
3 tablespoons chopped onion
⅓ cup Dijon mustard
¾ cup olive oil

3 loaves French bread (16 to 18 inches long, 2 inches in diameter)
1 pound top round, very lean, sliced no more than 1/16 inch thick

To make the herb butter, combine all the ingredients in a food processor. Put in a jar and cover well. Refrigerate until 1 hour before using. Soften to a spreading consistency.

Put all the sauce ingredients except the oil in the food processor. Chop coarsely and add the oil drop by drop through the tube until thick, like mayonnaise. Put in a bowl and cover tightly. Refrigerate.

To serve, cut the French bread into ¼-inch slices. Spread each with special herb butter. Put a piece of meat on top of each slice of bread. It is important to cover the bread completely with the meat. Spoon a little sauce on top of meat.

Snow peas with herb cheese.

Snow Peas with St. André
50 TO 60 HORS D'OEUVRES

This is a very popular hors d'oeuvre in my repertoire. Guests cannot believe that someone has actually stuffed a snow pea!

50 to 60 tender young snow peas
½ pound St. André cheese or Boursin or Boursault
Fresh mint (optional)

Remove stem end from snow peas, string them, and blanch in a large pot of rapidly boiling water for 30 seconds. Plunge them immediately into cool water to stop the cooking and preserve their beautiful green color.

With a small sharp knife, slit open the straight seam of each snow pea and pipe softened cheese into each one, using a small-tipped pastry tube, or spread with a small spatula. Garnish each pod with a small leaf of mint just poking out the top of the snow pea.

Pâté on Apple Slices

APPROXIMATELY 80 PIECES

The slight hint of apple in the pâté is complemented by serving the pâté on a slice of crispy apple. Prepare the pâté at least 2 days in advance to allow the flavors to mellow.

- 1 pound chicken livers
- 3 tablespoons chopped onion
- 1 medium Granny Smith apple, peeled and chopped
- ½ pound (2 sticks) unsalted butter, at room temperature, plus 1 tablespoon butter
- 1 teaspoon dry mustard
- ¼ teaspoon salt
- ¼ teaspoon grated nutmeg
  Dash each cayenne pepper and ground cloves
- 3 tablespoons clarified butter

- 5 crisp apples (Red Delicious, Yellow Delicious, McIntosh)
- 10 cornichons (sour French gherkins)

Trim the livers of all fat. Put in a small saucepan and cover with water. Bring to a boil, then reduce heat and simmer 20 minutes. Cool in the liquid and drain.

Sauté the onion and apple in 1 tablespoon butter over medium heat for 5 minutes.

In a food processor or blender, combine the livers, remaining ½ pound butter, onion, apple, and seasonings. Blend until very smooth. Pack into a terrine or earthenware bowl. Spread with melted clarified butter, which will preserve the pâté. Scrape off before using.

No more than 1 hour before serving, core the apples and cut in half lengthwise. Place each half cut side down and slice crosswise ¼ inch thick. (Slices will be crescent-shaped.) Spread pâté on the slices and decorate each with 2 or 3 thin slices of cornichon.

Above: *Pâté spread on crescents of crisp apple.*

Left: *Carpaccio on French bread slices, nestled in an old basket.*

Blini with Red Caviar and Sour Cream

APPROXIMATELY 40 BLINI

1 package active dry yeast
½ cup warm water
1 cup milk
1½ cups flour
3 egg yolks
½ teaspoon salt
Pinch sugar
6 tablespoons melted butter
3 egg whites
½ pint thick sour cream
1 small jar (3½ ounces) red caviar

Proof yeast in warm water for 5 minutes.

Put the yeast mixture, milk, flour, egg yolks, salt, sugar, and melted butter in a blender or food processor. Blend at high speed for 40 seconds. Turn machine off, scrape down, and blend another few seconds. Pour batter into a bowl that is large enough to accommodate the rising. Cover loosely and set in a warm place to rise for 1½ to 2 hours. Do not let batter rise much longer or blini will taste overfermented.

Beat egg whites until stiff. Fold into batter.

Heat a heavy skillet or griddle. Brush with butter. Drop blini batter by teaspoonfuls into hot pan. Turn when first side is lightly browned and cook briefly on second side. Keep pancakes on a heated platter until all the batter is used.

Arrange warm blini on a tray lined with a starched linen napkin. Put a small dollop of sour cream in the center of each, then a few grains of caviar. A strip of smoked salmon decorated with a sprig of dill may be substituted for the caviar, if desired.

NOTE: Blinis may be cooled, wrapped in foil and refrigerated for use the next day. Warm in 300° oven before serving.

VARIATION: Make blinis as directed, topping with a dab of sour cream, and substitute one 2-inch tip of freshly steamed asparagus for the red caviar.

Almond-Stuffed Dates with Bacon

60 HORS D'OEUVRES

1 pound pitted dates
1 4-ounce package blanched whole almonds
1¼ pounds sliced lean bacon

Stuff each date with one whole almond. Cut bacon strips into thirds and wrap a piece around each date. Secure with a round wooden toothpick.

Put the dates on a foil-lined baking sheet and bake in a preheated 400° oven until bacon is crisp (12 to 15 minutes). Drain on a rack or on paper towel. Serve warm.

NOTE: Prepared dates can be frozen in advance and baked unthawed in a preheated 400° oven until crisp.

Roquefort Grapes

50 HORS D'OEUVRES

1 10-ounce package almonds, pecans, or walnuts
1 8-ounce package cream cheese
⅛ pound Roquefort cheese
2 tablespoons heavy cream
1 pound seedless grapes, red or green, washed and dried

To toast nuts, preheat oven to 275°. Spread nuts on baking sheet and bake until toasted. Almonds should be a light golden brown color; pecans or walnuts should smell toasted but not burned.

Chop toasted nuts rather coarsely in food processor or by hand. Spread on a platter.

In the bowl of an electric mixer, combine the cream cheese, Roquefort, and cream and beat until

smooth. Drop clean, dry grapes into the cheese mixture and gently stir by hand to coat them. Then roll the coated grapes in the toasted nuts and put on a tray lined with waxed paper. Chill until ready to serve.

NOTE: Any leftover cheese mixture can be frozen and reused.

VARIATIONS: Roll grapes in softened Pâté (see recipe, page 45) or tinned mousse of foie gras.

Endive with Herb Cheese
50 HORS D'OEUVRES

Endive is usually omitted from everyday salads because of its expense. However, as an hors d'oeuvre endive goes a long way and is very versatile. The leaves provide a perfect base for a variety of fillings.

4 heads endive (try to find nice short, fat heads)
1 5-ounce package Boursin with herbs or similar soft cheese

GARNISH
Alfalfa sprouts or watercress

Trim bottoms of endive so that the leaves are 2 to 3 inches long. Soften the cheese and spread approximately ¾ teaspoon on the bottom of each leaf, using a pastry bag, teaspoon, or spatula. Garnish with sprouts or watercress.

Arrange on a platter and refrigerate until serving time.

VARIATIONS: Spoon sour cream and red caviar onto bottom of endive and garnish with a watercress leaf, or pipe softened smoked salmon mousse onto endive and garnish with a sprig of dill.

Above: *Roquefort grapes in an Oriental basket garnished with green grapes and slices of lime.*

Left: *A single spear of endive is covered with softened cheese and garnished with a bright leaf of watercress.*

47

Cocktails for Fifty: A Festive Occasion

THIS IS MEANT TO BE AN EX-traordinary cocktail party, for celebrating an extraordinary event like an engagement, a birthday, an anniversary, or a promotion. The menu is elaborate by design, making use of more expensive raw ingredients, and recipes that require more advance preparation as well as more last-minute preparations. Two or three people will be necessary to help make hors d'oeuvres, arrange trays, and serve.

For a formal occasion, nothing conveys a sense of importance like silver and white linens. Tables look beautiful decorated simply with shiny leaves and showy flowers, or with cabbages and flowering kales, crisp linen napkins wrapped around the wine bottles, and tiny linen napkins to pass with the hors d'oeuvres. Lacking a dowry of silver, you can always borrow or rent.

❧ MENU ❧

Gravlax on Whole Wheat Pumpernickel
Lamb on Skewers with Mint Sauce
Crab Claws with Cocktail Sauce   Endive with Herb Cheese
Fillet of Beef with Rosemary on French Bread
Smoked Trout Chevrons with Horseradish Cream
Phyllo Triangles Filled with Curried Walnut Chicken
Almond-Stuffed Dates with Bacon   Roquefort Grapes
Blini with Red Caviar and Sour Cream   Chinese Pearl Balls
Open Bar

Gravlax on Whole Wheat Pumpernickel

SERVES 50

Fresh salmon, marinated in dill, salt, sugar, and pepper, is cured 3 or 4 days in the refrigerator. Many people prefer this way of serving salmon to smoked sides of salmon. Gravlax is very easy to prepare, and much less expensive to serve.

1 4- to 5-pound piece of salmon, cut in half and boned; leave the skin on
¼ cup coarse salt
¼ cup sugar
2 tablespoons peppercorns (preferably white), crushed or coarsely ground
2 large bunches dill

2 loaves thinly sliced whole wheat pumpernickel bread

MUSTARD SAUCE
4 tablespoons Dijon mustard
1 teaspoon dry mustard
3 tablespoons sugar

2 tablespoons white vinegar
⅓ cup light vegetable oil
1 small bunch dill, finely chopped

To cure salmon, put half the salmon, skin side down, in a glass dish. Combine the salt, sugar, and pepper and sprinkle on the fish, covering the whole side. Spread the dill over the seasonings. Put the other half of salmon over the dill, skin side up. Cover with plastic wrap. Put a smaller dish on top of the salmon and weight down with a heavy object. Refrigerate for 3 to 4 days. Turn the salmon every day.

To make the mustard sauce, combine the mustards, sugar, and vinegar in a bowl or food processor. Add the oil drop by drop until mixture is thick. Stir in the dill. Refrigerate until ready to use, up to 3 to 4 weeks.

To serve, remove the fish from the marinade. Wipe clean and pat dry. Slice each side on the diagonal into thin pieces, much as you would smoked salmon. Serve on half-slices of whole wheat pumpernickel, topped with the sauce.

Left: *A zested orange is the centerpiece for spears of endive with Boursin.* **Below:** *Pale pink salmon gravlax garnished with fresh dill.*

Lamb on Skewers with Mint Sauce
80 SKEWERS

Delicately marinated lamb cubes, threaded on bamboo skewers, lightly grilled or broiled, and served with a fresh mint sauce.

- 4 pounds lean lamb, cut into ¾-inch cubes
- ½ cup olive oil
  Juice of 2 lemons
- 1 tablespoon salt
  Freshly ground pepper to taste
- 1 teaspoon thyme
- 2 tablespoons chopped fresh mint

MINT SAUCE
- 4 tablespoons water
- 2 tablespoons confectioners' sugar
- ⅓ cup finely chopped mint leaves
- ½ cup white vinegar

Put lamb and marinade ingredients in a glass or stainless steel bowl. Let stand for 3 hours or overnight in the refrigerator.

Using 6-inch bamboo skewers, put 3 lamb cubes on each. This can be done the morning of the party.

Grill meat over a charcoal fire or in a hot broiler, being careful not to burn the skewers. If they do begin to burn, cover the exposed portion of the skewers with a piece of aluminum foil.

To make mint sauce, boil the water and sugar. Cool and then add the mint and vinegar. The sauce is best made ½ hour before serving. Serve in a small bowl along with the hot skewered lamb.

Above: *Marinated lamb on skewers.*

Right: *Giant crab claws are a special treat.*

Crab Claws with Cocktail Sauce

Snow crab claws are a luxurious hors d'oeuvre. They are difficult to find, and many fish stores have to order them specially. They are sold frozen and must be kept frozen until serving. Thaw in their wrapping overnight in the refrigerator or 2 to 3 hours at room temperature, then be sure to keep them refrigerated.

These large pink claws with a succulent piece of meat at one end are ready to eat as soon as they are thawed. Serve them stuck into a melon or arranged on a tray around a bowl of dipping sauce.

Also available are "cocktail" crab claws packed fresh in tins—the poor cousins of the snow crab claws.

There are approximately 16 crab claws per pound; allow two or more per person.

Approximately 6 pounds snow crab claws

COCKTAIL DIPPING SAUCE
- 1 cup catsup
- 2 to 3 tablespoons horseradish, fresh or bottled

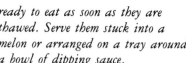

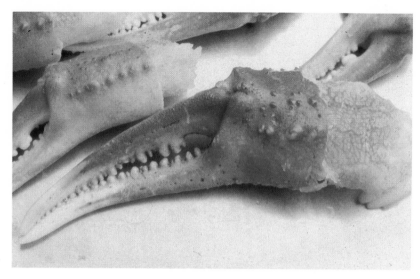

- 1 tablespoon Worcestershire sauce
- 2 to 3 drops Tabasco
  Juice of 1 lemon

Combine all sauce ingredients and chill until ready to use.

Endive with Herb Cheese
SEE RECIPE, PAGE 47

Fillet of Beef with Rosemary on French Bread
80 TO 90 HORS D'OEUVRES

This is a finger food of great elegance. A crispy diagonal slice of French bread is spread with herb butter, topped with a ¼-inch slice of rare fillet, which has been cooked with rosemary, and topped with a leaf of watercress.

- 2 3- to 4-pound beef fillets, trimmed of all fat (ask for thin fillets)
  Salt and freshly ground black pepper
  Sprigs of fresh or dried rosemary
- 4 to 5 loaves French bread
- ½ cup Herb Butter (page 92)
- 2 bunches fresh watercress

Preheat oven to 450°. Rub fillets with salt and pepper and rosemary.

Bake in hot oven for approximately 20 minutes. Let meat stand for at least 20 minutes before slicing. Beef can be cooked several hours before the party, and the hors d'oeuvres assembled right before serving.

To assemble, slice French bread into ¼-inch diagonal pieces. Butter one side with softened herb butter. Put a piece of fillet atop each piece of bread. Top each piece of meat with a watercress leaf.

Smoked Trout Chevrons with Horseradish Cream

30 TO 40 PIECES

1 8-ounce smoked trout
1 small red cabbage
1 cup heavy cream
¼ cup prepared horseradish, well drained

Fillet trout and separate into chevrons as illustrated. Arrange on a basket tray.

Hollow out the cabbage.

Whip cream until stiff. Stir in horseradish, mixing well. Spoon into cabbage and serve on tray with trout.

Whole trout.

With a sharp knife, remove fillets of fish from bones in 4 parts.

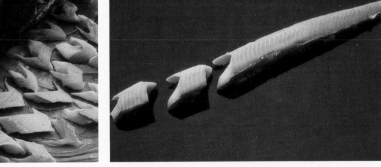

Whole trout, skin removed.

Each fillet breaks naturally into eight or ten 1-inch, V-shaped pieces.

Arrange chevrons in decorative pattern on a tray. Serve with horseradish cream.

Phyllo Triangles Filled with Curried Walnut Chicken

APPROXIMATELY 50 HORS
D'OEUVRES

Once you get the knack of working with paper-thin leaves of phyllo pastry, you will be able to make hundreds of these delectable morsels. The filling variations are endless, and they can be kept in the refrigerator, unbaked, for 2 days, or frozen immediately for future use. *To serve as an entree, use ¾ cup filling and whole sheets of phyllo to make large triangles.*

1 pound phyllo pastry

CURRIED WALNUT
CHICKEN FILLING
2 chicken breasts
2 tablespoons butter
2½ tablespoons flour
1 teaspoon curry powder
1 cup milk
½ teaspoon salt
½ cup chopped walnuts

1 pound (4 sticks) unsalted butter, melted

Thaw the phyllo dough overnight in the refrigerator, if frozen. To make the filling, bake chicken breasts in buttered aluminum foil in a 375° oven for 45 minutes. Unwrap and cool. Remove skin and bones, and cut meat into small pieces.

Heat 2 tablespoons butter in small pan. Add flour and curry powder and cook over low heat 2 minutes. Add milk and whisk until thick. Season with salt, stir in walnuts and chicken. Cool completely.

To assemble, melt and cool butter. Place 1 sheet of phyllo on flat surface and brush with butter. Top with 2 more sheets, buttering each. Cut sheet in half lengthwise, then cut each half crosswise into 6 equal parts. Spoon a teaspoon of filling onto end of each strip and form a triangle by folding right-hand corner to opposite side, as you would a flag. Continue folding until strip is used. Repeat whole process until all filling is used.

Preheat oven to 400°.

Place triangles on buttered baking sheet. Brush with melted butter and bake until golden brown, about 10 minutes.

Above: *Roquefort grapes on a bed of purple flowering kale.*

Left: *Phyllo triangles garnished with enok mushrooms.*

Almond-Stuffed Dates with Bacon

DOUBLE RECIPE, PAGE 46

Blini with Red Caviar and Sour Cream

DOUBLE RECIPE, PAGE 46

Roquefort Grapes

DOUBLE RECIPE, PAGE 46

Chinese Pearl Balls

DOUBLE RECIPE, PAGE 41

Cocktails for Two Hundred: Country Fare

*T*HE NECESSITY OF ENTERTAINING a very large group of people is a common dread, and every so often it becomes real. Few people in fact can escape for a lifetime a call to host a business or club affair, fête a friend or dignitary, or simply repay an ungainly accumulation of social debts. But although coping with a crowd of two hundred will never be a breeze, there are ways to make the task much less awesome than one would think. There are specific hors d'oeuvres that lend themselves to a large crowd; and there are specific ways of preparing those dishes in quantity in a home kitchen.

The first giant-sized cocktail party I did for the Museum of American Folk Art is an illustration of the relative ease possible

Freshly baked ham and cheese feuilleté.

❧ MENU ❧

Spinach-Cheese Quiche   Pissaladière
Ham and Cheese Feuilleté   Green Vegetables with Tarragon Cream
Baked Country Ham
Smoked Turkey on Blueberry Scones
Smoked Trout Mousse on Cucumber Slices
Baked New Potatoes with Dip
Tarragon Chicken Salad on Carrot Bread
Open Bar

with uneasy numbers. The setting was the Seventh Regiment Armory, the cavernous old brick fortress on Park Avenue and Sixty-seventh Street; the event, the benefit opening of the Fall Antiques Show. My charge was to prepare for two hundred patrons cocktail fare that could be as satisfying as a meal, since the show spanned the dinner hours (although the Armory was without kitchen facilities!); to articulate that year's theme, which was "Celebrate the Harvest"; and to keep myself within a budget of five dollars a head.

The entire occasion was inspired by the idea of the harvest and all the activities related to it. We served hearty farmtable fare—country cured hams and turkeys (which I had procured direct from an upstate farmer), chili, refried black beans, and chicken salad—but in dainty portions on biscuits, scones, and corn bread. There were mounds of crisp cooked seasonal vegetables, strawberries, figs, a huge wheel of New York State Cheddar cheese surrounded by apple slices, homemade fruit butters and breads, and a dazzling array of walnut, pecan, and mincemeat tarts, and other pastries. Arranged simply, the food itself had the exciting visual dynamics of a country roadside stand. We wrapped three long rented tables in brown paper, covered them with an inch of peat moss, and then positioned between trays of hors d'oeuvres antique mason jars of preserves, and pumpkins, squashes, cabbages, and eggplants hollowed into bowls to hold the fruit butters. Under tables and spilling out the door were bushel baskets of more vegetables, pails filled with "milk" (a fabrication of chalky water), and thirty antique poultry cages filled with an assortment of Bantam cochins,

My brother George and I cooked batter-dipped apple fritters at the Museum of American Folk Art's "Celebrate the Harvest" cocktail party.

Aracanas, lavender guinea fowl, and white silkies, which I had spirited away from my coop for the evening. All evening long, the roosters crowed their heads off.

It was an easy party because the fare itself was uncomplicated and was all prepared in advance, the decorating natural, and the presentation straightforward. This party could lend itself to a variety of occasions and a variety of sizes, and, in fact, would not require a professional caterer at the helm.

The following menu is slightly more sophisticated than the harvest fare I served at the Armory, and it suits any season. It has been carefully planned to make as light work as possible of large quantities. Although by my basic calculation of two of each hors d'oeuvre per person, one would estimate some 3,600 items to be produced (and one would despair), the mathematics in this case are misleading. Here is how the menu translated into practical terms: Three of the nine hors d'oeuvres here are pastry-based—the quiches, pissaladière, and feuilleté. As such, they can be enlarged in the simplest possible way—by making them on large cookie sheets instead of in individual quiche pans. Fashioned this way, comfortably in advance, they have then only to be reheated and cut into bite-size squares or triangles. And as one batch of the pissaladière will render eighty-two portions and one large quiche at least seventy-two, you are already on your way. To this, add one country ham, which, slivered and served on tiny scones, will serve two hundred; baked turkeys, similarly slivered and served, for two hundred; and two fresh vegetables dishes: green beans with an aromatic dip, and cucumber slices adorned with a piping of a very easy, ten-minute mousse of smoked trout.

In preparing quantities of food that are out of the ordinary, careful organization—of oven and refrigerator space as well as timing—is crucial. The larger the party, the more numerous and the more useful lists, checklists, and schedules will be. It is comforting, too, to have everything committed to paper. Most of the work of this party takes place in advance (if your party is a collaborative effort, this menu could easily be doled out among friends), with last-minute attention to detail. An hour before guests arrive, two people will be needed in the kitchen to assemble and decorate trays, and four are needed to pass trays of hors d'oeuvres. Four bartenders will keep an open bar running smoothly.

Wheels of New York State Cheddar cheese, whole apples, and apple wedges provided colorful and decorative edibles at the Folk Art party.

Spinach-Cheese Quiche
84 HORS D'OEUVRES

This hors d'oeuvre is baked on a large cookie sheet (17½ × 12½ inches) in a partially baked pastry shell and then cut into bite-size squares. Each sheet will make 84 squares.

PASTRY SHELL
- 1½ sticks unsalted butter
- 5 tablespoons unsalted margarine
- 3½ cups unbleached flour
- 1 teaspoon salt
  Ice water

FILLING
- 6 green onions, chopped
- 6 tablespoons butter
- 2 10-ounce packages frozen chopped spinach, thawed and drained
- 3 cups whipping cream
- 9 eggs
  Salt and pepper to taste
  Freshly grated nutmeg
- 1 cup grated Gruyère cheese

To make the pastry, cut the shortening into the flour by hand or in a food processor. Mix in the salt.

Add the ice water drop by drop until pastry forms a ball. It must not be sticky. Flatten into a rectangle and wrap in plastic wrap. Chill for at least 1 hour. Roll pastry on a floured board into a rectangle large enough to fill the pan. Press into the pan and flute the edges. Chill for ½ hour.

Preheat oven to 350°. Line pastry with aluminum foil, fill with weights (beans, etc.), and bake for 15 minutes. Remove weights and foil and bake 5 minutes longer, until pastry is cooked but not colored.

To make filling, sauté the green onions in butter. Add spinach and stir over high heat 2 minutes. Mix the cream with the eggs. Pour into spinach mixture and season with salt and pepper and nutmeg. Sprinkle cheese in bottom of tart shell and pour custard on top of cheese.

Bake in a preheated 350° oven until puffed and custard is set. Do not overcook. Cut into small squares and serve hot.

N O T E : Quiche can be frozen, uncut and well wrapped. Thaw in preheated oven until hot (approximately 20 minutes). Cut into serving pieces.

Pissaladière
84 HORS D'OEUVRES

This Provençal onion pie is related to pizza but has a more substantial base of yeast bread and is topped with onions, tomatoes, and olives.

YEAST PASTRY

9 tablespoons unsalted butter
3½ cups all-purpose flour
2 teaspoons salt
6 tablespoons tepid water
1 yeast cake
3 eggs, beaten

PISSALADIÈRE FILLING

3 pounds (16 to 18 medium) onions, peeled and coarsely chopped
¼ cup olive oil
8 ripe tomatoes, peeled, seeded, and chopped
2 cloves garlic, crushed (optional)
Salt and pepper to taste
¼ pound Niçoise olives, pitted and cut into quarters
1 cup anchovy fillets, drained and cut into thin strips
Fresh or dried oregano or marjoram

To make pastry, cut the butter into the flour. Add about 2 teaspoons salt. Dissolve the yeast in the water and mix with the eggs. Make a well in the center of the flour-butter mixture and pour in the egg-yeast mixture. Knead the liquid into the flour until the dough is smooth and no longer sticky. Add more flour or water if necessary. Shape dough into a ball, put in a floured bowl or pan, cover with a towel, and let rise until doubled (about 1 hour).

To make the filling, cook the onions in oil over low heat until soft

Pissaladière, or French pizza, can be made in flat rounds and cut into wedges.

and golden, about 45 minutes. Do not brown. Add the tomatoes and garlic and cook until the water from the tomatoes has evaporated. Season with salt and pepper. Remove from heat and cool.

Preheat oven to 400°. Butter a large (11 × 17-inch) cookie sheet with sides.

To form pie, pat down the dough, knead until smooth, and press the dough into the pan, pushing up the sides. Spoon in the filling. Decorate top with slivers of olives and anchovy strips. If you are going to cut the pie into small squares, plan your decorations accordingly. Sprinkle with herbs.

Let pie rise for 15 minutes before baking. Bake at 400° for 20 minutes, then reduce oven to 350° and continue baking 20 minutes or until crust is done. Serve hot or at room temperature.

Ham and Cheese Feuilleté
96 SQUARES

1 recipe Perfect Puff Pastry (page 237)
¼ cup Dijon-style mustard
1 pound thinly sliced boiled ham (lean, imported variety)
½ pound thinly sliced Swiss cheese
2 eggs mixed with 2 teaspoons heavy cream for glaze

Divide the pastry into 4 pieces. Roll 2 pieces into rectangles approximately 12 inches by 16 inches. Lay the pastry on two 12 × 16-inch baking sheets that have been sprayed with water.

Spread the pastry with a thin layer of mustard, leaving a 1-inch border around the outside. Layer the ham and cheese on top of the mustard, until it is used up. Fold the borders up over the filling. Brush with cold water, so that the pastry tops will adhere to the bottoms.

Roll the 2 remaining pieces of pastry into rectangles that are as large as the filled portions. Place directly on top of bottoms. With a sharp knife, trim edge of top pastry. With the tines of a fork, press down around the edges. With any scraps, cut decorative leaves, moons, etc.; brush lightly with water and arrange on top of the pastry. Chill for at least ½ hour before glazing and baking. Well wrapped, the rectangles can remain in the refrigerator a day or two.

Preheat oven to 450°. Brush egg glaze over top crust. Two applications give a better glaze. (Allow first coat to dry.) With the tip of a sharp knife, cut a pattern into the top pastry. Cut only partially through the pastry. Make 2 or 3 vent holes, and put in a hot oven. Bake until pastry has puffed and is a golden brown. Cool slightly before cutting into 1½-inch squares. This is best when eaten freshly baked.

Green Vegetables with Tarragon Cream
SERVES 200

A very simple hors d'oeuvre that is easy to prepare and complements the heavier cocktail fare in the menu.

- 12 pounds young tender asparagus or green beans
- 3 medium bunches fresh tarragon (or dill)
- 1½ quarts sour cream
  Salt, pepper, tarragon vinegar to taste

Blanch the vegetables a pound or two at a time in large kettles of boiling water. Cook until just tender (2 to 4 minutes). Plunge immediately into iced water, drain, and chill.

Strip the leaves of tarragon from the stems. Mince finely. Mix into the sour cream; add the salt, pepper, and vinegar to taste.

To serve, put the cream in a bowl set into the center of a large tray. Arrange the vegetables neatly around the bowl. Guests will pick up a stem and dip it into the sauce.

Baked Country Ham
200 OR MORE HORS D'OEUVRES

I have found 2 types of smoked hams that I especially like—Harrington's cob-smoked ham and Colonial ham, available in the supermarket. Glazed with a simple mixture of sherry, brown sugar, honey, and mustard, and slow-cooked to tenderness, these hams are delicious.

- 1 14-pound uncooked smoked ham
- 1 cup brown sugar
- ½ cup dry sherry
- ¼ cup honey
- ¼ cup Dijon mustard

Preheat oven to 300°. Put the ham, fatty side up, in a foil-lined metal baking pan. Cover with foil and bake for 3 hours. Combine remaining ingredients.

Remove ham from oven. Carefully trim away all but ⅛ inch of fat. Score with a sharp knife in a diamond pattern, making cuts ⅛ inch deep and 1 inch apart.

Pour excess fat from pan, line pan with new foil, and put ham in pan. Spoon glaze over ham and put in oven for 20 minutes. Raise oven temperature to 325° and glaze again. Bake an additional 20 minutes. Glaze once more and bake 15 minutes.

Cool before carving into thin slivers.

Country ham with mustard and fresh asparagus with dip.

Smoked Turkey
on Blueberry Scones

APPROXIMATELY 36
COCKTAIL SANDWICHES

*I came across this recipe for blueberry
scones late one summer on Martha's
Vineyard when the tiny wild
blueberries were ripe and everywhere.
The combination of pale pink smoked
turkey slivers and purple-studded
scones is a delight for the eye as well
as the palate.*

2 cups flour
½ teaspoon salt
2 teaspoons baking powder
¼ teaspoon baking soda
¼ cup (½ stick) butter
½ cup buttermilk
1 tablespoon molasses
1 cup fresh or dry-frozen
blueberries

½ pound thinly sliced smoked
turkey

Preheat the oven to 425° and lightly butter a baking sheet.

In a large bowl, sift together the
flour, salt, baking powder, and
baking soda. Cut the butter into
the dry ingredients with a pastry
cutter until the mixture resembles
coarse meal. Mix the buttermilk
with the molasses and add to flour
mixture; stir in the blueberries.
Work the mixture gently and
quickly with your hands until it
holds together; the dough should
be crumbly.

Pat the dough out to a ½-inch
thickness on a lightly floured
board. With a 3-inch floured biscuit cutter, cut out as many rounds
of dough as possible. Pat out the
scraps to make as many more
rounds as possible. Then, with a
sharp knife, cut each round into 4
triangular quarters. Transfer the
scones to the baking sheet and bake
them in the center of the oven for 8

to 10 minutes, or until they are
golden brown and puffed. Watch
carefully to prevent overbaking.

Cut the turkey slices into triangles
slightly larger than the scones. Using a sharp slicing knife, split the
scones. Fill each scone with 1 or 2
triangles of turkey to make little
sandwiches.

NOTE: To make large quantities of
scones, repeat recipe. Do not double.

VARIATION: Slivers of Baked
Country Ham (page 57) are also delicious on blueberry scones.

Smoked Trout Mousse
on Cucumber Slices

50 TO 60 HORS
D'OEUVRES

1 8-ounce smoked trout
1 cup heavy cream
 Salt and freshly ground
 black pepper
 Lemon juice
1 to 2 tablespoons fresh or
 bottled grated horseradish
2 8-ounce packages cream
 cheese, softened
4 cucumbers (preferably the
 seedless English type)

Carefully remove all skin and bones
from the trout. Put the flesh in a
food processor fitted with a steel
blade. Chop fine. Add the cream in
a steady stream until it is absorbed.
Season with a little salt and pepper,
lemon juice, and horseradish. Add
the softened cheese and blend until
thoroughly mixed and smooth.

Wash the cucumbers. Dry well and
cut in ¼-inch slices.

To serve, pipe 1 tablespoon of fish
mousse in the center of each cucumber slice, using a pastry bag fitted with a large star tip.

**Bite-size baked new potatoes
are a delicious hors d'oeuvre.
Here they are surrounded with
bowls of garnishes—sour
cream, chopped ham, scallions,
grated cheese, chopped parsley,
and sweet butter.**

Baked New Potatoes
1 PER PERSON

*Tiny baked new potatoes are a
satisfying, cheap, interesting hors
d'oeuvre. I put out great big trays of
steaming hot potatoes surrounded by
earthenware bowls filled with
toppings of crumbled crispy bacon,
sour cream, melted butter, grated
cheese, chopped ham, chopped
scallions, red caviar, herbs, salt,
and pepper. Buy the smallest, most
uniform, blemish-free new potatoes
you can find.*

Wash the potatoes and arrange in
one layer on baking sheets.

Bake in a 350° oven until tender.
Adjust quantities of toppings according to the number of potatoes.

N O T E : I discovered a fantastic
thing when preparing 1,500 potatoes for the Folk Art Show. We
baked the potatoes ahead of time,
intending to reheat them at the
party. We put the hot baked potatoes right into an insulated cooler
and took them off to the party.
Four hours later, when we went to
take the potatoes out to reheat
them, they seemed hotter than before. Although the skin was not as
crisp, the potatoes were perfectly
acceptable. Potatoes will stay hot
this way for as long as 6 hours. The
cooler was never the same (the interior plastic buckled a bit), but we
now use it just for potatoes.

Tarragon Chicken Salad
8 QUARTS

*White meat chicken, either cubed or
slivered, is flavored with lots of
fresh tarragon and a rich
mayonnaise. Pecans, grapes, or
chopped apples can be added for
variety.*

   Softened butter
2 onions, peeled and thinly
   sliced
   Fresh herbs—parsley,
   thyme, bay leaves, etc.
16 whole chicken breasts
   Juice of 2 lemons
   Salt and freshly ground
   pepper
4 to 5 tablespoons chopped
   fresh tarragon or 4 to 5
   teaspoons dried tarragon
¾ cup sour cream
¾ cup mayonnaise
4 cups finely chopped celery
3 cups chopped pecans
   (optional)

Preheat oven to 375°.

Butter a baking pan (or pans) very
generously. Scatter onion slices and
herbs in the pan and lay the halved
breasts on top, skin side up, in a
single layer. Sprinkle with lemon
juice and salt and pepper. Roast for
30 to 40 minutes, or until just
barely done. Do not overcook. Cool.

Remove the skin and bones from
the meat and cut or shred into
cubes or slivers. Put in a bowl and
mix with salt and pepper to taste
and tarragon.

Mix sour cream and mayonnaise together and stir into chicken a little
at a time until creamy but not wet.
Mix in more sour cream and mayonnaise if necessary. Taste for seasoning. Add the celery and nuts.

To serve, spoon chicken salad onto
thin slices of Carrot Bread (recipe
follows), or use thin rounds of
French bread or cucumber slices.

Carrot Bread
1 LARGE LOAF

A firm, slightly dense loaf that is an excellent base for open-face hors d'oeuvres (it doesn't crumble).

½ pound (2 sticks) unsalted butter, at room temperature
½ cup white sugar
½ cup brown sugar
3 eggs
2 cups all-purpose flour
1 teaspoon baking powder
1 teaspoon baking soda
1 teaspoon salt
2 teaspoons cinnamon
3 cups grated carrots
1 cup coarsely chopped walnuts

Preheat oven to 350°. Butter a large loaf pan.

Cream butter with white and brown sugar and beat until fluffy. Add eggs and beat well.

Sift together dry ingredients. Beat into the egg mixture. Fold in the carrots and walnuts. Mix thoroughly. Pour batter into prepared 9 × 5 × 3-inch pan. Bake for approximately 1 hour. Cool on rack.

NOTE: This recipe can be multiplied if desired.

Right: *When pissaladière and spinach-Gruyère quiches are baked on cookie sheets, they yield 168 bite-size pieces. A loaf of carrot bread, thinly sliced, will make more than 40 hors d'oeuvres.*

Below: *A hollowed-out pumpkin is the perfect container for asparagus crudités.*

CHAPTER THREE

The Crudité, Fruit, and Cheese Party

CRUDITÉS (OR CUT-UP VEGE-tables), fruits, and cheese—these are foods that stand on their own. Each, so complete in its natural state, demands no more than respectful handling and artful presentation. Each can constitute a course of a meal, or contribute to an hors d'oeuvre or buffet table. Together, the trio offers a very satisfying and very elegant alternative to a lunch or dinner.

I personally love the medium of crudités. The color, texture, shape, and taste of fresh vegetables are remarkable, and they offer the hostess the rare opportunity to be

63

both simple and elaborate, straightforward and imaginative. Of course, there is a world of difference between a careless and a careful presentation of crudités. Crudités are not just a haphazard bowl of cut-up carrot and celery sticks; they are closer to a good still life, an artful edible exhibit. Crudités have indeed become an art form among food professionals, so much so that each good caterer in New York is known for his particular way of arranging and serving them. Crudités change with each season, too. The look of a spring platter, based on asparagus,

Dips served in hollowed-out cabbages complement this abundant crudité display created as "landscape architecture."

peas and pea pods, and tiny young string beans, is very different from that of late summer, when you find cherry tomatoes, orange plum tomatoes, and a rainbow of lush, bright, and full-bodied squashes. The same seasonal differences are true with fruit arrangements.

Several years ago I began combining crudités, fruit, and cheeses, and found the resulting parties extremely successful. I realized that this was a new and important way to entertain; the food becomes a party in itself, for the visual dynamics set a mood. Besides that, it is enormous fun to prepare. Fruits and vegetables are not expensive and in shopping for them you can indulge every whim and fancy. Cheeses, while more costly, exist in such amazing variety these days—where only a few years ago there were two or three goat cheeses imported, now there are 40 or 50—that you will have a wonderful time sampling and choosing.

I have organized such parties for the Cooper-Hewitt Museum on Fifth Avenue in New York for three years now. The ease of advanced preparation and the spectacle of abundance were perfectly suited to large gatherings. Last June, in the setting of its graceful private garden, under strings of jumbo pink and white helium balloons, I covered two huge square tables with fresh vegetables, some whole, some cut up decoratively, some raw, and some cooked and cooled; seasonal fruits like strawberries, plums, apricots, black cherries, grapes, and melons as well as tropical varieties; some 23 different cheeses; and as many different breads and crackers. The food was an invitation to summer—festive, easy, evocative. It carried a message and made people gracious and lighthearted. Guests walked around and around the tables, looking and admiring before they decided what to eat. With only periodic refurbishing, the tables remained fresh and beautiful the entire night. As a way of extending the celebration, late in the cool evening we passed a tray of finger desserts. It was a party to remember, and a party to duplicate, in part or in whole.

Crudités

*T*HE IDEA OF CRUDITÉS CAME from Provence, the most magical of all the provinces of France. Here, the first fact of life is the sun, and sidewalk stands overflow with its products: diminutive green beans, big plump green artichokes and tiny dark-brown ones, skinny young leeks, baby carrots, red and green peppers, knobby celeriac, all sizes of tomatoes, squashes, and always olives, green and black, glossy and wrinkled.

Such is a Provencal's confidence in his raw staples that he will commonly offer as a special treat to a guest a simple plate of freshly washed radishes, still retaining their leaves, flanked only with olives and a mound of butter.

In America, our sun produces an ever-expanding array of produce, each year encompassing new hybrids and more and more Oriental vegetables. With air shipments and hothouse culture, many wonderful varieties are now available to us regardless of season. In Westport, I am fortunate to have a wonderful barn-sized greengrocery, that prides itself on its supply of less familiar items like

The garden of the Cooper-Hewitt Museum—the perfect setting for a summer evening crudité, fruit, and cheese party.

sunchokes, kohlrabi, straw mushrooms, flowering kale, okra, celery knob, fennel, and baby avocados. But even ordinary supermarkets are becoming more and more specialized these days, and most of the above make at least an occasional appearance. If you are lucky enough to have a garden plot, you can remain blessedly self-sufficient, and supply yourself with whatever produce suits your seasonal fancy.

In selecting produce, it is crucial to be sharp-eyed and to bring home only the freshest, crispest, most perfect-looking vegetables possible. And then, to prevent perfection from wilting before your eyes, it is important to store your selection properly in its raw state. Asparagus should stand up in a few inches of water. Cabbage, if it looks tired, should be revitalized in a cold water bath. Radishes and lettuce must be carefully washed, dried, and sealed in plastic bags in the refrigerator. All other vegetables should be bagged and refrigerated unwashed.

Of the dozens and dozens of varieties of vegetables, there are very few unsuitable to a crudité platter, namely:

BEETS	EGGPLANT	ARTICHOKES
OKRA	WINTER SQUASHES	KALE
POTATOES	RUTABAGA	

Of the remaining plentitude, there are those that are best washed and trimmed, but left otherwise as nature delivered them:

CHERRY TOMATOES	SUGAR SNAP PEAS	MUSHROOMS
PLUM TOMATOES	RADISHES	ENDIVE

These should be left raw but cut decoratively:

RED AND GREEN PEPPERS	CABBAGE—RED, WHITE, SAVOY, CHINESE	PURPLE-TOPPED TURNIPS
CUCUMBER		FENNEL
PURPLE AND GREEN KOHLRABI	YELLOW AND GREEN ZUCCHINI	CELERIAC SUNCHOKES

These are best when curled, feathered, or fanned:

CELERY	CARROTS	SCALLIONS	WHITE RADISHES

And these require a quick blanching to maximize their flavor and color:

ASPARAGUS	CARROTS	BRUSSELS SPROUTS
GREEN BEANS	SNOW PEAS	CAULIFLOWER
BROCCOLI		

Blanching is a simple high-speed operation, best done 4 to 24 hours before a party. Some vegetables, notably green beans, asparagus, and snow peas, require only a few seconds in vigorously boiling water, but even with fastidious draining and storage, they seem to fade overnight, and should therefore be prepared as close to the event as possible. Others—like the slow-maturing winter vegetables such as cauliflower, broccoli, and Brussels sprouts—require as much as two minutes, but then remain crispy for days. Like flowers, each vegetable has a particular timetable.

The Art of Crudité: The object of cutting up crudités is first of all practical: to fashion something that is neither too large to be eaten in one or two bites nor too tiny to be handled gracefully; and second, aesthetic: to create a pleasing shape. There are many different cutting techniques, ranging from the simple to the very elaborate, the latter of which results in fantastic scallion brushes, cucumber coils, and radish fans. Several years ago, in his wonderful book *La Technique,* Jacques Pepin demonstrated the art of creating tomato roses and lemon baskets. Now Oriental manuals, like *Japanese Garnishes,* have taught us how to make very beautiful curls and crisps and feathers with a few deft strokes of a (very sharp)

Counterclockwise from top left: *Dahlia blossoms add a touch of color to a Big Max pumpkin filled with asparagus; an antique copper gugelhopf mold holds a simple crudité arrangement decorated with fresh sage and red cranberries; a miniature Sussex trug basket contains just enough crudités for two; a Victorian flower basket holds a potpourri of endive spears, whole green beans, and snow peas mixed with purple cabbage, hyssop branches, and pattypan squash; an Irish teamer is the perfect background for an arrangement of whole baby carrots, sliced zucchini, and whole spring onions.*

67

Blanching Vegetables for Crudités

Many vegetables used for crudités benefit from a quick immersion in rapidly boiling water, or blanching. Blanching maximizes their flavor and color and makes them tender yet crispy. Use fresh, unblemished produce, and don't blanch vegetables before the day of the party and preferably no longer than six hours before serving.

Vegetables require varying amounts of blanching time:

CAULIFLOWER—5 to 6 minutes.

ASPARAGUS—3 to 5 minutes, depending on thickness of stalk.

GREEN BEANS—2 to 4 minutes, depending on freshness and size.

BROCCOLI—approximately 3 minutes to tenderize and brighten color.

CARROTS—approximately 3 minutes to brighten color.

SNOW PEAS—approximately 30 seconds.

BRUSSELS SPROUTS—approximately 8 minutes to tenderize.

Trim or peel vegetables if necessary, and cut asparagus into equal lengths.

Blanch a small quantity in rapidly boiling water.

Immerse immediately in ice-cold water to stop cooking and chill the vegetables.

Drain on racks. Gently pat with a towel if wet.

Store on racks placed on paper toweling. Cover with paper towels.

Wrap in plastic and refrigerate until ready to use.

knife. I have immersed myself in all these books, and inevitably I have revised my own techniques, for there is much to learn, particularly from the East. I used to *pull* the top and string off a pea pod, for instance, but I've learned that it is more efficient and exact to *cut* and pull instead. At the moment I like to cut carrots and zucchini into a variety of irregular diagonals, which is accomplished by simply giving a vegetable a quarter turn while cutting (I do *not* like to lose half the substance of a vegetable by cutting it into ovals, or stars, or fish). Green and red pepper strips have given way to pepper chunks. I am awed by the beauty of a paper-thin length of purple turnip rolled up and fanned out into a blossom, but I will probably use it as a flourish on an otherwise simple tray. The point is not to be precious or fussy, but decorative and provocative. Clearly, crudités have become an art form, but their best expressions are judiciously simple.

Crudités are a remarkably flexible medium; they can take hours or minutes to assemble, depending on your mood and interest. A platter of crudités can serve as a centerpiece for a dinner, or for a reception (in small baskets, placed on each table); it can be a part or the whole of a cocktail party. The kind and quantity of vegetables purchased depends entirely on the purpose and aesthetics of your arrangement, as well as on the season and the shops. Try to think in visual terms of bunches of ingredients rather than exact pound measures, and don't fear an oversupply, for the leftovers can always be turned into a wonderful soup or purée the following day. Some hostesses even make gifts of bags of extra cut-up vegetables at the end of a party, which is a nice gesture.

Any number of containers will serve to display your particular selection of vegetables. I tend to favor baskets, because they look natural, and because I have amassed a large collection; some are antique, but some are cheap Oriental imports sprayed with black lacquer. I also have

Irregularly-cut vegetables make a more interesting display.

discovered that certain vegetables themselves make exceptional containers, either for the crudités or for the dips. A pumpkin or a squash, for example, can be hollowed out and used, as can a giant zucchini, a pattypan squash, a giant pepper, a butternut squash, or a red, green, or savoy cabbage. Polish the vegetable with a soft cloth until it gleams like a jewel.

My style of arranging is asymmetrical. There is something very appealing and surprising, I feel, about an unbalanced platter. I also like to bunch vegetables of one kind together, using only three or four kinds per tray; to add sprigs of herbs (which add a scent to the table); and to mix cut vegetables with whole specimens. Not only is it dramatic to position a whole purple broccoli and a white scalloped pattypan squash, say, in a basket, and then surround them with pea pods and endive, but when your display is half consumed, it will still look quite lovely (and the intact vegetables can be eaten another day).

Dips: In her book *With Bold Knife and Fork,* M.F.K. Fisher spoke of her disdain for the American expression "dip," partly because it conjured up something messy, potato chips broken off in a big bowl of that old standby, sour cream with dry onion soup. My feelings are somewhat the same. But although we are stuck with the word "dip," in fact dips don't have to be tired and predictable. I have experimented with all sorts of ingredients—a homemade mustard, or honey to which I add a generous pinch of curry powder. The old sour cream, yogurt, or mayonnaise base takes a dozen different forms when you add herbs, capers, green peppercorns, anchovies, tomatoes, or cheese. A cold vegetable purée is an interesting alternative, too, especially served with zucchini or pumpkin bread. In wintertime, try a hot bagna cauda, or a cheddar cheese fondue (good with apple slices, as well as vegetables). Experiment too with different ways of presenting dips: hollowed-out vegetables are a personal favorite. There are no rules—only the dictates of taste.

Cucumber Sour Cream Dip
APPROXIMATELY 1 QUART

2 large cucumbers, peeled, seeded, and finely grated
2 pints sour cream
½ cup chopped herbs (parsley, chives, tarragon, mint, dill, etc., or a combination)
Salt and pepper

In a strainer, squeeze out excess liquid from the cucumbers. Mix with sour cream, herbs, and salt and pepper to taste. Refrigerate until ready to use.

VARIATIONS: Substitute 1 pint good-quality whole-milk plain yogurt for 1 pint of the sour cream. Omit herbs and add 1 clove minced garlic and approximately 1 tablespoon cumin, to taste. Or add 4 or 5 finely minced scallions, greens included. One to 2 tablespoons Dijon mustard can be added to either combination.

Brooke's Mustard Dip
APPROXIMATELY 1 QUART

½ cup dry mustard
¾ cup distilled white vinegar
½ cup white wine or dry vermouth
3 eggs
½ cup sugar
½ tablespoon salt

Mix mustard, vinegar, and wine in a porcelain or stainless steel bowl.

Cover and soak overnight.

Beat eggs with sugar and salt until very light and foamy. Add mustard mixture, and cook in a double boiler (or in a stainless bowl over a pot of simmering water) until thick, approximately 1 hour, whisking occasionally.

Cool and refrigerate until ready to use.

Honey Curry Dip
APPROXIMATELY 1 QUART

1 quart honey
¼ cup curry powder
½ cup homemade or good-quality store-bought mayonnaise

Heat honey and curry in a saucepan until curry is dissolved. Cool slightly. Whisk mayonnaise thoroughly into mixture. Refrigerate until ready to use.

Anchovy Mayonnaise
APPROXIMATELY 1 QUART

1 quart homemade or good-quality store-bought mayonnaise
8 to 10 oil-packed anchovy fillets, finely chopped
2 large cloves garlic, minced
4 hard-boiled egg yolks, sieved or riced
½ cup minced parsley
3 tablespoons capers, drained and minced
⅛ teaspoon cayenne (optional)

Mix all ingredients together and adjust seasoning. Chill until ready to use.

Cottage Cheese and Dill Dip
APPROXIMATELY 1 QUART

2 pounds small-curd, low-fat cottage cheese
½ cup chopped fresh dill
1 tablespoon grated onion
Salt and freshly ground pepper to taste

Mix all ingredients together and adjust seasoning. Chill until ready to use.

Bagna Cauda

APPROXIMATELY 3 CUPS

2 cups olive oil
½ cup (1 stick) unsalted butter
5 to 6 cloves garlic, minced
30 anchovy fillets, rinsed and drained (about two 2-ounce tins)
Salt to taste

Heat oil and butter together. When butter starts to foam, add garlic and sauté lightly. Do not allow it to brown.

Add anchovies and crush to a purée with a wooden spoon. Add salt, stirring to dissolve.

Serve immediately with a selection of raw vegetables. Keep warm over a small fondue flame, but do not allow it to cook further.

Taramasalata

2 CUPS

A thick creamy dip made from pale orange carp roe. The Greeks serve it with bread or with fresh vegetables.

4 slices white bread
¼ cup milk
½ cup tarama (available in **Greek** or **Middle Eastern** grocery stores)
4 tablespoons lemon juice
¾ to 1 cup olive oil
¼ cup vegetable oil

Remove the crusts from the bread and soak the bread in milk. Squeeze dry and blend with the rest of the ingredients in a food processor.

Serve at room temperature.

Dips look especially beautiful in hollowed-out Savoy cabbages, pattypan squashes, and radicchio.

Cheddar Cheese Fondue

3 CUPS

1 pound sharp cheddar, grated
1 cup beer
1 teaspoon paprika
Pinch cayenne
1 tablespoon mustard
Salt and pepper

Mix cheddar with beer in a fondue pot or crockpot. Heat slowly, stirring frequently, until melted. Add seasonings to taste.

Eggplant Caviar

APPROXIMATELY 3 CUPS

4 large eggplants
¾ cup olive oil
4 medium tomatoes
2 small onions, coarsely chopped
2 large cloves garlic, minced
½ cup fresh parsley, minced
Salt and pepper

Preheat oven to 350°.
Cut eggplants in half lengthwise, brush all sides with ¼ cup olive oil, lay face down in an oiled shallow pan, and roast until eggplant collapses and is tender, about 45 minutes. Cool, saving juices.

Peel the tomatoes by dipping in boiling water for 30 seconds and slipping off the skins. Cut in half and gently squeeze out the seeds. Chop fine.

Scrape eggplant from skin. Chop flesh finely on a large board. Add the onion and chop until it is well minced. Add the garlic and the tomatoes. Chop until the mixture is a fine consistency. Mix in the parsley, remaining ½ cup olive oil, and reserved juices; season to taste with salt and pepper.

Chill until ready to use.

Fruit

M*Y TRADEMARK HAS COME* to be a giant wicker gardening basket brimming with fresh strawberries. I used it at my first catered event, which was a home wedding, and I have used it many times since, at buffets and brunches. The basket is associated with a lot of important memories for me. It once belonged to the Baroness Hilla von Rebay, who for many years owned the property behind our house, which is now a bird sanctuary. I imagine she gathered peonies and giant dahlias in it and then looped it over her arm. It was kept in her barn, and one day after her death, it was passed on to me by her gardener, a man named Fred Specht, whose gardens and whose uncanny sensitivity to nature have been a profound source of inspiration to me. I think this kind gesture was meant as a form of encouragement.

I like to use fruits opulently, for a centerpiece, or as an element in a buffet or brunch, because it attracts the eye. I think, too, that people like the act of eating a whole fruit, and that when you have plump, radiant, perfectly ripe peaches, plums, pears, nectarines, cherries, strawberries, or grapes, it is more pleasing to present them in their natural state rather than cutting them up into a salad. For a very elegant wedding buffet, I once arranged six hundred summer peaches in colossal pyramids in the middle of the buffet table for decoration and saw every one of them devoured before the event ended.

Serving fruit is basically a matter of display. In the fall, a tray of all the wonderful seasonal varieties of green,

Left: *My signature basket is filled with hundreds of fresh strawberries.*

Right: *A small portion of my basket, tray, and bowl collection, which I use for fruit and crudité arrangements.*

yellow, and pure red apples looks very beautiful; in summer, the same tray can be loaded with an exotic parade of tropical fruits, decorated with only an orchid. Since many tropical fruits are mysterious and misshapen, I often cut several examples open to make the unfamiliar familiar to guests. Who would know without previous experience that a small brown fuzzy oval contains the luscious, sweet, lime-green kiwi fruit? Only exotic fruits, and larger native fruits, however, have to be cut. (If cut, an apple or a pear needs a brush of lemon juice to prevent its turning brown.) I will slice a pineapple horizontally, and arrange the rounds in overlapping concentric circles

Above: *Papayas, kiwis, and pomegranates intermingle with pineapple, blood oranges, mangos, and bananas, some sliced in half for display.*

Right: *A harvest of colorful Hudson Valley apples—Ida Reds, Macouns, Empires, Staymens, Winesaps, Mutsus, Tussetts, Romes, Northern Spys, Winter Bananas, Baldwins, and Cortlands.*

on a platter; or I might cut it vertically, hollow it out to within a half inch of its skin, cube the pulp, and pile this back in the newly created bowls. I slice cantaloupe thinly, and arrange the wedges decoratively on a bed of dill. Sometimes I add one blossom from the garden to the platter.

Cheese

TODAY THERE ARE SO many different cheeses available in specialty markets that one could spend years sampling a new one a day. In France alone, there is such variety that Charles de Gaulle once quipped, "How am I to be expected to govern a people that produces 370 different cheeses?"

Such a wealth can be alternately exhilarating and stupefying. In attempting to categorize cheese, the matter becomes more rather than less diffuse, for cheeses, at least the classic or fermented cheeses, are an individualistic lot, subject to the vagaries of animal, maker, and region. (I ignore the other two categories here—fresh cheese like ricotta and cream cheese, unless made into a crème or fromage blanc, which is not appropriate to a buffet or hors d'oeuvre table, and processed cheese, about which I defer to Clifton Fadiman: "The most I can say for it is that it is nonpoisonous; the worst, that it represents the triumph of the technology of science over conscience.") There are cow's milk cheeses, goat milk cheeses, and sheep milk cheeses; hard, semisoft, and soft-ripened cheeses, the last classified by their butterfat content or matière gras, 50 percent qualifying a double crème, 72 percent a triple crème, the elevation signifying richness. There are factory-made cheeses, and a few homemade or "farmhouse" cheeses. There are also special seasonal cheeses like Vacherin from Switzerland and Toma from Italy, that make short-lived annual appearances. And, as with other items deemed sophisticated, there are fads in cheeses, when fashionable food conversation suddenly pivots on the mention of "Explorateur" or "Mascarpone." In such circumstances, the most reliable course of action is tasting—at a cheese store and whenever the opportunity arises—and committing to memory the particular name and source of cheeses you like. From such field work, I have made a list of favorites that may serve as a base for exploration:

BRIE DE MEAUX— PERFECTLY RIPE	BRILLAT SAVARIN	REBLOCHON
	EXPLORATEUR	BANON
CHÈVRE—IN VARIOUS SHAPES AND SIZES	FROMAGE BLANC	GORGONZOLA
	ROQUEFORT	TOMA
	LOU PERALOU	ST. ANDRÉ
CAMEMBERT	LA BOUILLE	

As fabricants discovered long ago, the character of a cheese can be altered dramatically by the addition of certain elements—a coating of ashes or a wrapping of grape

A variety of imported cheeses are clustered around a great mound of fresh Normandy butter.

or oak leaves to a goat cheese, pepper or herbs to a Brie. Many of the popular commercial treatments of cheese can be duplicated, even improved upon, at home. A cylinder of Montrachet goat cheese, for example, can be marinated in a fine olive oil mixed with fresh rosemary. A Boursault can be rolled in cracked black or red peppercorns, or herbs. And a Fromage de Chèvre takes on an appealing tang when doused with cayenne pepper. Knowing that the French and Italians sometimes serve warm cheeses, I have also experimented successfully with oven-heating a Camembert or tiny rounds of goat cheese, just to the point when they begin to escape from their rind. A Fon-

tina, too, can be melted on a platter and served almost like a fondue.

For a cocktail table, I usually select three to six of these cheeses, depending on the size of the gathering, accompanied by whole-grain crackers or thin slices of homemade French bread. I avoid hard cheeses, which are difficult to cut in a crowd and dry out quickly, and cheeses with inedible rinds, for the accumulation of unsightly remains poses a problem for a hostess, and is more easily dealt with at a dinner party. I try to choose unusual, but not too pungent, varieties—a pepper Brie, a plain Brie, and an herb Brie, for example, or a Morbier, an Ex-

plorateur, and a goat cheese like St. Marcelene. I arrange them in a simple symmetry on a tray that I have covered with some decorative leaves—usually banana or lemon leaves—for protection and contrast.

On a buffet table, cheese invites a fruit accompaniment, for cheese brings out the sweet bite of grapes, pears, or figs, and the fruit reciprocates by emphasizing the flavor of the cheese, especially that of a Brie or a triple crème. Surrounding a whole cheese like a Brie with a wreath of grapes makes a very pleasing and tempting still life. I cut the grapes into manageable bunches with scissors. I save the wooden box that encases a Brie (or a Camembert or Coulommiers) and elevate the cheese on that and then mound the fruit around, thus preventing the grapes from tumbling into the cheese, or the cheese from oozing out of bounds.

Fresh figs suit a dry goat cheese like Bucheron. Unlike the heavy, overly sweet dried varieties, fresh figs have an interesting taste and an unusual texture, soft with a little crunch of seeds. Cutting figs into quarters or halves with a stainless steel knife will prevent discoloration. Then they too can be arranged in a border around a cheese.

With almost any cheese, a mound of strawberries, or a pretty bowl piled with pears and apples, completes the picture.

Opposite: *Half an Italian Fontina and two Toma cheeses make a spectacular display with quartered and whole fresh figs and rows of crackers.*

Left: *A big wheel of Brie, set on its box, is placed inside a copper tray and surrounded with small Bartlett pears, Bremer wafers, and bunches of seedless grapes.*

79

CHAPTER FOUR

The Omelette Party

*A*N *EGG IS PROBABLY ONE* of the most complete, versatile, and beautiful objects in itself in the whole world of cuisine.

Egg dishes have a kind of elegance, a freshness and allure, that sets them apart from any other kind of food. The omelette, that light union of several eggs deftly turned into a roll that may or may not enclose another ingredient or combination of ingredients, is special even within egg dishes. In France, early in this century, the delicate creations of a certain fortuitously named Mère Poularde drew attention to the dish. Gastronomes, it seems, would travel great distances to savor an omelette Poularde at her small auberge in Brittany. Then, in the

1930s, a Frenchwoman named Mme Romaine brought the omelette to New York. Her tiny downstairs restaurant-tearoom, which still serves 553 different kinds of omelettes, named for generals, writers, and historic places, has probably been responsible for thousands of introductions to the versatility of this dish. In the 1960s, after Rudolph Stannish began to market his special heavy-gauge aluminum omelette pans, cooks tried omelettes at home, and then for friends. Soon trend-setters were hiring caterers to mastermind large gala suppers serving omelettes made before one's eyes. Now, with the interest in lighter meals and with the popularity of the Sunday brunch, the omelette party enjoys a secure and

An outdoor omelette party is great fun for guests because they can choose a filling from among the variety on display and then watch the proceedings.

fashionable place in all home entertaining.

Despite all the talk of the art of the omelette, of light hands and heavy pans, omelettes are easy, and wonderfully suited to parties of almost any size. An omelette party is inexpensive; it is decorative, because the fare is in full view; it is interesting, because of the variety of fillings offered; it is festive—even a little flashy—because of the ongoing action; and it is convivial, for a guest is quite naturally flattered to participate in the selection and execution of his entree. And spontaneous though it looks, everything but the one-minute omelette operation can be done in advance. Thus, one even has time to indulge in some of the cosmetic pleasures of entertaining that are too often preempted by kitchen duty: to arrange flowers, roll napkins in an unusual way, or pull forgotten dishes out of the cupboard, for instance.

Omelette parties can be staged for almost any time of day—breakfast, brunch, lunch, late afternoon, dinner, midnight supper. To a certain degree, the time chosen determines the menu: a brunch, which in the country might take place outdoors in summer and autumn, is a combination meal, and so demands a more substantial offering than a midnight supper, which is an elegant snack. The season should also influence the fare: spring suggests an asparagus filling or a strawberry dessert; fall, ratatouille or apples, pears, and nuts as a filling.

The number of guests depends on your inclination, of course, the size of your house or apartment, and the number of people who will be making omelettes. One person reasonably adept at the operation can serve thirty people quite gracefully—approximately one a minute— making the duration of the actual serving half an hour. At the proper high temperature, an omelette pan works rapidly and systematically. An assistant, who can be a friend, teenager, or favorite baby-sitter, will ease the sit-

Eggs of all sizes, shapes, and hues from my Turkey Hill hens.

Master Omelette Recipe

There is no single technique for preparing light, fluffy, no-fail omelettes, but here is my method. However, if you are successful and more comfortable with another, there is no reason to change.

At large omelette parties I use either portable electric stoves (recommended for enclosed locations), propane gas burners, or small butane gas burners on tabletops to provide ample cooking and service space.

Clarified butter should be used in making omelettes as it tends to burn less easily than regular butter. It is simply melted butter skimmed of foam and strained, with any watery residue discarded.

MAKES ONE OMELETTE
1 tablespoon melted clarified butter
2 eggs, well beaten but not frothy
Salt and pepper to taste

Heat the omelette pan over high flame. Add clarified butter and heat until hot but not smoking.

Ladle eggs into pan.

Pull eggs away from sides of pan with a fork while moving pan constantly over the flame to prevent sticking.

Just before eggs are set, spoon ¼ to ⅓ cup filling into center of omelette.

Gently roll ⅓ of the omelette over the filling, tilting pan and using a fork.

Turn cooked omelette onto serving plate. Entire procedure should take less than one minute.

uation, or double the crowd capacity. (In New York and other major cities, for a reasonable fee it is also possible to hire professional omelette makers, who arrive with their own electric burners or propane stoves.)

The focus and fun of an omelette party is the act of making omelettes, so the chosen area of operation must be carefully conceived. It might be the kitchen, if you have an island stove, or a stove placed in a fluid space in which you can cook the omelettes, array the fillings, and serve without undue congestion. For most of my parties, I rent a two-burner tabletop unit and set it up on a table in the dining room, an entryway, or the living room. I plan five feet of table space to a cooking station, to allow for bowls of filling at each stove. In addition to the stove or electric burners, and a big table, the equipment necessary is quite simple:

AN IRON OR HEAVY ALUMINUM ALLOY OMELETTE
  PAN OR PANS

A SMALL PITCHER FOR CLARIFIED BUTTER

FORKS

EXTENSION CORDS, IF USING AN ELECTRIC UNIT

SERVING DISHES AND SPOONS FOR FILLINGS

A SMALL TRASH BASKET UNDER TABLE BY EACH
  STOVE FOR EGGSHELLS

A BOWL LARGE ENOUGH TO HOLD AND BEAT TWO
  DOZEN EGGS

A LADLE FOR DIPPING EGGS

POTHOLDERS FOR PAN HANDLES

PAPER TOWELS AND KOSHER SALT FOR CLEANING
  STICKY PANS

Your own dishes, possessions, and personality will determine the style and tone of the occasion. Some people can go to the cupboard and draw upon matched sets of the family Minton. Others will have a funky array of Depression glass and tinware. A collection of pottery bowls and baskets suggests a country party; crystal and silver, a more formal setting. Build upon what you have and like, and consider as possible containers for fillings and accompaniments:

BASKETS   TIN MOLDS
EARTHENWARE   MUSHROOM BASKETS
  BOWLS   LARGE SEASHELLS
ENAMEL DISHES

and as table coverings (washable in such an active situation), consider:

AN OLD QUILT   A RAG RUG
A LENGTH OF   A BED SHEET
  DAMASK OR CALICO   A NAUTICAL FLAG
AN OLD DRAPE   OR LENGTH OF
  OR BEDCOVER   SPINNAKER OR SAIL

The crucial issue of an omelette party of course is the making of the omelettes. A memorable omelette is often achieved by quite different methods from those advocated by professional chefs, and if you have an eccentric but successful formula, by all means use it, but do practice. If you are going to borrow a pair of novice hands for the event, teach them well before the party and ask them to rehearse at home.

Several years ago, during Christmas week, I was hired to cater a party for a thousand people to celebrate the publication of a new book. The setting was Cass Gilbert's palatial U.S. Custom House on Bowling Green in New York City, which at that moment was biding its time, majestic and vacant, until federal rehabilitation. In deliberating the choice of omelettes as the fare, I ran through the same checklist of virtues that any more reasonable homebound hostess might be drawn to: inexpensive, uncomplicated, suitable to advance preparation, easily transportable, highly visual. The mathematics of the party turned out to be amusing: we needed 3,000 eggs, 50 pounds of butter, 5 pounds of salmon caviar, 20 quarts of sour cream, 6 gallons of curried chicken, 12 pounds of cream cheese and 12 jars of ginger marmalade, 600 baby croissants and 600 baby brioches; we also needed 10 tables and 10 double burners, 8 bartenders, 10 servers, and 10 omelette chefs. It was entertainment by inflation. It was, more than any other event I can recall, theater.

I found a fledgling rock group, grateful for the exposure, to perform nonstop in the central rotunda, and for a small wood-paneled room in the wings, a woodwind quartet of young Juilliard students. I also found a local farmer who sold me an odd assortment of a hundred irregular Christmas trees, with birds' nests and pinecones still in their limbs. They made an inexpensive and very beautiful backdrop, and when the party was over, they all went home with someone. We filled the air with helium balloons, and as the coup de grace, we convinced a spirited lot of Fashion Institute of Technology students to dress themselves up in fairy costumes and position themselves around a fountain and in our erstwhile forest. One girl slept the duration of the party, from 8:00 P.M., until 1:00 A.M., curled up under a tree.

This production looked extravagant and expensive, but it wasn't, because the basic fare was eggs. Omelette parties of any size have both elegance and practicality. I have prepared each of the following menus many times for parties, so they are tried and true, but they are neither inflexible nor sacrosanct. Vary the fillings according to your own taste, budget, and availability of ingredients. Remember, too, that by the simple substitution of a batter for the beaten eggs, an omelette party can become a crêpe party. A stripe of velouté sauce or a tomato coulis added to the rolled crêpe completes the transformation. Crêpes and omelettes can also be happily combined, either produced simultaneously or sequentially, savory omelettes leading to a finale of sweet crêpes.

Tender asparagus tips peek out from the fold of this 3-egg omelette.

Sunday Omelette Brunch for Eight to Ten

*A*N *INTIMATE INFORMAL BRUNCH* transforms an ordinary Sunday into a special Sunday without sacrificing the nice, lazy, expansive quality of that day. By beginning the brunch early, around 11:00 A.M., the meal can extend naturally into a walk, or a tennis game, or a trip to a museum. By making dessert in advance, purchasing the croissants (if not home-baked) on an early morning walk, and assembling the omelette fillings—elegant but very easy—just before the called hour, you will have almost as much freedom as your guests to enjoy the event. The act of making omelettes can center on the kitchen table, where everyone can enjoy the operation at close range and have a hand in it.

This party is a good way to launch yourself into the medium of omelettes, to perfect the timing and coordination. With such firsthand experience, you will see how, with an additional working chef, or an investment of another ten minutes of cooking time, your small brunch might become a midnight supper for thirty.

MENU

Fresh Fruits   Brie and Parsley Omelettes
Asparagus Omelettes   Grated Gruyère and Bacon Omelettes
Croissants with Homemade Jams and Sweet Butter
Apricots Baked with Vanilla Sugar
Steamed Chocolate Pudding with Whipped Cream
Sugar Cookies
Bloody Marys, White Wine, Café au Lait

Omelette fillings of bacon and cheese (left) and Brie and herbs (right) are exquisitely simple and delicious.

Brie and Parsley Omelettes

For each omelette, remove the rind from 1 ounce ripe Brie, unless it is very fresh and tender. Roll the cheese in 1 tablespoon chopped fresh parsley. Fold the omelette over the cheese right before turning omelette onto serving plate.

Asparagus Omelettes
APPROXIMATELY 8 TO 10 OMELETTES

2 pounds fresh asparagus, thin stalks
4 tablespoons unsalted butter
   Salt and freshly ground pepper to taste

Cut asparagus tips into 3-inch lengths and steam over boiling water until crisp-tender, about 3 to 5 minutes. Toss asparagus tips in a sauté pan with the butter and season with salt and pepper.

Use 4 or 5 asparagus tips for each omelette.

Grated Gruyère and Bacon Omelettes
APPROXIMATELY 1 CUP FILLING FOR 4 TO 5 OMELETTES

1 pound good-quality sliced bacon, cut in 1-inch pieces
½ pound imported Swiss Gruyère cheese
   Salt and freshly ground black pepper

Cook bacon slowly in a skillet until it is brown and crisp. Remove from pan with a slotted spoon and drain on paper towel.

Grate Gruyère coarsely by hand or with the grating disk of a food processor. Mix cheese with bacon.

Season omelette with a bit of salt and pepper and place 3 to 4 table-spoons of cheese and bacon in each omelette before rolling onto plate.

Homemade Jams
SEE RECIPE, PAGE 133

Apricots Baked with Vanilla Sugar
SERVES 8

Make this dessert when apricots are in season, or substitute small ripe peaches.

2 tablespoons butter
8 fresh ripe apricots, cut in half with pits removed
¼ cup water
¼ cup vanilla sugar

GARNISH
   Cold yogurt, crème fraîche, or heavy cream

Preheat oven to 350°. Generously butter a baking dish just large enough to hold the apricots. Put the apricots in the dish, cut sides down. Add the water, sprinkle on the sugar, and dot with remaining butter.

Bake for 20 to 30 minutes until tender.

Serve warm with a spoonful of yogurt, crème fraîche, or a few tablespoons of heavy cream.

NOTE: To make vanilla sugar, store vanilla beans in a jar of sugar for several weeks.

Steamed Chocolate Pudding with Whipped Cream
10 TO 14 SERVINGS

This pudding has a light, cakelike texture and a rich chocolate-rum flavor. Served with a topping of whipped cream or crème Anglaise, a little goes a long way.

     Sugar
2½ cups light cream
1   whole vanilla bean
8   ounces semisweet chocolate
5   tablespoons butter
3   tablespoons flour
8   eggs, separated
¾   cup sugar
4   tablespoons dark rum

Butter a 2-quart pudding mold, including inside of the lid. Sprinkle mold with sugar and shake out excess.

Heat the cream with the vanilla bean. Add the chocolate and cook very slowly, stirring occasionally, until the chocolate is melted.

Melt the butter in a heavy sauce-pan. Add the flour and cook until blended. Do not brown! Stir in the cream-chocolate mixture, scraping the seeds from the vanilla bean into the mixture. Cook, stirring constantly, until thickened.

Beat the egg yolks with the ¾ cup sugar until thick and pale yellow. Gradually beat in the chocolate mixture, blending well. Add the rum.

Beat the egg whites until stiff. Fold ¼ of the whites into the chocolate to lighten the mixture. Then, very gently, fold in the remaining whites.

Pour the pudding into the mold. Cover and secure lid. Steam slowly on a rack in a covered kettle for 1½ hours. (Water should come halfway up the mold.)

Turn onto a heated platter right before serving. Serve with softly whipped cream or Crème Anglaise (page 257).

NOTE: The pudding can be made several hours in advance and left to sit in the hot-water bath.

Sugar Cookies
APPROXIMATELY FORTY
3-INCH COOKIES

4½ cups sifted flour
4 teaspoons baking powder
1 teaspoon salt
½ pound (2 sticks) unsalted butter
2 cups sugar
2 eggs
½ cup milk
½ teaspoon vanilla

Preheat oven to 375°. Butter baking sheets. Sift together dry ingredients.

Cream butter and sugar until fluffy. Add eggs and beat well. Add dry ingredients, 1 cup at a time, alternating with milk and vanilla, beating well after each addi-

Above: *Whimsically decorated sugar cookies in the shape of bows and hearts.*
Right: *Golden brown croissants.*

tion. Wrap and chill dough for at least 1 hour.

Divide dough into 4 pieces. Roll 1 piece at a time on a floured board and cut with large cookie cutters. Bake for 8 to 10 minutes.

Cool on racks.

NOTE: These cookies may be sprinkled with colored sugar or iced. See icing recipe (page 209).

Midnight Omelette Supper for Thirty

A LATE-NIGHT PARTY HAS A special elegance and drama. It might follow the performance of a play or concert; at holiday time, when late hours seem magical, or in summertime, when days are long and evenings warm and expansive, it can be an event on its own. There are a few particular considerations for nocturnal entertaining: be prompt serving supper, for social energy can wane with the hour. Invite guests for 10:00 P.M. (or directly following a performance) and start cooking omelettes at 11:00; serve undersized rolls, because they are lighter and daintier at night. Likewise, serve finger-size desserts to avoid the necessity of another plate.

Keep music going—rock, classical guitar, or flute concertos according to the mood of the party—for it is particularly important during late hours to provide a gracious background to fortify an event.

❧ MENU ❧

Cheese Tray with Fruits and Assorted Breads and Crackers
Creamed Spinach Omelettes   Swiss Cheese Omelettes
Red Caviar and Sour Cream Omelettes
Curried Chicken Omelettes   Creamed Leek Omelettes
Tiny Croissants and Brioches
Herb Butter   Homemade Jams
Lemon Curd Tartlets   Chocolate Victoria Tartlets
Chocolate Mousse   Alexis's Brown Sugar Chocolate Chip Cookies
Fresh Strawberries
Espresso, Decaffeinated Coffee, Teas

Creamed Spinach Omelettes

APPROXIMATELY 3 CUPS
FILLING FOR 9 TO 12
OMELETTES

3 pounds fresh spinach (or
  three 10-ounce packages
  frozen chopped spinach)
1 recipe Velouté Sauce (page
  92)
  Freshly ground nutmeg
  Salt and freshly ground
  black pepper
  Heavy cream (optional)

When using fresh spinach, wash the leaves thoroughly under cold running water. Steam until just tender, 5 minutes or less. Drain in a colander placed over a bowl.

When cool, press the leaves to remove excess liquid. Reserve ½ cup of the liquid for the sauce. Chop the spinach coarsely by hand. Frozen spinach need only be thawed, drained, and pressed in a colander to remove excess liquid. Save ½ cup of liquid.

Prepare the velouté sauce, substituting the spinach liquid for the chicken stock.

Stir the spinach into the sauce. Season to taste with salt, freshly ground black pepper, and freshly grated nutmeg.

Reheat in a heavy pan over low heat, stirring frequently to prevent scorching. If the mixture is too thick, thin with heavy cream (or milk or spinach liquid) a tablespoon at a time to reach desired consistency. As with creamed leek this mixture may be prepared a day or two in advance, covered and stored in the refrigerator.

VARIATIONS: Add shredded, sautéed scallions or thinly sliced sautéed mushrooms to spinach mixture.

Swiss Cheese Omelettes

APPROXIMATELY 4 CUPS
FILLING FOR 12 TO 16
OMELETTES

Use only best-quality, authentic imported Swiss Emmenthaler, Gruyère, or Appenzeller cheese. Grate 2 pounds of cheese coarsely by hand or with the grating disk of a food processor. Place 3 to 4 tablespoons of cheese in each omelette.

Red Caviar and Sour Cream Omelettes

APPROXIMATELY 4 CUPS
FILLING FOR 12 TO 16
OMELETTES

2 pints sour cream
1 7-ounce tin fresh salmon roe
  caviar

Fill a shallow bowl with the sour cream. Make a well in the center and fill with the caviar.

To serve, scoop a bit of caviar and about 4 tablespoons sour cream into each omelette.

Mary Emmerling's New York kitchen inspired me to create an omelette party with a country feeling—plaid cloths, yelloware bowls, and old baskets set the stage.

Curried Chicken Omelettes

APPROXIMATELY 4 CUPS
FILLING FOR 12 TO 16
OMELETTES

6 large chicken breast halves
  or 3 whole breasts
1 medium onion, sliced thin
6 parsley stems
1 bay leaf
  Juice of 1 lemon or ½ cup
  white wine
  Salt and freshly ground
  black pepper

CURRY CREAM SAUCE
¼ pound (1 stick) unsalted
  butter
4 tablespoons flour
2 tablespoons curry powder
  (more or less according to
  taste)
2 cups heavy cream, heated
  Salt and pepper

Preheat the oven to 375°.

Butter a shallow roasting pan in
which breasts will fit in one layer.
Scatter the onion rings and herbs on
the bottom. Put breasts skin side
up in the pan and sprinkle with
lemon juice and salt and pepper.
Roast chicken 30 to 40 minutes, or
until just done. Cool. Reserve pan
juices.

Remove skin and bone from
breasts. Cut or tear meat with your
fingers into bite-size pieces.

To make the sauce, melt the butter
in a heavy pan. Add the flour and
curry powder, mixing well. Cook
slowly 4 to 5 minutes. Cool slightly before whisking in the hot cream
and pan juices. Simmer the sauce
15 to 20 minutes, stirring frequently. Season to taste with salt
and pepper. Add chicken to the
sauce, mixing thoroughly.

VARIATIONS: Add ½ cup each
sautéed onion, apple chunks, currants or golden raisins, plumped in
water, to the mixture.

Creamed Leek Omelettes

APPROXIMATELY 4 CUPS
FILLING FOR 12 TO 16
OMELETTES

*This mixture may be prepared a day
or two in advance, covered, and
stored in the refrigerator.*

12 leeks (1½-inch diameter)
¼ pound (1 stick) unsalted
  butter
  Salt and freshly ground
  pepper

VELOUTÉ SAUCE
4 tablespoons (½ stick)
  unsalted butter
3 tablespoons flour
½ cup milk
½ cup chicken stock
  Salt, freshly ground white
  pepper, nutmeg
  Heavy cream (optional)

Split the leeks lengthwise and wash
carefully under cold running water
to remove all traces of grit. Trim
away the tough dark green upper
leaves. Slice crosswise into thin
pieces. Cook the leeks slowly in
butter in a heavy pan until tender,
about 30 minutes. Season to taste
with salt and pepper.

To make sauce, melt butter in a
heavy pan, add flour, and cook over
low heat, stirring with a wooden
spoon, for 3 minutes. Cool slightly. Heat milk and stock together,
whisk into flour and butter mixture, and cook over low heat until
it thickens. Allow to cook slowly,
stirring frequently, 15 to 20 minutes more, to cook the flour. Season
to taste with salt and pepper and a
pinch of freshly ground nutmeg.
Add a little cream if desired.

Stir leeks and any pan juices into
the sauce. Adjust seasoning. Reheat (in a heavy pan) over low heat,
stirring frequently to prevent
scorching. If the mixture is too

thick, add heavy cream (or milk or
stock) a tablespoon at a time to
reach desired consistency.

Herb Butter

1 POUND

*This herb-flavored butter always
gets compliments. It has many uses:
packed into a cabbage "bowl" and
decorated with flowers for a buffet,
or melted in loaves of hot crispy
bread.*

1 pound (4 sticks) unsalted
  butter, at room temperature
4 tablespoons finely chopped
  parsley
2 tablespoons finely chopped
  dill, chervil, or tarragon

Chop herbs in a food processor, add
soft butter, and mix together. Pack
into butter molds or crocks. Refrigerate up to 2 days. To keep longer,
freeze. Bring to room temperature
before using.

Lemon Curd Tartlets

TWELVE 3-INCH TARTLETS

1 recipe Perfect Plain Tart
  and Tartlet Crust (page 236)

FILLING
2 cups sugar
12 egg yolks, slightly beaten
  and strained
1 cup lemon juice
½ pound (2 sticks) unsalted
  butter
2 tablespoons grated lemon
  peel

  Lemon peel, crystallized
  violets, fresh raspberries
  (optional)

Make and bake the pastry shells,
following master recipe.

To make the filling, combine sugar
and egg yolks in medium-size
saucepan; stir in lemon juice gradually. Cook over low heat, stirring
constantly, until mixture coats
back of spoon and registers 168° on
candy thermometer; do not boil.
Remove from heat; whisk until
slightly cooled. Stir in butter and
grated lemon peel. Cool completely.

Fill pastry shells with lemon curd.
Garnish with lemon peel and violets or fresh raspberries.

Homemade Jams
SEE RECIPE, PAGE 133

Chocolate Mousse
2 QUARTS

12 ounces real chocolate chips
¼ cup water
5 egg yolks, slightly beaten

7 egg whites
Pinch salt

Melt chocolate chips and water in a stainless steel bowl in a 300° oven, or over simmering water. When melted, remove from heat and beat until smooth. Add the egg yolks and stir until smooth. Cool mixture 3 minutes.

Whip the egg whites with salt until almost dry. Fold into chocolate mixture.

Pour into a serving bowl or into individual serving glasses. Refrigerate for several hours before serving.

Chocolate Victoria Tartlets
12 TARTLETS

1 recipe Perfect Plain Tart and Tartlet Crust (page 236)

CHOCOLATE FILLING
8 ounces semisweet chocolate
⅓ cup sugar
2 cups whipping cream

Whipped cream and chocolate curls or candied lilacs (optional)

Make and bake tartlet shells, following master recipe.

To make filling, melt chocolate and sugar in a heavy saucepan, over low heat, stirring constantly until smooth. Stir in cream. Stir over heat until the mixture begins to thicken, 8 to 10 minutes. Cool.

Fill pastry shells with chocolate mixture. Refrigerate. Decorate with a dollop of whipped cream and chocolate curls or candied lilacs.

Alexis's Brown Sugar Chocolate Chip Cookies
THIRTY 4-INCH COOKIES

1 pound (4 sticks) unsalted butter
3 cups brown sugar
1 cup granulated sugar
4 eggs
2 teaspoons vanilla
3½ cups all-purpose flour
1½ teaspoons salt
2 teaspoons baking soda
1½ cups real chocolate chips

Preheat oven to 375°.

Cream butter until smooth; add sugars. Beat in eggs and vanilla.

Sift flour, salt, and baking soda and beat into above mixture. Add chocolate chips. Drop 2 to 3 tablespoons of batter onto greased baking sheet, 2 inches apart. Bake 8 minutes.

Remove from pans and cool on racks.

NOTE: If cookies become hard while still on the baking sheet, put sheet back into the oven for a few seconds to soften them for easy removal.

Alexis's chocolate chip cookies, lemon curd tartlets, chocolate mousse, and fresh strawberries displayed on the dessert rack.

Summer Omelette Brunch Outdoors for Sixty

A GENEROUS PATIO, AN expanse of lawn, or a formal garden invites a summer brunch. However, a porch, an awning, or the absolute assurance that the weather will be perfect is also prerequisite. Although a good client of mine has never taken these precautions and has been graced with beautiful sun for 20 years, I would never recommend that anyone else follow her example, unless their house could comfortably accommodate all the guests inside in an emergency. Set up a 16-foot buffet table, or a series of smaller tables, and, opposite, an 8-foot bar to serve drinks, perhaps an assortment of strawberry daiquiris, piña coladas, bloody Marys, and chilled wines. Desserts can be served, after omelettes, from the same buffet table, and coffee and tea from a moving tray or cart.

Choose colorful linens and tablecloths for out-of-doors. A dark green tablecloth with crisp white linens and a centerpiece of fresh strawberries provide a simple contrast to a garden of colorful flowers; a richer design scheme utilizing red and white polka dot linens, for instance, can be charming against a stand of plainer shrubs. The point is not to compete with, but to complement, nature. Plan for plenty of seating and remember that cushions, quilts and coverlets, and even straw mats can serve as well as tables and chairs. And if you have musical young friends, or access to a music school like Juilliard, consider adding a strolling guitarist or flutist to the scene.

Call the party for noon. Serve hors d'oeuvres until all the guests arrive, then begin cooking the omelettes. Make sure you have plenty of extension cords, an extra stove for emergencies (outdoors, you cannot resort to your kitchen), and screens to protect the omelette stoves if it is a breezy day. Help is imperative for this large a party. Two bartenders are required for fancy drinks, two omelette makers to serve sixty people, and one or two people to serve hors d'oeuvres and remove plates.

❧ MENU ❧

Almond-Stuffed Dates with Bacon

Shrimp Vinaigrette Wrapped with Prosciutto

Melon Wedges and Pineapple Slices

Glazed Virginia Country Ham

Smoked Salmon   Ratatouille Omelettes

Swiss Cheese Omelettes   Creamed Spinach Omelettes

Mushroom-Shallot with Madeira Omelettes

Red Caviar and Sour Cream Omelettes   Fines Herbes Omelettes

Vegetables in Mustard Vinaigrette

Butter Croissants, Chocolate Croissants, Sables

Iced Lemon Mousse   Pecan Sticky Buns

Open Bar, White Wine

Above: *Spikey dahlia flowers contrast with the delicate pink of smoked-salmon hors d'oeuvres.*

Left: *Vegetables arranged on terra-cotta platters are coated with an herb-flavored vinaigrette.*

95

Almond-Stuffed Dates with Bacon
DOUBLE RECIPE, PAGE 46

Shrimp Vinaigrette Wrapped with Prosciutto
DOUBLE VARIATION,
PAGE 42

Glazed Virginia Country Ham
SERVES 60 OR MORE

1   12- to 16-pound Smithfield-type ham
1   pound dark brown sugar
½   cup dry sherry

Soak ham for 10 to 12 hours in cold water to cover. Rinse ham and scrub rind thoroughly.

Put ham in a pot (a large fish poacher will work), skin side down. Cover with cold water. Bring to a boil, lower heat, and slowly simmer for 20 minutes per pound of ham.

Remove ham from water. Using a sharp knife, remove the tough outer skin, leaving a layer of fat around the ham. Score the surface of the ham with a sharp knife to make a decorative pattern.

Mix the sugar and sherry to form a thick glaze. Spoon the glaze over the ham. Bake in preheated 350° oven for 1 to 2 hours, or until the glaze is golden and crisp.

96

To serve, cut into thin slices. Ham may be served warm or at room temperature.

Smoked Salmon
FOR 60 GUESTS

Thinly sliced, garnished with fresh dill, and served on buttered bread rounds, smoked salmon will disappear quickly from the buffet table.

6½   to 7 pounds smoked salmon, sliced
1   pound Herb Butter (page 92)
    Freshly ground pepper
4   1-pound loaves of bread, thinly sliced

GARNISH
    Sprigs of fresh dill

VARIATION: Serve a whole side of salmon on a large board surrounded with slices of dark bread, bowls of softened herb butter, capers, cut lemons, and freshly ground pepper. Some shops will slice the side and reassemble it for you.

Ratatouille Omelettes
APPROXIMATELY 4
QUARTS FILLING FOR 48
TO 64 OMELETTES

Because ratatouille makes not only a wonderful warm filling for omelettes but also an excellent cold hors d'oeuvre or salad, it is a good idea to have ample amounts on hand.

6   medium yellow onions
8   to 10 small seedless Italian or Japanese eggplants or 6 large eggplants, unpeeled
6   large firm peppers (red, yellow, green)
6   to 8 small zucchini (1½ inches in diameter)
2   pounds tomatoes (5 to 6)
4   to 5 cloves garlic
1   small bay leaf
1   cup olive oil
¼   cup chopped fresh basil or 1 tablespoon dried basil
¼   cup chopped fresh parsley
1   tablespoon chopped fresh thyme or 1 teaspoon dried thyme
1   tablespoon coarse salt
    Freshly ground black pepper

Prepare the vegetables—peel and slice the onions; slice the small eggplants in ½-inch disks; cut the large ones into ¾-inch cubes; seed the peppers and cut into strips; cut the zucchini into ¼-inch disks; peel and chop the tomatoes, peel and crush the garlic.

Put the eggplant and zucchini in separate colanders. Sprinkle with coarse salt and toss. Leave to drain for 1 hour. Rinse and spread on towels to dry.

In a frying pan, sauté the onions in 3 to 4 tablespoons of hot olive oil. Toss over moderate to high heat for 10 minutes. Remove from the pan with a slotted spoon and put into a separate bowl. Repeat the process with the eggplant, peppers and zucchini, adding more oil when necessary.

Lower the heat, add a little more oil, and cook the tomatoes and garlic with the bay leaf for 10 minutes. Layer the vegetables in a heavy pan. Simmer uncovered until vegetables are just tender (30 to 40 minutes). If ratatouille is too soupy, drain the vegetables and cook down the

juices by half or more, or until syrupy.

Stir in the herbs and season to taste with salt and pepper.

Swiss Cheese Omelettes
DOUBLE RECIPE, PAGE 91

Creamed Spinach Omelettes
DOUBLE RECIPE, PAGE 91

A magenta-colored radicchio decorates a bowl of sour cream and salmon-roe caviar.

Mushroom-Shallot with Madeira Omelettes

APPROXIMATELY 6 CUPS FILLING FOR 24 TO 30 OMELETTES

¾ cup minced peeled shallots
½ pounds (2 sticks) unsalted butter
6 pounds mushrooms, washed or wiped clean, sliced very thin
3 to 4 tablespoons Madeira
½ cup finely chopped parsley

Salt, freshly ground black pepper, freshly grated nutmeg
Lemon juice

Using a large skillet, simmer the shallots in 4 tablespoons of butter until translucent. Set aside in a bowl.

In the same pan, melt 4 more tablespoons of butter over moderately high heat. When it begins to foam, add a layer of mushrooms and a few drops of lemon juice and sauté quickly. Remove from pan and put in a colander over a bowl. Add more butter to the pan and contin-ue to sauté batches of mushrooms until they are all done.

Return the accumulated mushroom juice to the pan, add Madeira, and reduce by ½ quickly over high heat. Mix in shallots, mushrooms, parsley, salt, pepper, and nutmeg. Toss over heat to combine flavors. Adjust flavor with salt, pepper, and lemon juice.

Red Caviar and Sour Cream Omelettes

DOUBLE RECIPE, PAGE 91

Fines Herbes Omelettes

APPROXIMATELY 32 OMELETTES

⅔ cup fresh chives cut crosswise in thin slices
⅔ cup fresh chopped parsley (or ⅓ cup parsley and ⅓ cup fresh chopped chervil)
⅔ cup fresh chopped tarragon

Mix herbs together; keep covered and chilled until ready to use.

Use 1 tablespoon per omelette.

Vegetables in Mustard Vinaigrette

3 heads cauliflowers, cut into flowerets
3 heads broccoli, cut into flowerets
4 pounds asparagus
3 pounds string beans
1 pound snow peas
3 pounds carrots, peeled and cut in quarter turns

MUSTARD VINAIGRETTE
1 cup tarragon vinegar or Japanese rice vinegar
1 cup Dijon mustard
3 cups olive oil (for a lighter dressing, use half vegetable oil)
   Salt to taste
   Freshly ground pepper
3 shallots, finely minced
   Chopped herbs: parsley, tarragon, chervil, dill (optional)

Blanche and chill the vegetables.

To make the mustard vinaigrette, whisk the vinegar and mustard together. Add the oil bit by bit, whisking vigorously. Season with salt, pepper, shallots, and herbs. Whisk before pouring over vegetables.

NOTE: Vinaigrette may be made in advance. Store in the refrigerator, but do not add the shallots and herbs until ready to use. If it solidifies, let it stand at room temperature until it can be whisked into a creamy dressing.

Sables

110 1¼-INCH COOKIES OR
50 2-INCH COOKIES

This rich, buttery dough is made in the food processor. It must be well chilled before it can be rolled. Glazed with egg and sprinkled with granulated sugar, these are the most delicate melt-in-your-mouth cookies! I often use this recipe to make round cookies with fluted edges, called sables in France. Omit the sprinkling of sugar if you want to be authentic, or, if you wish to be whimsical, sprinkle the cookies with colored crystal sugar.

12 tablespoons (1½ sticks) unsalted butter
⅔ cup sugar
2 egg yolks
2 cups flour
1 egg yolk beaten with 1 teaspoon water

Process the butter and sugar until creamy. Add the 2 egg yolks and mix for 30 seconds. Add half the flour and process until smooth. Add remaining flour and process until blended. Wrap dough in plastic wrap and chill until very cold.

Keep dough in the refrigerator until ready to use, and then roll only a third at a time on a very well-floured board. Roll about ⅛ inch thick. Cut into desired shapes with cookie cutters, or a 2-inch biscuit cutter, and transfer immediately onto a buttered baking sheet. Chill cut cookies until you have completed cutting all the dough.

Preheat oven 350°. Brush the top of each cookie with yolk-and-water glaze; sprinkle lightly with sugar. Bake 8 to 10 minutes, until cookies are pale golden. Remove to rack and cool.

Iced Lemon Mousse

4 QUARTS

2 packages unflavored gelatin
2 tablespoons water
1 cup lemon juice
2 cups sugar
   Grated rind of 2 lemons
14 egg whites
2 cups heavy cream

GARNISH
   6 paper-thin lemon slices and 6 mint leaves, or ½ cup heavy cream, whipped, and candied lilacs

Soften gelatin in water in small saucepan. Add lemon juice and sugar. Stir over low flame until gelatin is thoroughly dissolved. Add lemon rind and chill to syrup consistency. Gelatin mixture must be cool before being added to egg whites.

Beat egg whites until stiff. Beat in lemon-gelatin mixture. Whip cream until thick; fold into lemon-egg white mixture. Make sure all elements are thoroughly mixed, but take care not to deflate whites and cream.

Pour mixture into a 4-quart bowl and chill for 4 hours. Decorate with lemon slices and mint leaves, or with dollops of whipped cream and candied lilacs.

Pecan Sticky Buns

APPROXIMATELY 48
MINIATURE ROLLS

1 ounce fresh cake yeast, or 2 packages dry yeast
¼ cup sugar
½ teaspoon salt
¼ cup milk
½ cup sour cream
1 teaspoon lemon juice
   Grated rind of 1 lemon
½ teaspoon vanilla extract
2 egg yolks
3 cups flour
1 cup (2 sticks) unsalted butter, room temperature

FILLING
1 teaspoon cinnamon
¾ cup currants, plumped in 3 tablespoons brandy
½ cup light brown sugar
½ cup unsalted butter, melted
¾ cup light brown sugar
½ cup honey
¾ cup broken pecans

Cream the yeast, sugar, and salt until syrupy. (If you are using dry yeast, add 1 tablespoon of the milk to cream ingredients.) Add the milk, sour cream, lemon juice and rind, and vanilla and mix until smooth. Add the egg yolks and half the flour, blending well. Beat the softened butter into the dough and add the remaining flour. Turn onto floured board and knead until smooth and elastic, about 10 minutes. Form into a ball, place in a buttered bowl, and let rise, covered, in the refrigerator at least 4 hours.

Preheat oven to 350°.

To form sticky buns, turn the dough out onto a floured board and knead until smooth. Roll out into a long rectangle 4 inches wide and ⅛ inch thick. Spread cinnamon, currants, and ½ cup light brown sugar evenly over rectangle. Roll lengthwise into a tight cylinder and cut into ¾-inch thick slices.

Prepare miniature muffin tins by brushing each with melted butter. Combine brown sugar and honey and place a teaspoon of the mixture into each tin. Add a few nuts and cover with the cut slices of pastry. Brush tops with remaining melted butter and bake until puffed and golden brown, about 15 to 20 minutes.

Turn sticky buns onto cookie sheets immediately and cool completely before serving.

Opposite: *Miniature pecan sticky buns, crowded on a basket tray, are very popular at any party.*

CHAPTER FIVE

The Kitchen Party

*T*HE KITCHEN IS BECOMING, again, the hub of the house. Curiously, the success of technological advances like the food processor has attested to a greater rather than a lesser interest in cooking. These days there is rarely a new kitchen designed that isn't spacious and livable, that doesn't incorporate an island, a seating area, couches, a wood-burning stove, or a fireplace into its design. The warm social kitchen is in, and its equipment becomes more beautiful each day.

In the past, meals appeared as if by remote control from the servants' kitchen. Now what was once hidden is

With its large cooking top, warming ovens, and shelves, an old enamel range is the perfect place from which to serve a complete winter soup supper.

flaunted. Some cooks welcome any sort of company at any point in their preparations; they like to socialize while their hands keep busy, and they know that to see the raw ingredients of a meal, to witness the slicing, chopping, stirring, can be almost as intriguing as being on the inside of a magician's act. Others would choose a safer scene, in which the chances for error or mess are minimal. The following kitchen parties fall into the latter category, for they are either quick-cooking, like the tempura, or almost totally prepared, like the soup party.

If you have a kitchen with seating, some elbow room, and style (*any* style—High Tech or Americana,

1930s familial or bungalow quaint), a kitchen party can provide an easy and entertaining alternative to a more formal meal. The kitchen atmosphere itself breeds an easy conviviality. It lends itself to flexible numbers, for one can always pull up another chair (I don't give precise quantities in the following recipes for just that reason). Use your space thoughtfully, though, plotting out seating possibilities, setting up a bar, focusing on a few points of interest like a display of utensils or ingredients, a bowl of fresh fruit or a vase of herbs. And relax, for the hostess is master of ceremonies here. Her place is not in the wings, but center stage.

A Kitchen Salad Party for Thirty

A MEAL COMPOSED ENTIRELY OF cold salads quite naturally evokes summertime, when appetites are light, living is easy, and vegetables are in full bloom. It suggests a leisurely gathering—on a terrace, lawn, beach, or yacht—possibly a joint effort between friends. It could as easily be set indoors, in the family kitchen.

The challenge of assembling a riot of different salads is to make each with a distinctive taste and texture. Otherwise, however beautiful, such a meal would be boring. Here I have sought a balance between vinaigrette and creamy dressings, and relied on different herbs and fruits to impart singular tastes: basil for tomatoes; tarragon for broccoli; dill for cucumbers; raspberry vinegar for beets; raisins for grated carrots. Homemade breads and butters are a natural complement to this assembly, and rich desserts an appropriate finale.

Each one of these salads is so beautiful in itself that it must be presented confidently and simply. That way, the whole spectacle becomes one of glorious nature only a few steps removed from the garden. Fill a platter almost to overflowing with the beets, garnished with leaves of spinach; another with the carrots, bordered with red endive. (Additions of sprigs of herbs or a single flower provide a suggestion of flavor, or a small counterpoint of color or shape.) The perfect receptacle for salad is a large oval platter—white or glass—with sides deep enough to prevent spills but shallow enough to allow for a three-dimensional display. As a table covering, I like Chinese grass mats, which are natural, neutral colored, and sweetly scented.

Opposite: *Crisp heads of lettuce just picked from the garden.*

Right: *Cold beet salad.*

❧ MENU ❧

Carrot Salad   Salade Niçoise
Green Beans with Gruyère and Mushrooms
Broccoli and Red Pepper Salad
Cucumber Salad with Crème Fraîche Dressing
Potato Salad Vinaigrette   Cold Beet Salad
Marinated Mushrooms with Red Peppers
Pink Lentils Vinaigrette
Carrot Bread   Zucchini Bread
Homemade French Baguettes   Herb Butter
Apple Tart Normande   Iced Brownies
Wine

Carrot Salad
1½ QUARTS

½ cup raisins
¼ cup cider vinegar
2 pounds carrots, peeled and grated
¾ cup light olive oil (or mixture of vegetable oil and olive)
Salt and pepper
Dash of cinnamon or nutmeg (optional)
Finely chopped parsley

Soak the raisins in the vinegar for 30 minutes. Drain, reserve vinegar. Mix raisins with the carrots.

Add the vinegar to the oil, season with salt and pepper, add cinnamon or nutmeg for additional flavor, and mix with the carrots and raisins. Sprinkle with parsley.

NOTE: It is best to grate the carrots by hand on a coarse grater, but the job can be done quickly, and almost as effectively, in the food processor.

Salade Niçoise
12 SERVINGS

Salade Niçoise is the best known of "salades composées." Traditionally it is an assembly of cold green beans, tuna, olives, sliced new potatoes, hard-boiled eggs, tomatoes, and anchovies. Salade Niçoise makes a refreshing main course for a hot summer evening. Accompanied by crispy French bread, an exceptional cheese, chilled white wine, and a fresh fruit compote, this "meal in minutes" will delight all.

FRENCH VINAIGRETTE DRESSING
1 cup olive oil
2 tablespoons lemon juice

4 tablespoons wine vinegar
2 tablespoons Dijon mustard
1 clove garlic, finely minced
Salt and freshly ground pepper to taste
1 tablespoon each chopped fresh basil, tarragon, and oregano

SALAD
2 large heads of Boston or Bibb lettuce, washed, leaves left whole
8 new potatoes, steamed until tender, peeled and sliced and tossed with 1 tablespoon minced scallion, 3 tablespoons dry vermouth, salt and pepper to taste, and chopped fresh oregano
½ pound fresh green beans, blanched in boiling salted water 3 to 5 minutes, refreshed in ice water, dried and tossed with tarragon and vinaigrette
2 7-ounce cans Italian tuna, drained and flaked
3 tablespoons tiny capers
½ cup Niçoise olives (available at specialty stores)
1 2-ounce tin rolled anchovies
3 hard-boiled eggs, peeled and halved
4 ripe tomatoes, quartered, or 12 cherry tomatoes, halved, tossed with vinaigrette and basil

Combine vinaigrette ingredients and toss lettuce leaves with 2 tablespoons of the dressing. Arrange lettuce leaves on a deep round platter.

Arrange the potato slices in an outside ring on the lettuce.

Make a concentric circle of the green beans.

Put the flaked tuna in a mound in the center. Sprinkle the capers and olives around it.

Put the rolled anchovy fillets on top of the halved eggs and place around the tuna.

Dot the whole salad with tomato quarters or cherry tomatoes.

Spoon the remaining dressing over the whole salad and serve at once.

Green Beans with Gruyère and Mushrooms
SERVES 16

3 pounds tender young green beans

VINAIGRETTE
¾ cup light olive oil
¼ cup Japanese vinegar or sherry wine vinegar
4 tablespoons Dijon mustard
Chopped Italian parsley
Salt and freshly ground pepper to taste
½ pound Gruyère, coarsely grated
½ pound white mushrooms, trimmed and sliced thinly

Blanch and chill the beans.

Mix the vinaigrette, whisking or shaking it until creamy. Toss the beans with the vinaigrette until completely coated. Toss in the Gruyère and mushrooms.

Broccoli and Red Pepper Salad
3 QUARTS

4 bunches fresh broccoli
6 red (sweet) peppers
1 small bunch fresh tarragon or basil
1 pint sour cream
¼ cup Dijon mustard
½ cup tarragon vinegar
1¼ cups olive oil
Salt and pepper

Wash broccoli. Cut into small flowerets. Remove seeds from the red peppers and slice into slivers. Wash and mince the herb.

Blanch the broccoli in rapidly boil-

ing water until tender (4 to 5 minutes). Plunge into iced water to cool, and then drain well.

Combine the sour cream, mustard, vinegar, oil, herb, and salt and pepper. Pour over the broccoli and red pepper slivers and toss well.

Potato Salad Vinaigrette
6 CUPS

2 pounds new red potatoes
4 tablespoons dry white wine

VINAIGRETTE
2 tablespoons wine vinegar
1 teaspoon Dijon mustard
6 tablespoons olive oil
Salt and pepper
2 tablespoons finely minced green onion
3 tablespoons chopped dill

Boil the potatoes carefully so that they do not split and crumble. Cool slightly and cut in quarters. *Do not peel.* Pour the wine over the potatoes and toss gently.

Mix the vinaigrette, pour over the potatoes, and season. Serve while still warm, or chill.

Cucumber Salad with Crème Fraîche Dressing
1½ QUARTS

CRÈME FRAÎCHE (2 CUPS):
2 tablespoons buttermilk or sour cream
2 cups heavy cream

6 long cucumbers (seedless; English variety is best)
1 teaspoon coarse salt
¼ to ½ cup Japanese rice vinegar
Salt and white pepper
1 teaspoon sugar
1 bunch fresh dill, finely chopped

To make crème fraîche, add butter-milk or sour cream to heavy cream. Mix and let sit at room temperature 6 to 8 hours. Cover and refrigerate at least 24 hours before using.

Wash and slice the cucumbers ⅛ inch thick. Salt the cucumbers and let stand in a colander for 30 min-utes to drain. Rinse off the salt and pat dry with paper towels.

Add vinegar to crème fraîche and thin to desired consistency. Add salt and pepper and sugar. Mix into the cucumbers and blend well. Add the dill.

N O T E : Although crème fraîche can now be purchased in some gourmet shops, it is very easy to make at home. It is wonderful in salad dressings and as a topping for fruits and berries. It will keep in the re-frigerator for several weeks.

Cold Beet Salad
2 QUARTS

14 medium beets, unpeeled
6 tablespoons raspberry
    vinegar
1 cup olive oil
    Salt and pepper to taste

Preheat oven to 350°. Cut off all but 1 inch of the beet tops. Wrap the beets in a large piece of alumi-num foil and bake in the oven for 1 hour, or until tender. Cool and slip off the skins. Slice into thin rounds.

Make a vinaigrette of the vinegar, oil, and salt and pepper. Toss sliced beets with the vinaigrette and marinate at room temperature for at least 1 hour before serving. Top with chopped mint.

Clockwise from top left: *cucumber salad, cold beet salad, green beans with Gruyère and mushrooms, marinated mushrooms and red peppers, potato salad vinaigrette, carrot salad.*

Marinated Mushrooms with Red Peppers

SERVES 16

For this salad choose very fresh, white mushrooms of equal size. Rub off any soil with a damp paper towel.

MARINADE

- 1 cup light olive oil
- ¾ cup red wine vinegar
- ½ cup finely chopped onions (preferably red)
- ⅓ cup chopped parsley
- 2 cloves garlic, peeled and sliced
- 1 teaspoon sugar
  Salt and pepper to taste
- 2 pounds medium white mushrooms, stems cut off under caps
- ½ cup raw red pepper strips

Mix marinade ingredients and pour over cleaned mushroom caps. Marinate at least 2 hours.

Before serving, remove garlic slices and add pepper strips.

Pink Lentils Vinaigrette

SERVES 8

Lentils are best known as hearty winter fare, but they are delicious in summer salads. I prefer pink lentils, which are available in Indian shops.

- 1 pound pink lentils
- 2 tablespoons red wine vinegar
- 1 cup or more very good olive oil
- 1 cup finely minced shallots or very thinly sliced red onion
  Coarse salt and pepper to taste

Soak the lentils for an hour or two

in cold water. Drain and cook in fresh water until tender (30 to 45 minutes). Be careful not to overcook or they will become mushy.

Drain, cool, and mix with vinegar and plenty of olive oil. Add the shallots and season with salt and pepper. Chill before serving.

Herb Butter

SEE RECIPE, PAGE 92

Carrot Bread

SEE RECIPE, PAGE 60

Zucchini Bread

SEE RECIPE, PAGE 298

Apple Tart Normande

ONE 10-INCH TART

- 1 recipe Perfect Plain Tart and Tartlet Crust (page 236) or Perfect Sweet Tart and Tartlet Crust (page 237)
- 1½ pounds tart apples, peeled and cored
- ⅓ cup granulated sugar
- ½ teaspoon cinnamon

CUSTARD

- 1 egg
- ⅓ cup granulated sugar
- ¼ cup flour
- ¾ cup whipping cream
- 4 tablespoons Calvados or cognac
  Confectioners' sugar

Preheat oven to 375°. Prepare the pastry and line the tart pan according to master recipe, baking it for only 12 minutes.

Slice the apples into ⅛-inch lengthwise slices. Mix with the

sugar and cinnamon and arrange in concentric circles in the tart crust. Bake for 20 minutes at 375°, or until apples begin to color. Cool while preparing the custard.

Beat the egg and sugar until thick and pale yellow. Add the flour and beat until smooth. Add the cream and the Calvados and beat until smooth.

Pour mixture over the apples and return tart to the oven. After 10 minutes sprinkle top with confectioners' sugar. Continue to bake for 15 to 20 minutes, until custard is set and top is browned. Serve warm.

Iced Brownies

(16 BROWNIES)

- ½ cup (1 stick) butter
- 2 squares unsweetened chocolate
- 1 cup sugar
- 1 cup chopped pecans
- ½ cup flour
- 1 teaspoon baking powder
- 1 teaspoon vanilla
- 2 eggs

Preheat oven to 350°. Butter an 8-inch square glass pan.

Melt the butter and chocolate in the top of a double boiler or in a 300° oven. Remove from heat and stir well. Add all the ingredients except the eggs and stir thoroughly. Add the eggs and mix again.

Pour into buttered pan and bake 30 to 45 minutes, or until a toothpick comes out clean; do *not* overcook. They should still be moist and chewy in the middle. Cool thoroughly before cutting into 2-inch squares and removing from the pan.

NOTE: Before cutting, ice brownies with Chocolate Icing (page 256) for extra-fancy occasions. Brownies can be frozen, unfrosted and uncut, in pans. Thaw to room temperature before icing and cutting.

Homemade French Bread

My recipe for French bread is a variation of Julia Child's. This recipe will make 6 long thin loaves (baguettes), 2 braided loaves, 6 small round loaves (couronnes), or 36 little rolls (pistolets).

- 1 ounce fresh yeast or 2 packages dry yeast
- 2¾ cups warm water
- 7 cups unbleached white flour
- 4¼ teaspoons salt

Soften yeast in ¼ cup warm water.

Mix the flour and salt in a large bowl. Add the warm water and mix well. Add the yeast mixture. Blend into dough.

Turn onto floured board and knead until dough is smooth and elastic. If you have a heavy-duty mixer with a dough hook, this whole procedure will take only 4 to 5 minutes.

Put kneaded dough in a covered bowl and let rise until doubled in bulk. Punch dough down and let rise a second time until doubled. Punch down. Turn onto a floured board and shape as desired.

After forming the loaves, let rise covered with plastic wrap, until doubled in size. Long loaves must be slashed along top with a sharp razor.

Bake in a 400° oven for 25 minutes. To obtain a fine crust, spray the loaves with water 3 or 4 times during baking. Loaves are done when golden brown and crispy.

WREATHS

To form wreath, seal ends of one baguette together. Let rise.

Brush with egg wash. Sprinkle with poppy seeds. Cut points 3 inches long around wreath.

Pull points out from wreath and bake as directed.

BRANCHES

Use one long, thin baguette for each branch. Let rise.

Cut points 3 inches long using a sharp scissor.

Pull points out from baguette. Spray with water and bake.

BRAIDS

Seal 3 baguettes of equal length together at one end.

Braid the loaves evenly. Cover and let rise.

Brush risen braid with egg wash.

Sprinkle with poppy or sesame seeds and bake as directed.

◄ Homemade French breads of various sizes and shapes.

BAGUETTES

Divide dough into 6 equal pieces.

Pat dough into an oval and press down middle with edge of hand. Fold in half.

Seal edges with heel of hand, pressing hard to expel air bubbles..

Shape into long, even cylinder. Place in bread pan, cover, and let rise.

Uncover risen loaves. Make long cuts into surface with razor. Bake.

Tempura Party for Sixteen

ON MY LAST TRIP TO JAPAN, I was introduced to the art of tempura by Ten Masa, a chef who over the past 32 years has mastered the medium and earned a lofty reputation for himself. I spent a day with him in his restaurant in the heart of the commercial district of Akasaka, listening to him talk about different species of fish (he says he has studied fish for 60 years), watching him cut up an astounding variety of ingredients into precise little shapes, and tasting a finished product that was light, absolutely nongreasy, and extremely colorful. Ten Masa says his secret is his exclusive use of cottonseed oil (mixed with a little light sesame oil and used only once) for frying; the finest pastry flour for the batter; the steady heat of his gas-fired woks; and the variety and freshness of his ingredients (he visits the Tsjukiji market every morning for prawns, kissfish, sea urchins, nettles, pickled vegetables, ginger root, ginger root shoots, snow peas, lotus, and gingko). He is a fanatic about the size and quality of his fish—shrimps have to be precisely the length of the row of knuckles on his left hand—and the size and color of his vegetables.

Deeply affected by the passion of Ten Masa, I returned home to begin a similar quest for exceptional ingredients on native ground. I tried everything, from okra and radishes to clams and smelts. Reflecting on the restaurant setup I had seen in Japan—semicircular tables arranged around a tempura stove—I realized it was a form of entertaining easily adaptable to the American kitchen. So one night, I decided to invite a few friends over for a tempura party. I lined up all of my ingredients in rows on a counter top, so that guests could survey the choices and ask for "One of those,

please, and two of those." Then I dipped the pieces into a ready bowl of batter, quickly fried them at my stove, and served.

The most important concerns in giving a tempura party are (1) shopping well, casting the eagle eye of Ten Masa for freshness, color, and variety, and (2) cutting the ingredients into graceful, bite-size pieces. The rest is a matter of attractive display on a center island, counter top, or bread boards, and last-minute cooking. Have bowls of steamed rice and tempura dipping sauce ready for the table, and sake warmed and Japanese beer chilled for beverages. A bowl of fresh fruit—cut-up melon and mangoes—provides the appropriate dessert.

❧ MENU ❧

Tempura
White Rice
Dipping Sauce
Fresh Fruit
Sake, Japanese Beer

A kitchen with an island is the perfect setting for a tempura party.

Tempura
SERVES 16

Tempura was introduced to Japan more than four hundred years ago by Portuguese missionaries who ate a great deal of fried fish. The Japanese have made a great art of the cooking and presentation of tempura, and it has become a favorite food the world over.

OIL

Using the proportion of ¾ first-quality cottonseed oil or very light vegetable oil to ¼ light sesame oil, fill the wok about ⅔ full and heat the oil to approximately 180°. This temperature must be maintained throughout cooking, so it is important not to cook more than 3 or 4 pieces of fish or vegetables at one time.

BATTER
  1 yolk of large egg
1½ cups very cold water
  1 cup cake or pastry flour

Mix yolk with water using fat wooden chopsticks. Add the flour all at once and mix just slightly. There should be large lumps of flour and a rim of flour dust around the bowl. Overmixing will result in a heavy batter coating. It is best to mix the batter in this amount, and repeat as necessary. Prepare ingredients, dry them, and dredge lightly in flour before dipping in batter. (Don't dredge shiso, or seaweed.)

Blue-and-white Japanese plates hold freshly cooked tempura, made to order for each guest and served with individual bowls of dipping sauce.

INGREDIENTS FOR A TEMPURA PARTY

Medium-large shrimps, peeled but with tail left intact

Scallops

Clams on half shell

Sole or flounder fillets cut into 2-inch pieces

Asparagus tips 3 inches long

Eggplant cut into 1×3-inch strips

Sweet potato, peeled and sliced ⅓ inch thick

Zucchini, sliced on the diagonal, ⅓ inch thick

Carrots, peeled and julienned, cut into 2-inch pieces and wrapped in little bundles with seaweed

Oyster mushrooms

White mushrooms

Shitake mushrooms

Snow peas

String beans

Broccoli cut into flowerets

Onions, peeled, cut in half top to bottom, and sliced ⅓ inch thick (a toothpick holds the rings together)

Japanese radishes

Ginger shoots

Lotus root, peeled and sliced ¼ inch thick

Ginko nuts

Green peppers, each cut into 6 pieces

DIPPING SAUCE

1 cup dashi (¼ cup dried bonita flakes soaked in 1 cup warm water)

⅓ cup mirin (Japanese heavy sweetened rice wine)

⅓ cup light soy sauce

1 cup white Japanese radish (daikon), grated

1 or 2 teaspoons fresh ginger, grated

Mix the sauce ingredients together. Keep the sauce warm but not hot. Serve about 1 cup per person in 4- or 5-inch bowls.

Prepare the other ingredients; quantities will vary according to the number of guests. For this party we used 4 pounds shrimp, 2 clams per person, 3 pounds fish fillets, 2 pounds asparagus, 1 pound snow peas, 6 green peppers, 2 pounds white mushrooms, 3 sweet potatoes, 3 heads broccoli, 2 Japanese radishes, 2 bunches carrots. Ingredients will vary greatly according to season and location.

Shopping will take time and planning.

After ingredients are cut up and arranged, and guests are ready to eat, heat the oil. Test the temperature with a thermometer.

Mix up a batch of batter and begin cooking. Dip the item to be cooked, first in flour and then in the batter. Drop into the hot oil, 3 or 4 pieces at a time, and cook 30 seconds for mushrooms, 1 minute for shrimp, and 3 minutes for asparagus and onions. It will take some practice to tell when things are done, but *nothing* should cook longer than 3 minutes.

Skim the oil frequently with a skimmer to remove all signs of batter. This will keep the oil fresh and prevent it from darkening. The oil should not be used again for tempura.

Serve guests as you cook, taking orders for special items.

Vegetables for tempura should be chosen for their freshness and color.

Winter and Summer Soup Parties

I DON'T KNOW ANYONE WHO doesn't hold a special affection for soups. Soups as a genre are both very rudimentary—simple, digestible, economical—and very refined—sophisticated, European, poetic. On a cold winter night, a hot soup is somehow more substantial, more warming, and more hearty than a plateful of the same ingredients, and on a hot summer night, a cold soup is likewise more refreshing, more delicate, more interesting.

Soups are adaptable to a variety of situations and numbers: lunch, supper, kitchen party, picnic (beach, woods, tailgate, boat). A large jar of soup, supplemented with fresh breads, also makes a nice house gift. For a small gathering, one pot of soup is sufficient for a main course; for a larger crowd of, say, fifteen, a selection of two or three is interesting; and for more, three or four. Some of the soups here are more substantial than others—the borscht, for example, with its accompanying condiments of boiled potatoes, hard-boiled eggs, sour cream, and dill, is a full meal in itself, as is the onion soup, with its thick crust of toasted bread and melted cheese. The fresh pea and tomato soups, on the other hand, are relatively light, although quite filling. Each will be supplemented by homemade breads, butter, and perhaps cheese, and rich, wonderful desserts.

With a soup party, *everything* is made in advance. Last-minute responsibilities involve no more than enriching the vichyssoise with cream, or heating the bread. Even the presentation is easy, for the plain-speak of big caldrons of soup, or tubs of butter, is what creates an appealing scene. For the winter party, play up the homeness of your offering. Keep the soups simmering on the stove, for guests can taste-test and ladle out their selection themselves into soup bowls kept stacked and warm nearby. A Magic-Chef stove, old-fashioned enameled pots, and big ladles all heighten the mood.

With the summer soups, which are all chilled, try to position them in different corners of the kitchen—on tables and counters—and set up bowls, spoons, and stacks of fresh napkins around each, so that guests can move about the room and sample several kinds if they wish. The borscht looks spectacular surrounded by just its condiments; the pea and vichyssoise invite the addition of a small vase of fresh garden flowers.

WINTER SOUP MENU

Tuscan Tomato Soup   French Mushroom Soup   Onion Soup
White Bean and Escarole Soup
Vegetable Soup with Vermicelli   Fish Chowder
Homemade French Breads
Baked Apples   Baked Pears

Clockwise from upper left:
French mushroom soup, white bean and escarole soup, onion soup, fish chowder, Tuscan tomato soup, and vegetable soup with vermicelli.

Tuscan Tomato Soup

8 TO 10 SERVINGS

Signora Adorni in the town of Camaiore gave me her recipe for tomato soup using red, ripe tomatoes from the August garden. I use my home-canned tomatoes all winter long, with excellent results.

¼ cup olive oil
4 tablespoons (½ stick) butter
4 carrots, peeled and finely diced
4 stalks celery, finely diced
3 medium onions, finely minced
3 quarts canned tomatoes with juice or 14 large, ripe fresh tomatoes, peeled and seeded
½ cup finely chopped parsley
6 leaves fresh basil (optional)
Salt and freshly ground pepper

Heat the oil and butter in a heavy kettle. Cook the carrots, celery, and onions for about 20 minutes, or until very tender. Add the tomatoes and continue cooking over moderate heat for 25 to 30 minutes longer. Stir in the parsley and basil, season with salt and pepper, cook a minute or so longer, and serve hot.

VARIATION: This soup can be strained and thinned with light cream for a more elegant presentation. Stir a teaspoon of Pesto (page 143) into each bowl of soup and top with a dollop of sour cream.

French Mushroom Soup

12 SERVINGS

This is a fine, rich soup suitable for inclusion on a soup buffet or as the first course for a fancy sit-down dinner.

½ cup minced onion
¼ pound (1 stick) unsalted butter
6 tablespoons flour
12 cups rich chicken broth
2 sprigs parsley
½ bay leaf
Pinch thyme
3 pounds mushrooms, trimmed and sliced very thinly
½ teaspoon salt
1 teaspoon lemon juice
4 egg yolks
1 cup whipping cream

GARNISH
Finely chopped parsley

Cook the onions in 4 tablespoons butter until soft. Stir in the flour and cook over low heat for 4 minutes without browning. Add the broth, blending it completely with the flour. Add the parsley, bay leaf, and thyme and simmer for 20 minutes.

Melt remaining 4 tablespoons butter in a large pan. Toss the mushrooms in the butter with salt and lemon juice and cook 5 minutes. Add the mushrooms to the broth and simmer 5 minutes. If not to be used immediately, set aside.

Reheat to the simmer. Beat the egg yolks and cream until blended. Stir a cupful of the hot soup into the cream mixture. Add the cream to the soup and heat to below the simmer. (If the soup simmers, the yolks will curdle.) Taste for seasoning. Serve immediately, garnished with chopped parsley.

Onion Soup

16 SERVINGS

This is our favorite cold-weather soup. The onions cook for 2 hours in butter and oil to develop the rich golden color of the perfect onion soup. It helps if you have homemade beef or veal stock on hand.

5 pounds yellow onions, thinly sliced
6 tablespoons butter
2 tablespoons olive oil
½ teaspoon sugar
2 teaspoons salt
5 tablespoons flour
14 cups boiling beef or veal stock
1½ cups dry vermouth or dry white wine
⅓ cup cognac
2 French baguettes, sliced 1 inch thick
4 cups coarsely grated Swiss and Parmesan cheeses, mixed

Simmer the onions in butter and oil for 2 hours. Stir frequently, adding the sugar and salt after 15 minutes of cooking. Onions will turn a deep golden-brown color. Sprinkle on the flour and cook for 5 minutes longer. Add the boiling stock and the wine and simmer for 45 minutes longer. Skim if necessary. Correct the seasoning.

Before serving, reheat to boiling. Pour in the cognac. Serve in heated bowls with toasted rounds of French bread and generous servings of grated Parmesan and Swiss cheeses.

White Bean and Escarole Soup

8 SERVINGS

Of Italian origin, this soup is delicious served with a topping of freshly grated Parmesan cheese and crusty Italian bread.

1 pound navy beans
6 cups beef stock
1 large onion, minced
3 cloves garlic, minced
2 bay leaves
¼ pound pancetta (Italian raw bacon) cut into ¼-inch cubes

1 large head of escarole, washed and separated into leaves
Salt and freshly ground pepper

Soak the beans overnight, or boil for 3 minutes and soak for 1 hour.

Simmer the beans in the soaking water and stock with the onion, garlic, and bay leaves until the beans are tender (about 1 hour). Blanch the pancetta in boiling water for 5 minutes. Drain and add to the soup halfway through cooking.

When beans are thoroughly cooked, add the escarole leaves. Simmer for 2 minutes and season to taste with salt and pepper.

Vegetable Soup with Vermicelli

10 SERVINGS

This soup is a colorful addition to the buffet. It is also an excellent soup for a one-course supper served with home-baked bread and a green salad.

2 large onions, thinly sliced
½ cup olive oil
2 cloves garlic, minced
2 large red peppers, cut into 1 × ¼-inch strips
1 pound carrots, peeled and cut into ½-inch cubes
4 cups diced potatoes (cut into ¼-inch cubes)
8 cups rich chicken broth
2 pounds green beans, cut into 1-inch pieces
3 small zucchini, cut lengthwise into quarters and sliced ¼-inch thick
½ pound vermicelli
Salt and pepper
½ cup chopped parsley

In a heavy 6-quart casserole sauté the onions in the oil until soft. Add the garlic, red peppers, and carrots. Cook 5 minutes. Add the potatoes and stock and simmer until potatoes are almost tender.

Add the green beans and zucchini and simmer 5 minutes. Stir in the vermicelli and continue cooking until the vermicelli is al dente. Season with salt and pepper and sprinkle with parsley.

Serve piping hot.

Fish Chowder
10 SERVINGS

This hearty soup is simple to assemble. Fresh, fresh fish and rich homemade stock are the secrets to success.

¼ pound salt pork, cut into ⅛-inch cubes
1 large onion, finely chopped
1½ quarts Fish Stock (see below)
4 cups diced potatoes (cut into ¼-inch cubes)
2 bay leaves
1 pound bay scallops
1 pound shelled, deveined shrimp, fresh or frozen (30 count)
1 pound cod, cut into chunks
1 pound monkfish or other firm whitefish, cut into chunks
1 pint whipping cream
⅛ teaspoon cayenne pepper
Salt and white pepper to taste

Blanch the salt pork in boiling water for 10 minutes. Drain. In a heavy 4-quart casserole, cook the pork over low heat for 5 minutes. Add the onion and sauté until soft. Add the fish stock and bay leaves and bring to a simmer. Combine the potatoes with the stock mixture and cook until the potatoes are barely done. Add the scallops, shrimp, and fish and simmer for 5 minutes. Heat the cream and add it to the soup. Season with cayenne, salt, and white pepper. Serve very hot.

FISH STOCK

3 pounds bones of whitefish (flounder, fluke)
2 cups dry white wine
3 bay leaves
3 stems parsley
Sprig of thyme
1 teaspoon salt
2 quarts water

Put all ingredients into stockpot. Bring to a boil, reduce heat, and simmer for 25 minutes. Skim, cool, and strain through a fine mesh. Freeze any unused stock.

Homemade French Breads
SEE RECIPE, PAGE 106

Baked Apples
1 APPLE PER PERSON

As old-fashioned as apple pie, baked apples are a simple treat. Choose large, tart, firm apples such as Granny Smiths or Cortlands.

1 apple
1 teaspoon chopped pecans or walnuts
1 tablespoon brown sugar
1 teaspoon raisins
1 tablespoon unsalted butter
1 3-inch cinnamon stick

GARNISH
Whipped cream

Preheat oven to 375°. Cut the top off each apple. Core and seed the apple but do not cut through the bottom.

Fill apple with nuts, sugar, and raisins. Dot with butter. Put cinnamon stick in apple.

Butter a baking dish. Put apples in dish and add ¼ inch of water to dish. Bake in preheated oven until apples are soft but still retain their shape (about 25 minutes).

Serve hot or warm with softly whipped cream.

Baked Pears
1 PEAR PER PERSON

This simple dessert will become a favorite of pear lovers. The gentle baking in butter and poaching in cream brings out the flavor of pears like no other recipe. You should use Anjou pears for this.

1 Anjou pear
1 tablespoon sugar
2 tablespoons cream
Butter

Preheat oven to 375°. Peel each pear, cut in half lengthwise, and remove seeds.

Generously butter a baking dish just large enough to hold the pears. Sprinkle dish with half the sugar. Put pears cut side down in dish. Sprinkle with the remaining sugar and bake for 20 minutes. Remove from oven.

Pour cream over pears and return to oven for 15 minutes. Serve pears hot from oven or warm.

Baked apples and pears served right from the oven in which they were cooked.

❧ SUMMER SOUP MENU ❧

Vichyssoise

Iced Borscht

Sugar Pea Pod Soup

Homemade French Breads

Raspberry Tart in Puff Pastry Shell

Blueberry Tart in Walnut Crust

Red Currant Tart in Toasted Almond Crust

Vichyssoise
6 SERVINGS

An extremely smooth, creamy version of a very homey soup. Topped with chives, this iced soup is refreshing and delightful.

6 to 8 fat leeks (white parts only), cut crosswise

4 tablespoons (½ stick) butter

8 medium white potatoes, peeled and thinly sliced

1 tablespoon salt

5 cups rich chicken broth

2 cups half-and-half
Pinch freshly grated nutmeg
White pepper to taste

1 cup heavy cream

GARNISH
Fresh chives

Sauté the leeks in the butter for 10 minutes. Add the potatoes, salt, and broth and simmer until potatoes are tender, about 30 minutes. Purée potato mixture in food processor or blender, then put through a fine strainer to remove any lumps. Add the half-and-half, nutmeg, and pepper. Check the seasoning. Chill well.

To serve, stir in the cream. Top with fresh chives, whole or chopped.

Two cold soups with the flavors and colors of summer.

Left: *Chives float on top of a smooth, creamy vichyssoise.*

Opposite: *A beautiful pink iced borscht served in an old crackled bowl. Small bowls of garnishes—boiled potatoes, chopped cucumbers, hard-boiled eggs, fresh dill—surround it.*

Iced Borscht
10 SERVINGS

Once a humble peasant soup, borscht takes on a new delicacy when the ingredients are finely puréed. As part of a soup buffet, serve it iced with bowls of garnishes and thick slices of dark pumpernickel with sweet butter.

12 medium beets

2 medium yellow onions, peeled and minced

2 carrots, peeled and finely grated

1 tablespoon unsalted butter

2 teaspoons sugar

6 cups chicken or beef broth

3 tablespoons freshly squeezed lemon juice
Salt and pepper to taste

2 cups sour cream

GARNISHES
Boiled potatoes, peeled and cubed; chopped fresh dill; cucumber, skin on, cubed; hard-boiled eggs; sour cream

Wash unpeeled beets. Wrap in aluminum foil and put on a baking sheet in a preheated 350° oven. Bake until fork-tender, about 30 minutes. Cool, peel, and grate.

Sauté the onions and carrots in the butter for 10 minutes. Add the beets, sugar, and broth. Simmer for 20 to 30 minutes. Remove from heat. Purée in food processor or food mill. Stir in the lemon juice and season with salt and pepper. Chill.

Stir soup into the sour cream. Serve with bowls of garnish.

NOTE: Cooking beets this way is easy, it preserves the color and juice, and the skins just slip off when the beets cool. Use this method for beet salads, pickled beets, etc.

Sugar Pea Pod Soup

6 TO 8 SERVINGS

A bright green soup that gets its color from the addition of snow pea pods, puréed along with the peas. A chiffonade of Boston lettuce adds more green and an appealing crunch.

- 1 cup thinly sliced leeks
- 4 tablespoons (½ stick) unsalted butter
- 3 tablespoons flour
- 4 cups chicken broth
- 1 teaspoon salt
- 1 10-ounce package frozen peas
- 1 pound fresh snow peas (or sugar snap peas), strings removed
- 1½ cups water
- 1 scallion, chopped
- 8 large leaves Boston lettuce
- 1 cup milk
- ¼ to ½ cup whipping cream
  Salt to taste
  White pepper to taste

GARNISH
  6 leaves of Boston lettuce cut into thin strips (chiffonade)

Sauté leeks in 3 tablespoons butter for 10 minutes, or until tender. Add flour, mixing well. Stir in broth, salt, and frozen peas. Cook for 20 minutes over low flame. Purée cooked mixture in food processor. Set aside.

Cook snow peas, scallion, lettuce, and remaining 1 tablespoon butter with the water for about 15 minutes. Purée in the food processor and put through a strainer to remove any fibers. Add to the purée base, thin with milk, and chill.

To serve, enrich with cream, season with salt and white pepper, and garnish with lettuce chiffonade.

Sugar pea pod soup.

118

Homemade French Breads

SEE RECIPE, PAGE 106.

Raspberry Tart in Puff Pastry Shell

SERVES 10 TO 12

1 pound Perfect Puff Pastry (page 237)

EGG GLAZE
1 egg yolk beaten with 2 teaspoons water
2 cups Pastry Cream (page 182)
2 pints ripe raspberries

GLAZE
½ cup red raspberry jelly melted with 2 tablespoons cognac

Prepare puff pastry according to master recipe. Roll out into a large rectangle, about 20×16 inches. Cut pastry into an even rectangle 18 × 14 inches, and reserve trimmings. Place on a water-sprayed baking sheet. Use the 1-inch trimmings to build up the edges of the pastry shell by pasting the strips on the edges with water. Prick the bottom with the tines of a fork and line with aluminum foil. Weight the bottom with beans or rice, just as you would a tart shell. Refrigerate for at least 30 minutes.

Preheat oven to 400°. Brush the edges of the pastry with egg glaze and bake for 12 minutes, or until edges have puffed and are browning. Remove foil and weights and continue baking a few more min-

utes, until shell is light golden brown. Remove from oven and cool completely on rack.

Prepare pastry cream according to directions.

To assemble the tart, spread the pastry cream in the bottom of the shell. Top with even rows of raspberries and brush with a light coating of glaze. This should be done no more than 2 hours before serving.

Blueberry Tart in Walnut Crust

SEE VARIATION, PAGE 241

Red Currant Tart in Toasted Almond Crust

SEE VARIATION, PAGE 241

Below: *A luscious blueberry tart in a crunchy walnut crust and a raspberry tart in puff pastry shell.*

A Chinese Banquet for Ten to Twelve

MY DAUGHTER, ALEXIS, INTRO-
duced me to the pleasures of preparing Chinese food at home. She
loves to browse in old cookbooks and new food magazines, and,
like many young people, is particularly attuned to the fresh combinations of flavors and textures in Chinese food. She likes the
names, too—lions' heads, gold coins, strange-flavor fish. She
found and made sesame-flavored scallion bread and pearl balls on
her own, and at thirteen she executed her first Chinese banquet, for
an anniversary surprise for Andy and me.

Chinese food is easy and fun to prepare, and very well suited

❧ MENU ❧

Watercress Soup   Chinese Pearl Balls
Scallion Bread   Sesame Noodles   Gold Coin Eggs
Lions' Heads Meatballs
Sweet and Hot Cabbage Pickles
Strange-Flavor Eggplant   Strange-Flavor Fish
Rice   Cucumber Pickles   Dipping Sauce
Almond Cookies   Fruit
Chinese Teas

**The parlor table set with
blue-and-white Oriental dishes.**

to the relaxed atmosphere of the kitchen. It requires mainly ultra-organization, for many dishes have to be cooked quickly at the last minute, so their ingredients must be cut, assembled, and ready for the wok. When the action begins, it is fast and furious, but brief. In this menu, the soup and bread, the lions' heads meatballs, the sesame noodles, and the pickles are ready in advance—and the hors d'oeuvres are ready for quick heating. All the components of the other dishes should be carefully and decorously ordered on counter tops or in mounds on plates.

When guests arrive, serve drinks. When most of them have gathered, complete and serve the hors d'oeuvres. Then, after a course of soup and scallion bread, heat the lions' heads and serve them, laying the rice and pickled dishes on the table, too. When everyone has sampled these, cook the other two dishes. There will

be no awkward waits, for there is plenty of food on the table and there is entertainment in the spectacle at the stove. It is as fascinating to watch an assortment of exotic ingredients come together into a beautiful entree in a matter of minutes as it is rewarding to taste the freshness and purity of the end product. That is what Chinese cuisine is all about. The rhythm of a Chinese banquet, fluid, familial, leaves room for conversation and appreciation.

It is not difficult to contrive a table setting with Oriental overtones with just plain white dishes and plain white napkins, if you add chopsticks, a celadon-green side dish, or flowered teacups, and perhaps a stark, serene centerpiece—a single peony, a convoluted branch, a spray of flowering quince. For an authentic touch, Chinese accessories—rice bowls, soup bowls, or teacups in various patterns—can be purchased inexpensively.

Watercress Soup
SERVES 10 TO 12

3 quarts chicken broth
2 teaspoons salt
2 bunches watercress
1 cup shredded Chinese cabbage leaves
4 tablespoons cornstarch, dissolved in 4 tablespoons water
12 dried Chinese mushrooms, soaked for 10 minutes in 1 cup very hot water; discard stems
4 tablespoons dry sherry
2 scallions (green and white parts), thinly sliced
1 cup pressed tofu (bean curd), cut in 1-inch cubes (optional)

Boil broth. Add salt, watercress, and cabbage; simmer 2 minutes. Stir in cornstarch; cook 1 minute.

Stir in mushroom caps with liquid; add sherry, scallions, and tofu.

NOTE: To make Alexis's chicken broth, poach broiler chicken in 6 cups canned chicken broth. Save the cooked chicken for salad.

Chinese Pearl Balls
SEE RECIPE. PAGE 41

Far left: *Slicing scallions into "flowers" to garnish the watercress soup.*

Left: *Chinese cooking requires great organization: Lexi plans each step of the dinner and arranges all ingredients beforehand. Here she prepares gold coin eggs.*

Scallion Bread
SERVES 12

4 cups unbleached flour
3 teaspoons baking powder
⅔ cup cold water
6 teaspoons kosher salt
⅔ cup boiling water
4 teaspoons sesame oil
½ cup thinly sliced scallions (green and white parts)
1 cup peanut oil (or other light vegetable oil)

Sift 2 cups of flour with the baking powder. Stir in the cold water and knead until smooth; let rest.

Combine remaining flour with 2 teaspoons of salt. Stir in boiling water; mix well. The dough will be very sticky. Knead the hot dough together with the cold dough until smooth. Oil a glass bowl with 1 teaspoon of sesame oil. Put dough in bowl; cover and let rest 2 hours.

To form the breads, knead the dough 3 to 4 minutes. Divide into 6 parts. Roll each part into a flat circle 7 to 8 inches in diameter. Brush the top of each circle with ½ teaspoon sesame oil. Sprinkle each circle with salt and scallions. Roll up each circle into a cylinder, pinching the ends closed. With the palms of your hands, roll each cylinder until it is about 12 inches long. Coil each cylinder like a snake and let it rest. Roll all the coils into 7-inch circles with a rolling pin.

Heat a thin layer of peanut oil in a large skillet. Fry each circle 8 to 10 minutes, turning midway, until each side is golden and the breads are slightly puffy. Transfer to a heated platter and keep warm until all the bread is cooked. Serve hot, cut into wedges.

Divide bread dough into smaller portions for rolling.

Roll out to 7-inch circle, brush with sesame oil, and sprinkle with scallions.

Roll the circle into a cylinder and coil, pinching ends together.

Sesame Noodles
SERVES 10 TO 12

Make this dish the day before serving.

2 pounds Chinese egg noodles
½ cup sesame oil
½ cup black soy sauce
3 tablespoons black Chinese vinegar
3 tablespoons sugar
1½ tablespoons salt
2 tablespoons hot pepper oil
½ cup finely sliced scallions (green and white parts)

In a large pot of boiling water, cook the noodles (thawed if frozen) 1 pound at a time. Boil 4 to 5 minutes, until just tender. Drain, rinse well under cold running water until chilled, and drain again. Put in a large bowl.

Combine remaining ingredients. Stir into cold noodles, mixing well (use hands to distribute sauce evenly). Chill overnight.

Gold Coin Eggs
SERVES 10 TO 12

SAUCE
¼ teaspoon dried red pepper flakes
2 scallions (green and white parts), finely chopped
1 teaspoon minced fresh ginger
½ teaspoon sugar
4 teaspoons rice vinegar
½ cup hot water
4 teaspoons light soy sauce
2 teaspoons sesame oil

8 large eggs, hard-boiled
8 teaspoons cornstarch
Oil for frying

Mix together ingredients for sauce; set aside.

Peel eggs; slice into ¼-inch slices. Coat with cornstarch.

Heat a thin layer of oil in frying pan. Fry egg slices on both sides until golden. Arrange cooked slices on serving platter. Add sauce ingredients to oil in pan and heat. Pour over eggs; serve immediately.

Lions' Heads Meatballs
SERVES 10 TO 12

5 pounds Chinese cabbage
1 1-inch piece fresh ginger
⅔ cup cold water
3 teaspoons dry sherry
½ teaspoon freshly ground pepper
2½ pounds ground pork (3 parts lean to 1 part fat)
1½ cups vegetable oil
2 teaspoons coarse salt
2 tablespoons cornstarch
4 tablespoons cold water
4½ cups rich chicken broth

Remove 5 outer leaves of cabbage. Cut off crinkly tops of rest of cabbage and reserve for another dish. Cut the thick white ribs into 2½-inch-wide pieces.

Crush the ginger with the dull edge of a cleaver. Soak it in ⅔ cup cold water for at least 15 minutes. Discard the ginger and reserve the water. Combine the ginger water, sherry, and pepper in a large mixing bowl. Add the pork and mix very well with your hand.

Heat a large wok. Add 5 tablespoons oil and heat until hot. Add the sliced cabbage and stir-fry for 1 minute. Add the salt and continue cooking for 2 to 3 minutes. Arrange the cooked cabbage in the bottom of a heavy 8-quart earthenware casserole.

Mix the cornstarch and water. Dipping your hands into this mixture,

roll the pork mixture into 16 meatballs. Set balls on a baking sheet.

In a heavy skillet, fry the meatballs in 2 to 3 tablespoons hot oil. Carefully turn the meatballs to brown them evenly. Add more oil if necessary.

Arrange the browned meatballs on top of the cooked cabbage in the casserole. Pour the chicken broth over the meatballs. Cover with the whole cabbage leaves and simmer, tightly covered, for 3 hours. Serve hot, each meatball accompanied by some cabbage and broth.

Sweet and Hot Cabbage Pickle
SERVES 10 TO 12

This is best made at least 2 days before the party.

4 pounds Chinese white cabbage
1 tablespoon kosher salt
2 tablespoons vegetable oil
1 teaspoon red pepper flakes
½ teaspoon Szechuan peppercorns
1 tablespoon finely chopped peeled fresh ginger
4 teaspoons light soy sauce
5 tablespoons sugar
1 tablespoon cider vinegar

Trim outer cabbage leaves of leafy green parts (reserve for Watercress Soup, page 123). Cut heart into eighths; you should have a pile of ribs and pieces of heart.

Put trimmed cabbage pieces in a glass or stainless steel bowl. Sprinkle with salt; mix well. Let stand at least 6 hours. Rinse and drain well.

In wok, heat oil. Add red pepper, peppercorns, and ginger. Cook, stirring over low heat, 10 seconds. Add cabbage. Cook, stirring over medium heat, 30 seconds. Add soy sauce, sugar, and vinegar; cook 2

minutes longer. Remove from wok, cool, and chill at least 1 day before serving.

Strange-Flavor Eggplant
SERVES 10 TO 12

Good hot or cold, this dish is best made from the small, seedless Italian or Japanese variety of eggplant.

3 pounds ripe, firm eggplant
2 tablespoons finely minced garlic
1½ tablespoons finely minced fresh ginger
1 teaspoon red pepper flakes
6 tablespoons chopped scallions
4 tablespoons light soy sauce
2 teaspoons rice wine vinegar
4 tablespoons brown sugar
2 tablespoons hot water
4 tablespoons vegetable oil
2 teaspoons sesame oil

Preheat oven to 450°. Lightly oil a baking dish and put the whole eggplants in the dish; prick skin with a fork. Bake for 25 to 30 minutes, until the eggplants are soft to the touch. Cool and peel the eggplants, tearing the flesh into small strips.

In a small bowl mix the garlic, ginger, red pepper flakes, and scallions. In another bowl, mix the soy sauce, vinegar, sugar, and water.

Heat wok until hot. Add the vegetable and sesame oils and heat over a high flame. Add the garlic mixture and cook 1 minute, taking care not to burn it. Add the soy sauce mixture, bring to a simmer, and stir in the eggplant. Cook over high heat until the eggplant is hot. Season to taste and serve hot, room temperature, or cold.

VARIATION: Add 2 red peppers, very thinly sliced, to the wok 1 minute before the addition of the eggplant.

Strange-Flavor Fish
SERVES 12

SAUCE

3 tablespoons finely chopped peeled fresh ginger

4 cloves garlic, peeled and finely chopped

4 tablespoons finely chopped scallion (green and white parts)

2 teaspoons red pepper flakes

4 tablespoons light soy sauce

4 teaspoons black Chinese vinegar

4 tablespoons sugar

1 cup water

4 whole porgies (2 to 2½ pounds each), heads left on, cleaned and scaled

1 tablespoon kosher salt

2 cups peanut oil

In a large bowl, combine all the sauce ingredients. Stir to dissolve sugar. Set aside.

Wash the fish and pat dry. Score each side to within ⅛ inch of bone with diagonal cuts. Sprinkle with salt and let sit for 30 minutes. Rub off excess salt.

In a large skillet, heat the oil until sizzling. Brown the fish, one at a time, in oil 2 minutes; reduce heat and cook 3 minutes more, spooning oil over the fish. Turn fish; raise heat and cook 2 minutes. Reduce heat and cook 3 minutes longer, until done. The fish will be opaque, firm, and easily flaked.

Repeat until all the fish are cooked. Add more oil if necessary.

Remove fish to platter. Pour off all but 2 tablespoons of oil from the pan. Add the sauce and simmer 2 to 3 minutes; pour over the fish. Serve immediately.

Almond Cookies
36 COOKIES

These cookies are the perfect ending for a Chinese dinner. In fact, they are so good we often make them just for the cookie jar.

½ cup (1 stick) butter

1 cup lard

1½ cups sugar

2 eggs

2½ tablespoons almond extract

3¾ cups flour

2½ teaspoons baking soda

¾ teaspoon salt

36 whole blanched almonds

Preheat oven to 350°.

Cream butter, lard, and sugar until fluffy. Add eggs and almond extract and continue beating until smooth.

Sift flour, baking powder, and salt together, and stir into butter mixture. Knead a bit with your hands to make a stiff, smooth dough.

Form dough into 1½-inch balls, and place 3 inches apart on a buttered baking sheet. Flatten with the palm of your hand, and center a whole almond on each cookie. Bake 10 to 12 minutes, until lightly browned on bottom but very pale on top. Cool on racks.

Scoring a whole porgy with a Japanese cleaver for strange-flavor fish. The diagonal cuts permit the flavors of the sauce to penetrate the flesh of the fish.

CHAPTER SIX

The Buffet

ONCE A BUFFET WAS JUST a piece of furniture, a sideboard. Now it is also a meal served from that sideboard. By nature it is an authentic movable feast and a boon to entertaining. It is the fastest, easiest way to entertain without a staff of servants or a banquet hall. It is a complete meal, to be served on only one plate. It is adaptable to many moods, many styles, many menus, and can as easily be a Southern barbecue as a Russian feast, a salad bar as a country breakfast.

It is curious that the buffet in America seemed to be associated with the development of the chafing dish; many people never progressed beyond chicken fricassee or turkey divan, made in huge quantities and kept warm over a tiny candle. I suppose the prospect of a crowd naturally conjures up the steam table and the cafeteria line,

The public beach in Rye, New York, was the setting for this luau. My husband, Andy, was reponsible for cooking the suckling pigs.

but the casserole is to the buffet what the onion soup dip is to the cocktail party—a tired old cliché.

I have a friend who every spring gives what I consider to be the ultimate buffet dinner. She covers an 18-foot harvest table with so many choices there is not a glimpse of mahogany beneath. Beginning on the left, there are hors d'oeuvres, seven kinds of olives, cold meats, shrimp, and pâtés, then salads of all descriptions, which progress to vegetables and meat dishes; and on the right, cheeses and desserts. It is almost enough just to look at her spread, a veritable groaning board, with all the different textures of breads and vegetables and the riot of color.

Another such spectacle is the French *garde manger,* the buffet on which great transatlantic ships and great hotels used to pride themselves. The international cruiser LaFrance still carries on the tradition, in which dozens of chefs create entrees that look like heroic eighteenth-century paintings, formal, dramatic, a little outrageous: a pair of spiny lobsters à la parisienne, performing a contredanse, their claws joined aloft with a ruffled bow; a glossy turbot decorated with delicate vegetable flowers on aspic; a whole pheasant retaining its proud head and full plumage, reigning over a covey of quail breasts stuffed with foie gras, truffles, and aspic; tables full of pâtisserie, each one a work of art.

Today's buffet has become simpler, less ostentatious, and, in a way, more confident. A good buffet does not have to overwhelm. Opulence has as much to do with variety and sensitive display as with ostentation. It is possible to create a varied menu and a spectacle of plenty on any number of themes within a simple format.

There are at least as many themes as national cuisines. Indeed, a meal organized around a particular ethnic cuisine and style provides the same sense of adventure as going into a restaurant in Chinatown or Little Italy does, and also gives a special shape to a meal. By happy coincidence, many of the most interesting and flamboy-

ant affairs are also the least expensive and the least demanding. And because of the unusual ingredients and provocative display, they are entertainments in themselves.

Several years ago, I staged a commemorative *Festival Romano* to commemorate the opening night of Shakespeare's play *Julius Caesar* at Stratford. Because it was summer and the party was outdoors in a tent, we chose a cold buffet. To ten cold pasta salads we added huge platters of antipastos, Italian breads and cheeses, and a colossal array of Italian desserts, all cut into finger-size portions: cannolli, panettone, polenta cakes, ricotta cheese-cakes, and, of course, amaretti. Enjoying the essential theatricality of the event, we rummaged through Stratford's prop rooms and extracted suits of armor, busts of ancient rulers, staffs, flags, banners, and 75 tiki torches for decoration. To indulge the mood we were creating—something that comes easily when you are a hired impresario, and *should* come just as easily at home, given a sense of fun—we hired acrobats, and musicians to play ancient music on their ancient instruments.

For the advertising firm of Wells, Rich, Green, I created a Tex-Mex dinner for a hundred fifty guests. Billed as "Tijuana Cheap," it enabled us to *be* cheap in the name of art and spoof. The menu was impressive in length and diversity and included guacamole and tortilla chips, scallops seviche on shredded lettuce, pork, beef, and chicken empanadas, turkey mole, refried red beans, black beans with sour cream and chopped onion, corn and wheat tortillas, jalapeño corn bread, buttermilk pie with lemon crust, chocolate pudding, and sour lemon tarts.

Although the display was extravagant, the ingredients were inexpensive. I served the hot entrees directly from great cooking vats, and others from big pottery bowls, all arranged on plastic checkered tablecloths. A bartender made margaritas and oversaw the dispensing of sangria and Mexican beer; he and the other helpers wore peasant outfits assembled from what hung in their closets. Everywhere there were plastic pots of plastic flowers, and plastic dime-store birds, chirping away a synthetic song. At the center of the table were suggestions of the hosts' concerns of the hour: a tray of Alka-Seltzer tablets and a piñata stuffed with Purina Dog Chow.

Within the great wide realm of the buffet, everyone can find a theme and a menu appropriate to his budget, space, and style. The following parties—a country breakfast, a clam bake, and a handful of ethnic dinners—are just the beginning. Whatever the theme, the fixed conditions of a buffet—the sideboard principle—determine its planning and organization. A menu has to lend itself to advance preparation, and the fare has to be able to be reheated or to sit gracefully for an hour or so. While this does not dictate turkey tetrazzini, it does eliminate fragile deflatable concoctions and cooked-to-order individualized dishes, which in any case would not be practical for a crowd. Filet mignon, for example, would not be suitable, and yet a whole fillet of beef, or a butterflied leg of lamb, would, for they can be carved at the table, and remain delectable at room temperature, or even cold. The only times I indulge in last-minute cooking is with shish kebab or barbecued meat, when an informal mood makes it easy to bring the main course to the table with a certain flourish. At an outdoor party, I sometimes even place hibachis directly on the table and serve from grill to plate. If you enjoy activity, it is also perfectly feasible to mix freshly cooked pasta or assemble a mammoth Caesar salad before your guests' eyes, bringing to the buffet table some of the theater of the omelette party.

Because guests will serve themselves, it is important that your food be easy to handle. Many dishes come in individual portions: stuffed chicken breasts, chicken Pojarsky, crêpes, and coquilles St. Jacques. In other cases, the proper serving utensil will facilitate a graceful portioning of poached fish or moussaka. Roasts can be completely or partially precarved. With a little ingenu-

ity, other more cumbersome foods can be made suitable for a crowd—a soup, for example, can be ladled into mugs or balloon goblets in advance. All the food need not be offered simultaneously; sometimes I serve hors d'oeuvres separately, or clear the table and give desserts a fresh new presentation.

The following recipes are designed for large groups, because the point of a buffet is to accommodate more people than would usually sit down to dinner. However, there is no reason the recipes can't be halved or quartered.

Individual servings of Russian borscht look beautiful on the buffet table in large balloon goblets.

A Country Buffet Breakfast for Forty

THE DISTINCTION AND JOY OF this breakfast is that it is not Continental (croissants and brioches) or English (kippers and toast) or chic (omelettes aux fines herbes), but old-fashioned, rib-sticking all-American. It is also Country, not strictly because of its menu, but because of its presentation, which calls for gingham, yellowware bowls and earthenware crocks, and bushel baskets of flowers. The occasion for the original party was a breakfast meeting hosted by a designer about to launch a new collection of country fabrics. The place was a cavernous loft in downtown Manhattan; on the walls were racks of fresh plaids, small prints, and checks. We covered a central serving table with an antique crib quilt and in baskets stacked napkins cut from cloth in various patterns. As guests served themselves scrambled eggs and sausage, country ham, scones and buttermilk biscuits, homemade jams and fruit butters, and wandered about the displays, business and pleasure seemed to merge beautifully.

❧ MENU ❧

Fresh Orange Juice with Champagne   Bloody Marys

Scrambled Eggs   Sausage Patties   Sausage in Puff Pastry

Baked Country Ham

Buttermilk Biscuits   Currant Scones   Ginger Muffins

Homemade Jams

Applesauce   Apple Butter   Honey   Sweet Butter

Navel Oranges

Hot Coffee and Tea

Scrambled Eggs
SERVES 40

Ever since I was small I have loved scrambled eggs, but generally only as my mother made them—fresh eggs, lightly beaten with a fork and cooked in melted sweet butter— nothing added.

80 eggs
 1 pound (4 sticks) unsalted butter
    Salt and pepper to taste

A dozen at a time, break the eggs and lightly whisk them. Heat 3 tablespoons butter in a very large skillet until very hot. Pour the eggs in all at once and move them around with a wooden spoon. Cook the eggs quickly, and do not overcook.

Remove each batch to a heated, ovenproof shallow dish. Brush tops of cooked eggs with butter to keep them from hardening. Keep warm in the oven until all the eggs are cooked.

Repeat the process until all the eggs have been cooked.

Sausage Patties
30 PATTIES

It is simple and fun to make your own old-fashioned sausage meat. Experiment with various seasonings.

 2 pounds pork, finely ground
 1 pound pork fat, finely ground
 2 teaspoons salt
 1 teaspoon freshly ground pepper
 2 teaspoons leaf sage, crumbled
 1 teaspoon ground coriander
    Pinch freshly grated nutmeg

Combine all the ingredients, mixing well. Sauté a bit of the mixture in a hot frying pan and taste for seasoning. Roll mixture into 1½-inch balls, and flatten.

Place patties on foil-covered cookie sheets and cook in hot 375° oven until brown (about 20 minutes). Drain on paper toweling and serve hot.

N O T E : Patties may be made ahead and frozen. To cook, thaw slightly and bake as directed.

Sausage In Puff Pastry
APPROXIMATELY 100 HORS D'OEUVRES

I often made saucisson en croute for dinner parties or lunches, but could not think of a way to use this combination for large-scale cocktail parties. Dorian Leigh, the famous "Fire and Ice" model, showed me her way, and we now make this delicious puff pastry by the hundreds.

 1 pound Perfect Puff Pastry (page 237)
 1 pound ground pork
 2 teaspoons ground cumin
 1 teaspoon thyme
 3 cloves garlic, peeled and crushed to a purée
    Salt and pepper to taste
 1 egg yolk mixed with 1 tablespoon cream

Roll the puff pastry into a rectangle ⅛ inch thick. Cut into lengthwise strips about 3 inches wide. Put on baking sheets sprayed with cold water. Refrigerate.

Mix the meat with the spices, and garlic, and salt and pepper. Divide into as many portions as you have strips of pastry. Roll each portion of sausage into a cylinder as long as the pastry strips. With a pastry brush, lightly paint the surface of each strip of pastry with water. Put the sausage meat near one long edge and roll up, patting the closing edge firmly to seal it.

You can refrigerate the rolls for a day, until ready to bake, or wrap well and freeze for several weeks.

To bake, preheat oven to 375°. Cut the rolls into ½-inch sections. Put on water-sprayed baking sheets, 2 inches apart. Paint with egg wash and bake until puffed and golden brown, about 12 to 18 minutes. Serve hot.

N O T E : You can bake these rolls to a light golden brown (10 to 12 minutes) and store until just before the party, reheating before serving.

Baked Country Ham
SEE RECIPE, PAGE 57

Brush the tops with heavy cream and bake in the oven 13 to 15 minutes. Do not overcook. Cool on racks.

NOTE: Biscuits can be baked ahead and frozen. Put the biscuits in single layers between sheets of waxed paper in plastic bags or in plastic tubs with close-fitting lids.

VARIATION: Add ¼ cup chopped chives or dill to the dough before refrigerating.

Currant Scones
APPROXIMATELY FORTY
1-INCH SCONES

These scones are excellent as 2½-inch rounds for teatime consumption or as tiny 1-inch hearts for hors d'oeuvres with smoked turkey or ham.

4½ cups flour
 2 teaspoons baking powder
 ½ teaspoon baking soda
 2 tablespoons sugar
 ½ pound (2 sticks) unsalted butter
 ½ pint heavy cream
 1 cup dried currants
 3 tablespoons brandy or sherry

Sift the flour with the baking powder, baking soda, and sugar. Cut in the butter with a pastry cutter or in the food processor. Stir in the cream and mix until dough holds together. Add 1 cup dried currants plumped in 3 tablespoons brandy or sherry to the dough. Wrap in plastic wrap and chill well.

Preheat oven to 375°. On lightly floured board, roll out dough ½ inch thick for tiny scones, ¾ inch for larger rounds. Place close together on a lightly buttered baking sheet. Brush tops with heavy cream for a glazed finish and bake in a hot oven until puffed and golden brown (13 to 15 minutes).

Heart-shaped, currant-studded miniature scones are served in an old tin scoop.

Buttermilk Biscuits
75 TO 80 1¼-INCH
BISCUITS

 6 cups sifted unbleached flour
 ¼ cup baking powder
 1 teaspoon baking soda
 ¼ cup sugar
 2 teaspoons salt
 2 cups solid vegetable shortening, or 1 cup each butter (2 sticks) and shortening

1¼ cups buttermilk
 ¼ cup heavy cream

Preheat oven to 400°.

Sift the flour, baking powder, baking soda, sugar, and salt together into a large bowl. Cut the shortening into the dry ingredients with a pastry cutter until texture resembles rolled oats. Cover and chill the mixture in the refrigerator for at least 20 minutes.

Make a well in the center of the mixture. Pour in the buttermilk and stir in quickly with your hands or a large spoon until just combined. It does not matter if there are bits of unincorporated flour left in the bowl. Turn the mixture out onto a lightly floured surface and divide in two. Shape the dough lightly into rough rectangles. Place 1 piece on top of the other. Transfer right onto a buttered 17½ × 11½-inch baking sheet, preferably without sides. Roll the dough out quickly and gently and take care not to overwork it. Pat the edges to make them straight. Cut into 1¼-inch squares for cocktail biscuits or 2-inch squares for dinner biscuits.

Ginger Muffins
48 TINY MUFFINS

We bake these muffins in the miniature muffin tins. As an hors d'oeuvre topped with ginger cream cheese or a breakfast bread dipped in spicy apple butter, they are superb.

- ½ pound (2 sticks) unsalted butter
- 1 cup molasses
- 1 egg
- 1 cup granulated sugar
- 2¼ cups all-purpose flour
- 1½ teaspoons baking soda
- 1½ teaspoons ground ginger
- 1½ teaspoons cinnamon
- ½ teaspoon freshly grated nutmeg
- ½ teaspoon ground cloves
  Grated rind of 1 large orange
- ½ cup boiling water
- 4 tablespoons sour cream
  Pinch salt

Preheat oven to 350°. Butter or vegetable-spray pans.

Melt butter in molasses in a small saucepan. Cool. Beat egg and sugar until fluffy. Sift dry ingredients together. Add to the egg mixture alternately with the butter and molasses, stirring well. Add the rind, boiling water, salt, and sour cream. Blend well.

Fill muffin tins half full. Bake in preheated oven until puffed (about 15 minutes). Turn muffins onto rack to cool.
N O T E : These muffins can be made in quantity and frozen between layers of waxed paper in plastic containers. To use, thaw in covered container.

Homemade Jams

Jams should be made when the fruits are in season and abundant. Packed

Buttermilk biscuits with bowls of apple butter and jams.

in sterilized jars and topped with melted paraffin, jams will last 6 months or more. I prefer to make jam without pectin, the old-fashioned way, but either gives satisfactory results.

RASPBERRY JAM
- 4 cups crushed raspberries
- 3 cups sugar

APRICOT JAM
- 4 cups chopped unpeeled apricots
- 3 cups sugar
- 2 teaspoons lemon juice

SOUR CHERRY JAM
- 4 cups pitted, chopped sour cherries
- 3 cups sugar

Crush the fruit. Add sugar (¾ cup to 1 cup fruit). Stir over low heat until sugar is dissolved, then bring to a rapid boil and stir constantly until jam is thick and a teaspoonful dropped onto a saucer stays in place. The faster it thickens, the brighter the color and fresher the flavor.

Cook jams in small quantities—4 cups of fruit at a time.

Pour jams into hot, sterilized jars and seal immediately with melted wax, or use standard metal lids and rings.

Applesauce
APPROXIMATELY 2 QUARTS

- 8 pounds tart apples (McIntosh, Macoun, etc.)
- ½ cup water
  Sugar to taste
  Cinnamon to taste
  Grated rind of 2 lemons (optional)

Core and quarter apples. Put in a heavy saucepan with a closely fitting lid, add water, and cook over low heat until very soft.

Purée through a food mill and add sugar and cinnamon. Often I add no sugar at all, just a bit of cinnamon and lemon rind.

Apple Butter
APPROXIMATELY 5 PINTS

- 4 pounds tart apples, quartered
- 1 cup water
- 1 cup apple cider
  Brown sugar as needed
- 2 teaspoons cinnamon
- 1 teaspoon ground cloves
- ½ teaspoon allspice
  Grated rind and juice of 2 lemons

Cook the apples in the liquid until soft. Pass through a food mill. Add ½ cup brown sugar for each cup of purée. Add the spices, rind, and lemon juice and cook over very low heat until thick and dark brown. This may take 3 to 4 hours, or overnight on a flame tamer.

If not to be used within a week or two, pour into hot sterilized jars and seal tightly.

Clam Bake for Thirty

THE TRADITIONAL CLAM BAKE would begin near dawn on a stretch of beautiful beach. Here a crew of strongarms dig a six-foot-deep pit in the sand, set it ablaze with hardwood, and, hours later, when the pit is glowing with coals, load in a layer of seaweed, burlap bags of potatoes, corn on the cob, clams and lobsters, and more seaweed on top. While the feast steams, the time is whiled away with drinks, hors d'oeuvres, volleyball, swimming, and general seaside merriment.

Last year, for a large clam bake on a little private island in Long Island Sound—formerly the domain of Billy Rose—I discovered an alternative to pit-digging, which seemed simple and rustic enough to be acceptably authentic. In view of our rocky beach site, and limited time (and manpower), I asked Andy to build me eight large wooden boxes, with bottoms of rabbit wire, sized to fit exactly on top of the Big John grills I rent for such events. We covered the grills with six inches of seaweed picked off coastal rocks, stacked up boxes of lobsters and steamers lined with seaweed on top, and relegated the onions and unhusked corn to a direct fire, along with chicken and ribs. The boxes functioned like a series of individual pits, and as the heat rose up through the seaweed, extraordinary smells caught the breeze. Fresh clams and guacamole and tortilla chips staved off hunger until the moment the steamers were judged open, the lobsters a respectable red. Then, with enormous ease, we transferred the boxes to a nearby picnic table, added platters of the barbecued ribs and chicken, and a ready accompaniment of potato salad, French bread, and melted butter. Later on, we passed bowls of fresh fruit, and giant cookies of many kinds.

A clam bake is ideally staged with at least a view to, if not access to, the water. The informality and expansiveness of a beach scene is perfectly suited to this finger fare, to paper plates, and attendant ball games. And a bonfire, marshmallows, and a sing-along guitar are possible extensions. Our situation on Tavern Island was unusual, yet given a reliable source of fresh seafood (and seaweed, which can be ordered from fish stores), an adventuresome person in the Berkshires or Kansas City should and would be able to stage a clam bake. It is a festive, easy party, and with the box method, adaptable to anywhere.

❧ MENU ❧

Fresh Clam Bar   Guacamole and Tortilla Chips
Barbecued Ribs   Barbecued Chicken   Lobsters
Steamers   Coal-Roasted Corn on the Cob
Homemade French Bread   Potato Salad
Fresh Fruits   Sugar Cookies
Beer, White Wine, Iced Tea

Steamer clams cook on the grill.

Steamer boxes of fresh lobsters atop a Big John grill.

Guacamole

SERVES 30

6 ripe avocados
4 tomatoes, peeled, seeded, and chopped
3 to 4 hot green chilies, seeded and chopped
1 small onion, grated
3 teaspoons fresh coriander, chopped
1½ teaspoons kosher salt
¼ teaspoon freshly ground pepper
   Lime juice

GARNISH
   Sprigs of fresh coriander

Peel, pit, and mash avocados. Combine with tomatoes, chilies, onion, and coriander. Season with salt and pepper, and squeeze lime juice over top to prevent turning brown. (Bury the avocado pit in guacamole to help prevent the dip from darkening. Remove before serving.)

Decorate with sprigs of fresh coriander and serve with store-bought tortilla chips.

VARIATION: Use as a dip for freshly cooked shrimp served on bamboo skewers.

A metal plant tray holds the ingredients for a fresh clam bar.

Barbecued Ribs

30 SERVINGS

Racks of pork ribs are marinated for 2 days, then grilled atop charcoal fires. Hack them into individual ribs with a cleaver on a board.

MARINADE
1½ cups light soy sauce
6 tablespoons bean paste
1½ cups hoisin sauce
½ cup dry sherry
1 tablespoon sugar
3 tablespoons catsup
3 tablespoons grapefruit juice
2 tablespoons honey
9 cloves garlic, peeled and crushed

2 8-pound racks of ribs, well trimmed of excess fat

Mix all the ingredients for the marinade together. Rub over the ribs and refrigerate for 2 days, turning 3 or 4 times.

To grill, cook over a well-made fire for approximately 40 minutes, turning and basting with marinade. Be careful not to char the ribs.

A box of bright red lobsters with the protective seaweed removed.

Barbecued Chicken

32 PIECES

Use broiler chickens (2½ pounds each). The barbecue sauce is also a marinade.

4 broiler chickens
½ cup olive oil
½ cup chopped onions
1 cup water
½ cup wine vinegar
3 tablespoons Worcestershire sauce
½ cup lemon juice
4 tablespoons brown sugar
2 cups catsup
   Chili powder to taste
   Black pepper and salt
1 tablespoon paprika

Cut each chicken into 8 pieces.

Sauté the onions in the oil until soft. Add the remaining ingredients and simmer for 20 minutes. Cool sauce before adding the chicken. Marinate 24 to 48 hours in the refrigerator.

Grill over charcoal fire, cooking slowly and evenly, basting frequently with the sauce.

Lobsters

At a clam bake everyone wants lobsters, so allow 1 per person. Each lobster should be about 1¼ pounds.

1 lobster per person
   Lots of melted butter (5 pounds for 30 guests)
   Lots of lemon wedges

Line the wooden boxes with a layer of seaweed. Arrange the lobsters on top of the seaweed and if there is room for a second layer put seaweed between. Top with a final layer of seaweed.

Steam on the grills at least 35 to 45 minutes. Check 1 lobster for doneness. It is wise to rearrange the boxes 20 minutes after beginning to cook so the lobsters will cook evenly.

Steamers

30 SERVINGS

30 pounds steamer clams
4 pounds melted butter

Wash the steamers very well under cold water. Arrange in shallow lay-

Potato Salad

6 CUPS

This is one of my favorite potato salads for summer picnics. Double or quadruple the recipe as the guest list demands.

2 pounds waxy new potatoes, boiled in skins, peeled, and sliced
1 cup freshly made mayonnaise thinned with whole milk
2 green onions, finely minced
Salt and pepper

GARNISH
⅓ cup finely chopped parsley

When boiling the potatoes, take care not to overcook them. Peel and slice them while they are still warm. Pour on the mayonnaise and mix carefully to coat every slice. Add the onions. Season to taste and garnish with parsley.

Sugar Cookies
SEE RECIPE, PAGE 89

Above: *Spicy barbecued chicken.*

Right: *Summer corn cooking in the husk.*

ers in the wooden boxes. Cover with seaweed.

Place boxes on a layer of seaweed atop the grill. Steam until the clams open.

Serve with bowls of melted butter.

Coal-Roasted Corn on the Cob

A simple way to roast corn at a clam bake: the corn is put directly over the coals, unhusked. The natural juices remain locked in the corn, and as each guest shucks his corn, a bowl of melted butter flavored with lime juice and a sprinkling of cayenne pepper is passed, with a brush for painting the corn. Allow at least 1 ear per person.

Homemade French Breads
SEE RECIPE, PAGE 106

Italian Buffet for Fifty

THIS MEAL BEGINS WITH AN opulent antipasto and then continues with samplings of an array of tempting pastas.

The components of the antipasto—many kinds of sliced cheese, pickled and marinated vegetables, many kinds of Italian olives, meats and sausages—are so rich in color and texture that they invite a wildly imaginative display. Although it is more time-consuming than mere stacking, arranging vegetables and sausages in large unusual patterns on trays and rolling sliced meats and cheeses into fans or cornucopias will create a table as beautiful as a painting. Because it is a random arrangement, such a presentation will stay beautiful and fresh-looking as it dwindles.

This menu was the offering at a very sophisticated party held at a large contemporary house in Connecticut. The occasion was the twentieth reunion of Proctor & Gamble's marketing division. The interior of the house was all High Tech white, so we covered long tables with shiny waterproof fabric in the same circus colors as the hostess's Hellerware, for lively contrast. The decorations necessarily had little to do with Italy, and everything to do with Proctor & Gamble. Gigantic blowups of its products were placed outside along the route to the house (by eleven o'clock, all had been removed by would-be art collectors). All over the house were reminders of the corporate state: oversized photographs of other P&G parties; graphics pointing the way to men's room, ladies' room, and coat room; on waiters, T-shirts bearing photographs of company presidents; by the pool, an eight-foot bar of Zest; and in the pool, a huge cake of Styrofoam Ivory. The hostess went to extremes to be interesting, and the party turned out to be not only a high-spirited celebration, but an exemplary illustration of how entertaining a business affair can be.

❧ MENU ❧

Antipasto
Egg Spaghetti with Pesto
Tomato Fettuccine with Snow Peas Alfredo
Tortellini with Broccoli and Pesto
Lasagna with Spinach and Smoked Ham
Whole Wheat Tagliatelli Primavera
Spinach Tagliatelli with Fontina and Parmesan
Focaccia   Italian Garlic Bread
Figs and Melons
Italian Wines

White linens and dishes set off the colors and textures of pasta.

Above: *The completed antipasto—a bountiful arrangement of meats, cheeses, vegetables, and condiments for guests to pick from. Everything should be bite-size: Sliced meats can be rolled into cornucopias, large peppers cut into strips, and cheeses julienned and rolled.*

Right: *Antipasto ingredients lined up for assembly. (Left to right): hard salami, provolone, pepperoni, Genoa salami, braided mozzarella.*

Antipasto

I purchase ingredients for antipasto at a little Italian grocery in Westport. Greek food shops also have many of these items, as do gourmet food shops.

An antipasto can contain all of the following items. Of course, you can substitute your favorites or add more. I find that variety rather than quantity makes an antipasto fascinating.

If you have the time, marinate your own mushrooms, eggplant, artichoke hearts, and roasted peppers, and crack and season your own green olives.

Artichoke hearts, marinated in
   oil and herbs
Spanish olives
Calabresi olives
Salad olives with pimentos
Sicilian olives
Calamata olives in olive oil
Pepper strips
Cherry peppers
Chickpeas (ceci) in vinaigrette
Whole mushrooms, marinated in
   oil and herbs
Hot peppers
Roasted red peppers
Whole sweet peppers
Marinated roasted eggplant
Sweet crisp yellow peppers
Lupini beans

Pepperoni—hot and sweet, big
   and little
Pepperoncini
Prosciutto
Soppressata
Capicola—hot and sweet
Genoa salami
Hard salami

Mortadella
Provolone
Mozzarella

Homemade Pasta

8 SERVINGS

To make egg pasta, here is a simple recipe for the hand pasta machine, readily available in large department stores.

3½ **cups sifted all-purpose**
    flour
5 **large eggs**
1 **teaspoon salt**
1 **tablespoon olive oil**

Make a mound of flour in the center of a large board. Make a well in the center of the flour. Break the eggs into the well. Sprinkle on the salt and add the oil. With the fingertips of one hand, or with a fork, slowly mix the eggs into the flour, gradually breaking away the walls of the well. When all the eggs are mixed with the flour, knead the dough until it is smooth and elastic. It will be very firm, and should be quite smooth. The kneading will take about 10 minutes.

Cover the dough with an inverted bowl to prevent it from drying out while shaping the pasta.

To make fettuccine, follow the di-

rections which come with the pasta machine. Cut the dough into small pieces with a sharp knife and roll it into long strips. Dry the strips slightly on a broomstick stretched between 2 chairs, or a wooden laundry rack. Do not let strips dry too much or dough will be too brittle to cut into pasta.

Adjust machine to thickness desired and cut the pasta. Dry on racks until ready to use, or sprinkle lightly with cornmeal and cover with plastic wrap until

ready to use. Fresh pasta may be frozen in its soft state if well wrapped. To use, just drop frozen pasta into boiling salted water and cook only until al dente, or just cooked. Fresh pasta cooks much faster than dry pasta and care must be taken not to overcook it.

The whole process of making enough pasta for 8 persons will take about 2 hours. The taste and texture of homemade pasta is incomparable and well worth the effort.

A wire-bottomed wooden tray is perfect for drying homemade pastas. Whole wheat, tomato, and spinach are easy variations of basic egg pasta.

To make tomato pasta, add 4 tablespoons rich tomato paste to egg pasta.

To make spinach pasta, add ½ cup finely puréed spinach to egg pasta.

To make whole wheat pasta, substitute 2 cups whole wheat flour for 2 cups white.

Egg Spaghetti with Pesto

SERVES 16 TO 25 AS
PART OF BUFFET

4 pounds egg spaghetti
(commercial or homemade)
2 cups Pesto (page 143)
½ pound pine nuts (pignolia
nuts)
Olive oil, grated cheese,
fresh basil leaves (optional)

Put cooked egg spaghetti (it can be hot or cold) in a large bowl. Toss with the pesto, pine nuts, and oil and cheese as needed. Season with salt, pepper, and additional oil or cheese, if desired.

Arrange pasta on a platter, decorate with basil, and serve.

Above: *Egg spaghetti dressed with a flavorful homemade pesto and garnished with basil leaves.*

Right: *To make pesto by hand, chop all ingredients together into a coarse, thick paste.*

Pesto
APPROXIMATELY 3 CUPS

Genoese cooking has contributed this very versatile uncooked basil sauce, historically made in a mortar and pestle (hence the name pesto). When made in a mortar, pesto is thick and has a unique texture. Chopped on a wooden board as they do in Tuscany, the texture is quite similar. Prepared in a blender or food processor, the texture and taste are somewhat different, but this method is surely the most simple.

½ cup pignolia nuts
4 cloves garlic, peeled
1 teaspoon kosher salt
½ teaspoon freshly ground pepper
3 to 4 cups fresh basil leaves
¼ pound freshly grated Parmesan cheese
¼ pound freshly grated Pecorino or Romano cheese
1½ to 2 cups fine olive oil

To make by hand, chop the nuts and garlic with the salt and pepper until fine. Add the basil, chopping until very fine. Put in a bowl and add the grated cheeses. Add the olive oil, drop by drop, mixing until creamy and smooth.

To make in the food processor, grind all the ingredients until fine with ½ cup of the olive oil. Add the remaining oil and process until smooth and creamy.

VARIATIONS: Walnuts, a little butter, parsley, or cooked spinach may be added.

NOTE: To preserve pesto, omit the cheese and add enough olive oil to come ½ inch above the pesto. Covered this way, pesto will remain fresh throughout the winter. Pesto can be frozen in usable quantities in plastic bags, or stored in glass jars in the refrigerator.

Focaccia
TWO 10-INCH ROUND
FLAT BREADS

I make these thin, flat crusty breads in a variety of shapes—rectangles, circles, ovals—and I flavor them with salt, olive oil, and herbs—rosemary or sage. They are best right out of the oven, hot and crispy, but they can be made in advance and reheated.

4 cups unbleached flour
⅔ cake yeast dissolved in ⅔ cup warm water
10 tablespoons olive oil
⅓ cup water
2½ teaspoons salt
10 sage leaves, coarsely chopped; or 1½ teaspoons fresh rosemary; or 1 tablespoon coarse salt

Mix 2 cups flour with the dissolved yeast. By hand, or in the mixer with a dough hook, knead the dough for 10 minutes. Shape the dough into a ball, and put in a floured bowl to rise until doubled in bulk (about 3 hours).

Punch down, put on floured board, and knead again, incorporating the remaining flour, ⅓ cup olive oil, salt, and water. Knead until smooth and elastic. Let rise again in a covered bowl for another 3 hours.

Preheat oven to 400°.

Divide the dough in half and roll on a well-floured board into circles ½ inch thick. Brush with remaining olive oil and press the sage, rosemary, or salt into the top of the breads. Bake on a baking sheet until golden brown, about 20 minutes. Serve warm or at room temperature, cut in wedges.

Italian Garlic Bread

12 thick slices whole wheat Italian bread (bought or homemade)
5 cloves garlic, crushed and peeled
½ cup green olive oil
Salt and freshly ground pepper

Preheat the broiler. Toast the bread on both sides until light golden brown. Rub 1 side with crushed garlic. Brush generously with olive oil, soaking 1 side lightly. Sprinkle

Above: *Focaccia, a flat bread rubbed with olive oil and garlic and studded with herbs, is excellent with Italian meals and wines. Here it is surrounded by whole and quartered figs.*

with salt and pepper and serve warm.

NOTE: Italian whole wheat bread can be made by using half white and half whole wheat flour in the Homemade French Bread recipe (page 106).

Tomato Fettuccine
with Snow Peas Alfredo
SERVES 25 AS PART OF
BUFFET

This is a delightful pasta dish—it combines the creaminess of the traditional Alfredo with the crunchiness of snow peas. An added attraction is the use of tomato noodles.

4 pounds tomato fettuccine
2 cups whipping cream
4 egg yolks, lightly beaten
1 cup grated Parmesan cheese
6 tablespoons butter
   Salt and pepper
1 pound snow peas, blanched
   1 minute in boiling water

Cook the pasta in a large kettle of boiling, lightly salted water. Drain.

In a heavy skillet or sauté pan, heat the cream to a simmer. Stir a bit into the egg yolks, then add the yolks to the cream. Do not boil or the eggs will curdle. Over low heat, stir in the cheese and butter, and season with salt and pepper.

Gently toss the cooked pasta with the sauce, coating the noodles. Add the snow peas and serve from a heated bowl or platter.

Tortellini with
Broccoli and Pesto
SERVES 50 AS PART OF
BUFFET

8 pounds tortellini (half
   spinach, half egg)
3 bunches broccoli, cut into
   small flowerets

Tomato fettucine and snow peas.

1 cup Pesto (page 143)
1 cup French Vinaigrette
   (page 104)
   Salt and freshly ground
   pepper to taste

**Grated Parmesan cheese
(optional)**

Cook the tortellini in small batches in large kettles of boiling salted water. When done, drain in colanders and spread in thin layers on oiled baking sheets to cool, tossing lightly in the oil to prevent sticking.

Blanch the broccoli in boiling water for 3 to 4 minutes. Immerse in iced water to cool; drain well on racks.

Mix the pesto with the vinaigrette and correct seasoning. Toss broccoli and tortellini with the dressing. Add cheese if desired. Serve hot, or as soon as possible.

NOTE: Do not let the tortellini cool completely before tossing with the dressing.

VARIATION: To serve cold, immerse cooked tortellini in cold water, drain immediately, and toss with oil.

Lasagne with
Spinach and Smoked Ham
SERVES 25 AS PART OF
BUFFET

This is an unusual pasta—the broad noodles are layered, uncooked, with a rich tomato sauce, thin slices of smoked ham, ricotta, mozzarella, and steamed spinach leaves. Be sure to use fresh, uncooked pasta, about 3 inches wide, or the thin lasagna noodles made by Barilla, which need no precooking. I have always found the chore of cooking ordinary lasagna noodles messy and time-consuming—and they are much thicker and less delicate than the noodles I suggest.

8 cups homemade tomato sauce

1½ cups chopped parsley, basil, and/or oregano

4 pounds fresh noodles, 3 inches wide

3 pounds whole-milk ricotta, mixed with 2 egg yolks and 1 teaspoon freshly grated nutmeg

3 pounds mozzarella cheese, grated

1½ cups grated Parmesan or Pecorino cheese

2 pounds smoked ham, thinly sliced

4 pounds fresh spinach, leaves only, washed and steamed for 1 minute, and drained well
Salt and pepper

Preheat oven to 350°.

Spread a thin layer of tomato sauce in 2 large baking pans or Pyrex baking dishes. Sprinkle lightly with herbs. Layer pasta, cheeses, ham, and spinach, seasoning lightly as you complete each layer. Spread sauce and sprinkling of herbs between each layer. Top with a final sprinkling of mozzarella and Parmesan.

Bake for 45 to 60 minutes, until cheese has melted. Cool slightly before cutting into squares.

NOTE: This can be made in advance and reheated; or assemble lasagne the day before the party and bake just before serving.

Whole Wheat Tagliatelli Primavera

SERVES 25 AS PART OF BUFFET

4 pounds tagliatelli

3 carrots, peeled and diced

12 small zucchini, diced

12 stalks fresh asparagus, cut into 1-inch pieces

¾ pound string beans, cut into 1-inch pieces

1 large head cauliflower, broken into flowerets

1 head broccoli, broken into flowerets

2 green peppers, diced

3 Jerusalem artichokes, peeled and sliced

½ cup olive oil
Salt and pepper to taste

½ cup each chopped basil and parsley
Grated Parmesan cheese (optional)

Cook the tagliatelli until just tender. Drain, rinse with cold water, and drain again. Cook the vegetables (except for the green pepper and Jerusalem artichokes) separately in boiling water until they are tender but still crunchy. Cool in ice water and drain. Additional vegetables can be added or substituted for the ones suggested. It is important that the mixture be colorful.

Toss the cold tagliatelli with the vegetables. Add oil, salt and pepper, basil and parsley along with the green pepper and artichokes. Grated cheese can be added for flavor.

Spinach Tagliatelli with Fontina and Parmesan

SERVES 25 AS PART OF BUFFET

2 pounds mushrooms, sliced

2 pints heavy cream

⅓ cups cubed Fontina cheese

⅓ cups Parmesan cheese

12 eggs

16 slices prosciutto, cut into slivers
Salt, pepper, freshly ground nutmeg to taste

4 pounds spinach tagliatelli

To make the sauce, cook the mushrooms in the cream in a heavy skillet. Add the cheeses and cook over low heat until cheeses are completely melted. Cool slightly. Add the beaten eggs and put the mixture back on low heat, stirring constantly. (If mixture boils or becomes too hot, the eggs will curdle.) Season with salt, pepper, and nutmeg, and add the prosciutto. Keep warm over low heat while cooking pasta.

In a large kettle of lightly salted, boiling water cook the tagliatelli al dente. Drain.

Place freshly cooked hot pasta on a large platter and spoon sauce over top. Serve with additional grated cheese, if desired.

Below left: *A colorful assortment of crisp cooked vegetables brightens a dish of whole wheat tagliatelli.*

Below right: *Spinach tagliatelli (tinted with the addition of finely puréed spinach) with Fontina and Parmesan cheeses, slices of mushrooms, and slivered prosciutto.*

Russian Buffet for Twenty-four

RUSSIAN FOOD IS PROBABLY ONE of the least familiar cuisines in America. In New York, there are many more Thai or Korean restaurants than Russian, and the few Russian outposts invariably carry names like the Big Bear or the Troika, which somehow convey the message that inside awaits a heavy meal fit for a Siberian logger. Russian food such as I know it (there are very few Russian chefs around to transmit their knowledge) is not intrinsically heavy, but interesting, colorful, and adaptable to many situations. And for someone who operates best in a controlled situation, the following buffet offers distinct advan-

Opposite: *A fifth of Russian vodka is put into a half-gallon milk carton, filled with water and sprigs of flowers, and frozen for 24 hours. To serve, peel off carton and set vodka in a deep tray.*
Below: *Dark damask and silver enhance a hearty Russian buffet.*

tages, for everything but the chicken Pojarsky, which is quickly sautéed at the end, is prepared in advance, over the course of several days. And everything can be served informally from a dining-room table; thus the problems of both time and space are virtually eliminated. I proved this recently when I prepared this menu for twenty-four in a five-room apartment with a tiny kitchen.

This meal begins with miniature piroshki, and tiny blini laden with asparagus, both served from a tray lined with a starchy white napkin (to keep the blini warm and absorb butter). Then a thin lovely cold borscht served in goblets. For the entrees: a coulibiac of bass, which I make in a long rectangle of puff pastry (instead of brioche or pâte à choux dough), for lightness, and the Pojarsky, which is accompanied by a light chicken-based sauce spiced with paprika, and my versions of stuffed cabbage. For dessert: a pashka, a rich native cheesecake that resembles a crunchy coeur à la crème with raisins, and a kulich. The perfect beverages for this buffet are iced vodka and Uncle Vanyas, a delicious drink made with lime juice, vodka, and blackberry liqueur.

❧ MENU ❧

Piroshki   Blini with Asparagus
Borscht in Goblets   Coulibiac of Bass
Chicken Pojarsky   Stuffed Cabbage
Individual Stuffed Cabbage Leaves
Pashka   Kulich
Uncle Vanyas, Iced Vodka, Hot Tea

Piroshki

24 PIROSHKI

The filling of these little "hand pies" (as I call them) is highly seasoned and the pastry short, crispy, and glazed before baking for a beautifully shiny finish.

Piroshki traditionally accompany borscht, but they can also be served alone as an hors d'oeuvre.

PASTRY

2 cups all-purpose flour
½ cup (1 stick) unsalted butter
4 tablespoons lard
1 teaspoon salt
4 tablespoons ice water

FILLING

1 medium onion, finely chopped
2 tablespoons olive oil
1 large clove garlic, finely minced
2 cups shredded cabbage
2 cups cooked pork cut into small cubes, or 1 pound lean ground beef
1 large potato, peeled, diced, and cooked
¼ cup heavy cream
1 tablespoon caraway seed
2 tablespoons snipped fresh dillweed
1 teaspoon salt
½ to 1 teaspoon freshly ground pepper

EGG GLAZE

1 egg yolk beaten with 2 teaspoons water

To make pastry, follow directions for Perfect Plain Tart and Tartlet Crust (page 236).

To make filling, sauté onion in oil in a large skillet until soft. Add garlic and cook 1 minute. Stir in cabbage and cook 10 minutes over medium heat, stirring occasionally. (If using ground beef, cook with onion and garlic for 5 minutes before adding cabbage.) Remove from

heat and stir in remaining ingredients. Adjust seasonings. Cool. Preheat oven to 375°.

To assemble, roll pastry to ⅛-inch thickness. Cut into 2½-inch circles with a glass or biscuit cutter. Put 1 to 2 tablespoons filling in center of circle, fold in half, and seal edges well, crimping with tines of a fork. Place on buttered baking sheet and glaze with yolk mixture. Pierce piroshki with 2 or 3 vent holes. Bake for 20 to 30 minutes, until golden brown. Serve warm.

NOTE: Piroshki can be prepared in advance and frozen unbaked. To serve, bake frozen pies in 375° oven until golden brown.

Blini with Asparagus

SEE VARIATION, PAGE 46

Borscht in Goblets

SERVES 24

This peasant soup can be eaten unrefined, unstrained. But for the Russian buffet the soup is strained, and additional grated beets are added to the clear soup.

4 pounds beets
½ cup wine vinegar
1 teaspoon sugar
½ cup (1 stick) butter
3 tablespoons oil
1 small head green cabbage
3 large onions, sliced
¼ cup minced shallots or green onions
3 green or red peppers, thinly sliced
1 pound zucchini, unpeeled, thinly sliced
1 pound carrots, thinly sliced
16 cups homemade stock
Salt and freshly ground pepper

GARNISH

3 cups sour cream

Peel and grate beets. Put ¼ of the beets into a bowl with the vinegar and sugar. Cover and set aside. Slice cabbage very thinly and chop.

In a heavy stockpot, melt the butter with the oil. Sauté onions and shallots until soft. Add the other vegetables except the beets and cabbage. Cover and cook for 10 to 15 minutes, until tender but not soft. Add remaining beets to the pot, along with the cabbage. Pour in the stock and bring to a boil. Reduce heat so liquid is simmering, cover

partially, and cook for 2 hours. Cool. Skim off any fat and strain. Add salt and pepper to taste.

Reheat the strained borscht with reserved beets and the liquid in which they were soaking; cook gently for 15 minutes; do not boil.

Serve hot, in goblets, with dollops of sour cream.

NOTE: Any root vegetable, such as turnips, celeriac, or parsnips, can be added to or substituted for the other vegetables (except, of course, the beets and cabbage).

Coulibiac of Bass

SERVES 24

This is a complicated recipe but if you allow 2 days for preparation you will feel less rushed. Make the bass filling, dill crêpes, egg and rice mixture, and puff pastry one day, and assemble the coulibiac on the day of the party.

Traditionally, the bass is encased in brioche dough, but I prefer a lighter and very pretty covering of puff pastry.

Coulibiac of bass—my version of a classic Russian-French creation.

2 pounds Perfect Puff Pastry
(page 237)

BASS FILLING
3 tablespoons minced shallots
2 tablespoons unsalted butter
2 pounds striped bass fillets
½ pound fresh mushrooms,
wiped clean and thinly
sliced
¼ cup fresh dill, finely
chopped
2 teaspoons salt
Pepper to taste
1 cup dry white wine
1 cup Velouté (page 92) made
with fish stock
5 egg yolks, lightly beaten
Juice of 1 lemon
Large pinch cayenne pepper

EGG AND RICE FILLING
1 tablespoon tapioca
½ cup cold water
1 medium onion, minced
2 tablespoons unsalted butter
½ cup rice
1½ cups rich chicken broth
3 hard-boiled eggs, sieved
4 tablespoons chopped parsley
1 teaspoon salt
Pepper to taste

DILL CREPES (18 CREPES)
1¼ cups all-purpose flour
4 eggs
1 cup milk
1¼ cups cold water
3 tablespoons melted butter
½ teaspoon salt
6 tablespoons finely chopped
dill

GLAZE
2 egg yolks mixed with 2
tablespoons cream

Prepare puff pastry according to master recipe.

To make bass filling, preheat oven to 350°. Cook shallots in butter until tender. Place bass in a shallow casserole, and add shallots, mushrooms, dill, salt, and pepper. Pour wine over fillets, cover casserole with foil, and bake 20 minutes.

Cool fish in cooking liquid. Re-move from casserole and reserve liq-uid. Using 3 tablespoons butter and 3 tablespoons flour, prepare ve-louté according to directions. Add the poaching liquid to velouté.

Pour a bit of velouté into the light-ly beaten yolks; whisk until smooth. Add yolks to remaining velouté, cook over low heat, and stir in lemon juice and cayenne pepper. Spoon velouté over cooked fillets and refrigerate until firm.

To make the crêpes, put all ingre-dients except dill in blender. Blend at high speed 30 seconds. Scrape down sides and blend 30 seconds more. Pour into bowl, mix in dill, and refrigerate 1 hour.

To make 6-inch crêpes, spoon 2 ta-blespoons batter into a hot buttered crêpe pan. Cook over medium heat until surface is bubbly; flip crêpe and cook until golden brown. Re-move from heat and stack until ready to assemble coulibiac.

To make egg and rice filling, soften tapioca in water for 5 minutes. Cook over low heat until tapioca is thick, 6 to 8 minutes. Cool and drain in fine sieve for 10 minutes.

Sauté onions in butter until soft but not browned. Stir in rice and cook, stirring constantly, until rice is transparent. Add stock, reduce heat, cover, and cook until rice is done, about 18 minutes.

Combine tapioca, rice, sieved eggs, and parsley. Mix lightly and season.

To assemble the coulibiac, roll 1 pound puff pastry into a rectangle 14×22 inches and ⅛ inch thick. Lay 6 crêpes on the pastry, leaving a 2-inch border around the edge of the rectangle, overlapping the crêpes slightly if necessary. Sprin-kle a third of the egg and rice fill-ing over crêpes, and spread half the bass filling evenly over the rice. Lay 6 more crêpes over the bass, and cover with half the remaining rice mixture. Spread the remaining bass filling, sprinkle with the rest of the rice, and top with the last 6 crêpes.

Refrigerate until top pastry has been rolled out.

Roll the second pound of puff pas-try into a 14×22-inch rectangle. Fold the 2-inch border of the pastry base over the filling and measure the coulibiac (it should be approxi-mately 10×18 inches). Cut the top rectangle slightly larger than that measurement. Brush the pastry border with iced water and cover with top pastry. Seal edges well. Use the trimmings for decorative cutouts, affixing them to the top pastry with water. Crimp pastry edges. Refrigerate until ready to bake, at least one hour.

To bake the coulibiac, preheat oven to 400°. Brush the top with the yolk-cream glaze. Cut two small vents in the pastry and insert two aluminum foil funnels in the holes to allow steam to escape. Bake until pastry has puffed, then reduce tem-perature to 350° and continue bak-ing for approximately 1 hour, until pastry is golden brown. Slide onto rack to cool slightly before cutting into serving pieces.

Chicken Pojarsky
16 CUTLETS

Golden cutlets of ground, juicy breast of chicken, flavored with nutmeg and sauced with a light paprika-thyme sauce. Chilling the cutlets between shaping, breading, and cooking maintains the shape of the cutlets. Double this recipe if needed. Any extra cutlets can be frozen, uncooked.

4 chicken breasts, skinned
and boned
¾ pound (3 sticks) unsalted
butter
Salt and freshly ground
pepper to taste
½ teaspoon freshly grated
nutmeg
1 cup flour

2 eggs, lightly beaten
3 to 4 cups fresh white bread
crumbs
¼ cup vegetable oil

PAPRIKA-THYME SAUCE
1 large yellow onion, chopped
2 tablespoons unsalted butter
4 teaspoons medium hot
paprika
2 tablespoons flour
1 teaspoon fresh thyme or ½
teaspoon dried thyme
1 cup chicken stock
1 cup heavy cream
Juice of 1 lemon
Salt and freshly ground
pepper to taste
2 teaspoons brandy
½ cup sour cream

Chill the chicken breasts. Chop finely in meat grinder or food pro-cessor. Melt 1½ sticks butter and stir into the ground chicken. Sea-son with salt, pepper, and nutmeg.

Chill the chicken mixture in the re-frigerator or freezer until very cold. Using ½ cup of the chicken mix-ture at a time, shape into cutlets, ¾ inch thick. Put on waxed paper and chill until ready to bread.

Dip each cutlet first into flour, then egg, then bread crumbs. Put on waxed paper and chill again un-til ready to sauté.

Heat the remaining 1½ sticks but-ter with the oil until hot but not smoking. Cook the cutlets on each side until light golden brown (ap-proximately 8 to 10 minutes). Keep cutlets warm on heated plat-ter in turned-off oven.

To make the sauce, cook the onion in butter for 5 minutes; add the pa-prika, flour, thyme, and stock and simmer for 5 minutes. Add the cream, lemon juice, salt, pepper, and brandy. Strain sauce through a fine sieve. Set aside until ready to use. Before serving, return to the heat, add the sour cream, and bring to a low simmer. *Do not boil.* Serve spooned around the cutlets or sepa-rately in a heated bowl.

Stuffed Cabbage
SERVES 16

This way of serving stuffed cabbage is unusual in that the entire head of cabbage is stuffed, reassembled, and cooked. Sliced, it presents a layered wedge of cabbage and filling that is very appealing.

- ½ pound ground pork
- ½ pound ground veal
- ½ cup kasha, cooked according to directions on box
- 2 large eggs
- ¼ cup shallots, minced and sautéed in 1 tablespoon butter until transparent
- 2 teaspoons thyme
- 1 teaspoon coriander
- ½ teaspoon freshly ground pepper
- 1 teaspoon salt
- 1 large green cabbage, preferably a hard winter variety
- 1 large onion, thinly sliced
- 1 tablespoon butter
- 1 tablespoon caraway seeds
- 2 cups beef stock

Combine the pork, veal, kasha, eggs, shallots, and seasonings. Mix.

Cut out core of the cabbage and steam until the leaves are tender and easy to handle without tearing. Separate the leaves, carefully stacking in order of size. Select a colander or sieve just big enough to contain the entire head of cabbage and a covered casserole or Dutch oven big enough to hold the colander without touching the bottom.

Line the colander with a double thickness of cheesecloth. Starting with the three largest, outermost leaves, line the colander by overlapping the leaves, stem ends up. Spread a thin layer of filling over the leaves. Line the colander with 3 more leaves, spread more filling, and continue until a solid shape

fills the colander. Pull the ends of the cheesecloth tightly around the cabbage and tie. Trim off any excess cloth to make a neat bundle. Tie around the circumference of the ball to secure the shape. Place the cheesecloth-wrapped cabbage in the colander, round side up.

In the casserole, sauté the sliced onion in the butter until tender. Add any leftover cabbage leaves, chopped finely, and the caraway seeds and stock. Bring to a boil, reduce heat, and place the colander over the stock. Cover the pot tightly and simmer slowly for 1½ hours. Check the liquid in the casserole several times, adding water if necessary.

Turn the wrapped cabbage ball onto a platter. Remove the cheesecloth. Invert onto a heated platter. Surround with the chopped cabbage and any extra cooking liquid.

Individual Stuffed Cabbage Leaves
SERVES 24

I learned to make our family's stuffed cabbage rolls from my Grandmother Kostyra. A few years ago in New York, I ate this type of stuffed cabbage—rounds filled with veal, pork, rice, and dill—and have been making it ever since.

- 1 head winter cabbage, cored
- 1 pound ground veal
- 1 pound ground pork
- 1 cup rice cooked until just tender
- 2 eggs, lightly beaten
  Salt, pepper, sweet paprika to taste
- ½ cup fresh dill, finely chopped
  Freshly grated nutmeg to taste
- 1 15-ounce can whole plum tomatoes in purée

- ½ cup dry white wine
- 1 bay leaf
  Sprigs of fresh thyme
  Small bunch parsley

Steam the cored head of cabbage. As the outer leaves cook, remove them and set aside until entire head is dismantled. Cut away the rib from center of each leaf, taking care not to cut through the leaf.

Combine the meats, rice, eggs, salt, pepper, paprika, dill, and nutmeg.

Preheat oven to 350°.

Place a cabbage leaf on a 14-inch square of cheesecloth. Spoon about ⅓ to ½ cup of the filling onto the center of the leaf. Pick up the corners of the cheesecloth and twist until the cabbage is in the shape of a flattened ball and the outside edges of the leaf are tightly folded over the filling. Remove the "ball" from the cheesecloth and place in a large baking dish, folded side down. Repeat until all the filling has been used. Pour the tomatoes, purée, and wine over the balls; add the herbs and an additional sprinkling of salt and pepper. Bake, covered, for 1 hour, or until the cabbage is very tender.

Serve with the sauce and a dollop of sour cream.

Pashka
2½ QUARTS (16 SERVINGS)

A traditional Russian dessert composed of cottage cheese, cream, hard-boiled egg yolks, and almonds, among other things. In Russia it is made in a four-sided, truncated pyramidal mold, but we make it in a cheesecloth-lined chinois (a large metal cone-shaped sieve), which enables the whey to seep out. Some people use a clay flowerpot.

- 1 pound unsalted butter
- 1½ cups sugar
- 1 vanilla bean
- 7 hard-boiled egg yolks, sieved or riced
- 4⅔ cups large-curd cottage cheese
- 3 tablespoons finely chopped toasted blanched almonds
- 3 tablespoons plus 2 teaspoons finely chopped candied citron
- 2 teaspoons lemon juice
- 1 teaspoon vanilla extract
- ¼ teaspoon grated lemon peel
- ⅛ teaspoon salt
- ⅔ cup heavy cream
- ⅔ cup sour cream

Almond-studded pashka garnished with brightly colored flowers.

GARNISH

½ cup unblanched whole almonds, fresh flowers

Line the mold of your choice with a large piece of cheesecloth.

Cream the butter and sugar until smooth and fluffy. Chop the vanilla bean very finely and add to the butter mixture. Beat the sieved egg yolks and cottage cheese into the butter. Mix very well. Add the toasted almonds, citron, lemon juice, vanilla, lemon peel, and salt.

Whip the cream and fold into the mixture along with the sour cream. Pour into the lined mold. Fold excess cheesecloth over the top of the pashka and put a flat plate on top. The pashka must then be refrigerated until firm, at least 24 hours.

To serve, unfold cheesecloth, reverse onto a serving platter, and unmold. Remove cheesecloth carefully and decorate with almonds

Kulich

2 LOAVES

This yeast cake is baked in two 1-pound tall coffee cans. The traditional decoration consists of white royal icing and a pink rose.

¼ cup milk
2 tablespoons unsalted butter
¼ cup all-purpose flour
1 egg
1 package dry yeast
1 cup sugar
¾ cup (1½ sticks) unsalted butter
½ teaspoon salt
8 egg yolks
1 vanilla bean, very finely minced
¼ cup candied citron, finely chopped
¼ cup golden raisins
¼ cup currants
¼ cup blanched slivered almonds

⅛ teaspoon cardamom
⅛ teaspoon nutmeg
⅛ teaspoon leaf saffron
¼ cup milk
1 tablespoon vodka
3 to 4 cups all-purpose flour

ROYAL ICING

1 cup confectioners' sugar
1 egg white
Lemon juice

Heat the milk and butter until the butter melts. Add the ¼ cup flour and stir in the egg. Cool.

Proof the yeast for 5 minutes in ¼ cup water (105°) to which 1 teaspoon of sugar has been added. Add to the flour mixture. Let "sponge" rise for 30 minutes, covered, in a warm place.

Cream the sugar and butter until light and fluffy. Add the salt and egg yolks and beat well. Add the vanilla, fruits, nuts, flavorings, and liquids to the egg mixture. Add the sponge. Using a mixer with a dough hook, add enough of the flour to make a smooth, elastic dough. Put dough in a well-buttered bowl, cover loosely, and let rise until doubled in bulk—about 3 hours.

Butter two 1-pound coffee cans. Line bottoms and sides with waxed paper. Butter the paper linings. Divide the dough in half. Put into the lined tins, cover, and let rise to the tops of the cans—about 2 hours.

Preheat oven to 350°. Bake the cakes for 45 to 60 minutes, until golden brown. Cool slightly, on their sides, before removing cakes from cans. Tear off the paper. Cool upright on a rack.

To make icing, mix confectioners' sugar with enough egg white and a few drops of lemon juice to make a runny icing. Pour over the cakes. When the icing dries, stick a rose in the top of each cake.

Royal icing decorates a kulich.

Hawaiian Luau for Twenty

*T*HIS PARTY GERMINATED FROM a hostess's affection for orchids, and her desire to entertain her friends in an unusual and colorful way in late November. Her greenhouse, an extension of the dining room, was the ideal place to serve a buffet inspired by Hawaiian cuisine and based on the flavors of the East (ginger, curry, soy) and the tropics (lime, coconut, pineapple). With a backdrop of her orchids, supplemented with succulent houseplants and spring flowers, the mood was exotic, a little dreamlike, and almost as affecting as if everything had been set up outdoors, which of course it could be in another season.

This meal is a hybrid, for apart from one spectacular entree, a 19-pound oven-roasted suckling pig with steamed rice, we served finger food that might suit a cocktail buffet: chicken wings with bananas, lime-marinated salmon, rumaki, coconut shrimp. Barbecued clams, miniature steak satés, and Dungeness crabs cooked on small tabletop hibachis.

Our hostess had a collection of lotus plates and big clam shells, which were the perfect receptacles for this food. (Any collection of oversized beach shells will do nicely.) We added melon-colored napkins. We devised a decorative way of cutting watermelon and found a bromeliad of matching hues for a garnish, and then adorned the fruit salad with bits of New Zealand star fruit, which had just appeared in the market. (When cut, this tart fruit falls naturally into perfect stars.) The pig wore a necklace of star fruit.

The essential element of this party is the overall feeling of carefree, sunstruck, island fun. Although orchids are impressive,

Batiks and exotic flora provide the backdrop for an indoor luau.

the authenticity of details is subordinate to the spirit of the details. Houseplants, dime-store leis, grass skirts, Hawaiian music, even a hula dancer are possibilities, for this party is meant to be amusing. The drinks set the tone—fresh, colorful, exotic—variations of Trader Vic's inventions. To serve them, you might use coconuts halved with a hacksaw, or heavy balloon goblets.

MENU

Roast Suckling Pig with Steamed Rice   Marinated Scallops

Salmon Poupous   Mock Drumsticks

Chicken Wings with Bananas   Coconut Shrimp

Rumaki   Barbecued Clams   Dungeness Crab

Gingered Flank Steak Satés

Pineapple with Star Fruit   Tropical Fruit Salad   Watermelon

Tropical Drinks

Roast Suckling Pig
APPROXIMATELY 30 SERVINGS

A luau is not authentic without the inclusion of a suckling pig, roasted until the skin is crunchy and the flesh very tender.

1 18- to 20-pound suckling pig
   Salt, pepper, thyme
   Vegetable oil

Preheat oven to 325°.

Season the cavity of the pig with salt, pepper, and thyme. Stuff the cavity with crumpled aluminum foil, to prevent the pig from losing its shape during roasting. Set the pig upright in a roasting pan large enough to hold the pig on its stomach with its feet curled under its body. Prop it up with balls of aluminum foil if necessary. Put a small ball of foil in its mouth to hold the shape.

Roast pig for about 3 hours, brushing occasionally with oil, until the skin is an even golden brown and the juices from the thickest part of the body run clear. If it is browning too much, reduce temperature and cover with foil.

Remove to a serving platter, discard the foil props, and decorate with star fruits, cranberries, apples, kiwis, etc. Serve warm or at room temperature. Carve one side at a time into small pieces. Try to include a bit of the skin with each serving.

NOTE: For a large outdoor barbecue I often prebake the pigs for about 2½ hours and then put them on the hot grills to finish the cooking and create a spectacle for the guests. To prevent charring, use aluminum foil to protect the skin from too-hot fires.

Marinated Scallops
APPROXIMATELY 60

1½ pounds fresh (not frozen) bay scallops

MARINADE

½ cup fresh lime juice
⅛ teaspoon Tabasco
½ teaspoon salt
½ teaspoon white pepper

SAUCE

1 cup grated coconut (fresh, packaged, or unsweetened)
¾ cup boiling water
½ cup sour cream
3 tablespoons finely chopped scallions

In nonmetal bowl, combine marinade ingredients; stir in scallops and cover. Marinate in refrigerator at least 2 hours.

Stir coconut into boiling water, strain through double layer of cheesecloth and cool liquid completely.

Combine cooled coconut liquid with sour cream and scallions; stir. Add drained scallops with 1 teaspoon marinade; stir.

Salmon Poupous
APPROXIMATELY 60

3 medium tomatoes, peeled, seeded, and chopped
1 cup fresh lime juice
½ cup finely chopped onions
⅛ teaspoon Tabasco
2 teaspoons sugar
1 tablespoon salt
1 teaspoon pepper
2 pounds fresh salmon
   Cherry tomatoes, halved

In nonmetal bowl, combine all ingredients except salmon and cherry tomatoes. Remove bones and skin from salmon and cut into 1-inch squares. Stir salmon into the marinade, cover, and marinate in the refrigerator at least 6 hours, up to 48 hours. This "cooks" the salmon.

Drain salmon. Using 4-inch bamboo skewers, thread 2 to 3 salmon chunks on each skewer. Top with cherry tomato half.

Chill; serve cold.

Mock Drumsticks
40 HORS D'OEUVRES

40 chicken wings

BATTER

1½ cups flour
2 tablespoons cornstarch
2 tablespoons baking powder
1 teaspoon salt
½ teaspoon pepper
¾ cup iced water

APRICOT SAUCE

1 cup apricot preserves
½ cup cider vinegar
1 teaspoon paprika
   Salt to taste, pinch of cayenne pepper

   Light vegetable oil for frying

Cut tip and middle joint from each wing, save for Chicken Wings with Bananas (below). With boning knife, loosen meat around large joint: push meat gently down bone, turning inside out.

Prepare batter ½ hour before using. Mix all ingredients, stirring until smooth.

To make the sauce, heat all the ingredients over low heat.

In deep skillet, heat 2 inches oil to 375°. Dip chicken in batter; fry 4 or 5 pieces at a time about 5 minutes, until crisp. Drain on paper towel. Serve on platter around bowl of apricot sauce for dipping.

Chicken Wings with Bananas
40 PIECES

8 tablespoons (1 stick) butter
40 chicken wing tips (saved from Mock Drumsticks, above)
   Salt and pepper to taste
4 unripe bananas, in ¼-inch-thick slices

In heavy skillet, heat 2 tablespoons butter; sauté chicken wing tips, 8 to 10 pieces at a time, turning so they brown nicely. Sprinkle with salt and pepper. When chicken is cooked through (12 to 15 minutes), remove to serving platter with slotted spoon and keep warm. Repeat with all the chicken until cooked, adding butter as necessary.

Sauté banana slices 3 to 4 minutes in skillet in which chicken was cooked; arrange over chicken.

Coconut Shrimp
35 HORS D'OEUVRES

35 extra-large shrimp, shelled, deveined, with tails intact

MARINADE
¼ cup fresh lemon juice
½ teaspoon salt
1½ teaspoons curry powder
½ teaspoon ground ginger

BATTER
2 cups flour
1⅓ cups cold milk
2 teaspoons baking powder

1½ cups grated coconut

Light vegetable oil for frying

With sharp knife, split shrimp lengthwise; do not sever halves.

Combine marinade ingredients and add shrimp. Marinate in refrigerator at least 2 hours.

Combine batter ingredients, stir.

Drain shrimp; stir marinade into batter.

Lightly toast the coconut in a 375° oven.

In skillet, heat 2 inches of oil to 375°. Dip shrimp in batter and fry 3 to 5 minutes, until golden brown. Dip into toasted coconut; serve warm.

Mock drumsticks with apricot sauce, pineapple with star fruit, and dungeness crab.

Rumaki

APPROXIMATELY 36 HORS
D'OEUVRES

½ cup light soy sauce
½ cup packed brown sugar
½ cup water
2 tablespoons minced fresh
   ginger root
1 3-inch cinnamon stick
1 large garlic clove, peeled
   and minced
8 star anise (available at
   Oriental food shops,
   gourmet centers)
3 bay leaves
1½ pounds chicken livers,
   trimmed, washed, patted
   dry, and halved
16 to 18 slices lean bacon, cut
   in half
16 to 18 water chestnuts (fresh
   or canned), halved

In heavy saucepan, combine soy
sauce, sugar, water, ginger root,
cinnamon, garlic, anise, and bay
leaves. Bring to boil, stirring constantly. Reduce heat, add livers,
and simmer 2 to 3 minutes. Livers
should be pink inside. With slotted
spoon, remove livers to platter.

Wrap half slice of bacon around
both a piece of liver and water
chestnut; fasten with toothpick.
Chill on foil-lined baking sheets
until cooking time.

Preheat oven to 400°. Bake 12 to
15 minutes, until bacon is crisp.
Drain on paper towel. Serve warm.

Barbecued Clams

48 SMALL CLAMS

BARBECUE SAUCE
1 cup catsup
½ cup chili sauce
½ cup packed brown sugar
¼ cup apple cider vinegar

2 tablespoons prepared Dijon
   mustard
1 medium onion, chopped and
   sautéed in 1 tablespoon oil
   for 5 minutes
1 teaspoon minced fresh
   ginger root
1 teaspoon grated lemon peel

Combine sauce ingredients and let
stand at least 1 hour.

Bake clams on baking sheet in preheated 450° oven 2 to 3 minutes,
until they open. Remove from
oven; cool.

With point of sharp knife, remove
top shell from each clam. Replace
clams in bottom shells on baking
sheet; top each with ½ teaspoon
barbecue sauce.

On hibachi, grill each clam over
coals about 3 minutes; in broiler,
heat 2 to 3 minutes, taking care not
to burn clams.

Dungeness Crab

*These are a seasonal treat, and were
in season when we gave the indoor
luau party. However, some fish-
mongers keep a supply, cooked and
frozen. Allow to thaw slowly to
room temperature. Serve ½ crab per
person as part of a buffet, or 1 per
person as a luncheon dish. The legs
should be cracked and the back shell
cut in slices for easy eating.*

To cook, follow directions for boiling lobster (page 284).

Serve with an herb-flavored homemade Mayonnaise (below).

Herb Flavored Mayonnaise

APPROXIMATELY 2½ CUPS

HOMEMADE MAYONNAISE
2 eggs
¼ teaspoon dry mustard

¾ teaspoon salt
2 tablespoons freshly squeezed
   lemon juice
1 cup olive oil
1 cup vegetable or safflower
   oil

½ pound spinach leaves
2 tablespoons chopped shallots
¼ cup watercress leaves
¼ cup chopped parsley
1 to 2 tablespoons fresh
   tarragon leaves

To make mayonnaise, mix eggs,
mustard, salt, and lemon juice in a

food processor or blender. Add the
olive oil, drop by drop, until the
mixture begins to thicken. Add the
remaining oil in a steady stream
and mix until smooth. Taste for
seasoning. Add more salt or lemon
juice if necessary. Refrigerate.

Bring a small pot of water to boil.
Add the greens and herbs and boil
1 minute. Drain and rinse with
cold water. Drain well and pat dry
with a towel.

Chop herb/greens mixture in a food
processor and blend into mayonnaise.

Opposite: Unusual containers can be imaginatively used for serving: Lotus plates holds coconut shrimp and pineapple with star fruit; scallop shells contain marinated scallops; tropical fruit salad is spooned into a hollowed-out coconut.

Gingered Flank Steak Satés

40 TO 50 HORS D'OEUVRES

If you partially freeze the steak for 10 to 15 minutes, you will find it much easier to slice.

- 1 flank steak (about 2 pounds), trimmed of all fat
- 1 fresh hot chili, 3 to 4 inches long, seeded and chopped
- 1 medium onion, minced
- 3 teaspoons grated or minced fresh ginger root
- 3 tablespoons fresh lime juice
- 2 tablespoons salt
- 2 tablespoons soy sauce
- 2 tablespoons vegetable oil

Holding knife at a slant, cut flank steak across grain in long thin strips, about ¼ inch thick, so that slices will be about 1 inch wide.

In nonmetal bowl, combine remaining ingredients. Add meat and marinate at least 2 hours, or preferably overnight in refrigerator.

Remove meat; reserving marinade. Using 6-inch bamboo skewers, weave 1 meat strip onto each skewer. Put skewered meat in shallow pan; pour reserved marinade over skewers. (This can be done several hours before the start of the party.)

When ready to cook, on hibachi or in broiler, broil skewered meat 4 to 5 minutes. Serve hot.

VARIATION: 3 pounds boneless chicken breast, cut in ¾-inch cubes, can be substituted for the flank steak. Marinate and cook as directed.

Pineapple with Star Fruit

- 3 fresh pineapples
- 4 kiwi fruits, peeled and sliced crosswise
- 4 star fruits, sliced crosswise
- ½ cup orange-flavored liqueur

With large, sharp knife, quarter each pineapple, cutting through foliage and fruit. With small, sharp knife, cut flesh away from skin, following contour of pineapple quarter; then slice crosswise. Leave slices in place so pineapple quarters appear whole.

Arrange kiwis and star fruits on top of pineapple quarters. Sprinkle generously with liqueur.

Tropical Fruit Salad

SERVES 20

Flesh of 2 cantaloupes, cut in small pieces or scooped into balls
Flesh of 1 honeydew melon, cut in small pieces or scooped into balls
Flesh of 2 pineapples, cubed
- 3 bananas, peeled and sliced crosswise
- 4 New Zealand star fruits, sliced crosswise
- 1 pound seedless green grapes
  Strawberries, hulled (optional)
  Kumquats (optional)
  Kiwi fruits, peeled and sliced (optional)

SAUCE
- 1 cup sour cream
- ¼ cup grated fresh coconut
- ¼ cup apricot preserves
- 2 tablespoons dry white wine
- ½ cup chopped macadamia nuts

Combine all fruits in giant clamshell or large bowl.

In another bowl, combine sauce ingredients; stir.

Serve sauce separately in hollowed-out coconut shell or bowl.

NOTE: Star fruits can be purchased fresh in season at Oriental groceries. Kumquats can be purchased fresh at specialty groceries or canned in gourmet shops. Kiwi fruits are available fresh in big-city supermarkets and greengrocers almost all year round. These fruits can also be ordered from Trader Vic's Food Products, P.O. Box 8603, Emeryville, CA 94608.

Watermelon

Choose a large ripe melon. Chill in ice or in refrigerator until party time.

To cut melon as in photograph, make vertical slices halfway through melon. Next, cut horizontally to sever the slices from lower half of melon. Each slice will be half-moon-shaped. Pull alternating slices out on each side of melon to create decorative effect.
Garnish with fresh flowers.

Ocean Sunrise
MAKES 1 GENEROUS
DRINK

Recipe can be doubled or tripled to make more than 1 drink.

Juice of 1 lime
1½ ounces cranberry juice
1½ ounces tequila
Crushed ice

Put all ingredients in cocktail shaker; shake well. (Or put in heavy-duty mixer and mix well.) Pour into balloon goblet or wine-glass.

Mango Daiquiris
SERVES 4

1 cup ripe mango
3 large strawberries
½ cup light rum
Juice of 2 limes
2 tablespoons superfine sugar
2 cups crushed ice

GARNISH
Strawberries

In electric blender, blend all ingredients (except garnish) until smooth and frothy. Serve in chilled glasses garnished with strawberries.

Virgin Island
MAKES 1 DRINK

The fresh pineapple taste of this nonalcoholic drink is reminiscent of a piña colada. Recipe can be doubled or tripled to make more than 1 drink.

3 ounces unsweetened
pineapple juice

2 slices or spears pineapple
(fresh if possible)
2 teaspoons canned coconut
cream
¼ ounce lemon juice
1 teaspoon superfine sugar
1 scoop finely crushed ice

GARNISH
Pineapple star

Put all ingredients in blender and blend until frothy. Pour into glass. Garnish with pineapple star.

Kiwi Cooler
SERVES 4

2 to 3 cups crushed ice
¾ cup vodka
2 tablespoons canned coconut
cream
Kiwi fruit, peeled and sliced
Juice of 2 lemons
¼ cup superfine sugar

GARNISH
Additional kiwi fruit slices

In the electric blender, blend all ingredients (except garnish) until frothy. Serve in chilled glasses, garnished with kiwi fruit slices.

Mai Tai Cocktail

Double or triple recipe to make more than 1 drink.

1 ounce light rum
2 ounces mai tai mix
3 ounces orange juice
Finely crushed or shaved ice

GARNISH
Lime slice

Fill a double old-fashioned glass with ice, add mai tai mix and orange juice, and mix well. Garnish with lime slice.

NOTE: Mai tai mix may be ordered from Trader Vic's Food Products, P.O. Box 8603, Emeryville, CA 94608. Write to them for details.

Papaya/Banana/Rum Shake
SERVES 2 TO 3

1 peeled, seeded ripe papaya
1 medium banana
Juice of 1 lime
1 tablespoon honey
2 egg yolks
½ teaspoon vanilla extract
1 cup milk, ice cold
⅓ cup rum, chilled (optional)
2 egg whites

In electric blender, blend all ingredients except egg whites until smooth. Beat the egg whites until stiff. Fold into the blended mixture. Pour into balloon glasses. Drink at once.

Cranberry Cocktail
SERVES 1

Recipe may be doubled or tripled to make more than 1 drink.

1 ounce cranberry juice
1 ounce apple juice
1½ ounces light rum
1 ounce vodka
½ ounce coconut cream
Juice of 1 lime
Dash of grenadine syrup
Finely crushed ice

GARNISH
Skewered cranberries

Put all ingredients except cranberries in blender and blend just until frothy. Pour into glass and garnish.

NOTE: You can substitute 2 ounces cranapple juice for cranberry and apple juices.

The exotic tone of a Hawaiian luau is enhanced with mouthwatering tropical drinks. Here, an array of colorful cocktails is garnished with fresh fruit, flowers, and mint.

CHAPTER SEVEN

The Dinner Party

T*HE MOST COMMON FORM OF* at-home entertaining is the sit-down dinner. Whether small or large, impromptu or formal, it is a figurative extension of the family table. This is my own personal favorite, for a sit-down dinner is a leisurely occasion, where there is time to savor and appreciate food, to have deep, old-fashioned conversations, to establish friendships. Dinner parties in hotels or at large benefit evenings can be boring because they are impersonal, but I can think of very few lackluster events set in the context of a home. Although I know that many hostesses concern them-

Hepplewhite chairs, grandmother's plates, old silver, and long-stemmed Italian poppies grace the dining table set on our porch.

161

selves with the liveliness of a dinner party, and so rearrange tables between courses and sometimes even change rooms to keep things moving, I honestly believe this is unnecessary. There is no need for cagey socializing at a home dinner. If a hostess plans the cocktail hour carefully, seats guests sensitively, and presents an interesting dinner, she has no need to act like a shipboard social director.

The cocktail hour is a prologue to dinner, a time of introductions and general socializing, made easier and more colorful by means of drinks and light snacks. Thoughtful decisions about this early fare can set an interesting tone right from the start. Offering a special drink as an option—iced Russian or Polish vodka, your own perfect martini, a piña colada, a pitcher of margaritas, or a vessel of hot toddies—adds an element out of the ordinary. Choosing a particularly interesting vintage, if you are serving a wine aperitif, or adding a strawberry or a slice of orange instead of lemon to a spritzer, is also a nice gesture. Even the extra effort of serving cocktails in balloon goblets, glass mugs, or colorful kitchen glasses can make a difference. As for cocktail food, I generally limit it to something light that will not subvert a good appetite for dinner: *fresh* salted nuts, or homemade puff pastry straws rolled in cayenne, poppy seeds, sesame seeds, black peppercorns, red peppercorns, or cheese. Sometimes, however, particularly with a small group, it is nice to serve the equivalent of a first course in the living room—a slice of pâté on a plate, or melon and figs. If you are having trouble getting dinner together, don't hesitate to transfer the appetizer, if it is transportable (like a leek quiche or a puff pastry shell of crabmeat), to the living room, rather than prolong dinner. I generally opt for a short cocktail hour because I don't want guests drinking too much or becoming restless. Cocktails that last much longer than an hour jeopardize the shape and momentum of the whole evening.

Planning a dinner menu is fun. Classically, courses should grow bigger as the meal progresses, and move from mild to strong. A dramatic spicy taste or a heavy soup is therefore an inappropriate way to begin a dinner. (Only if something light follows should a first course dominate.) I happen to like delicate hot soups or light pasta dishes as a first course in winter, and cold soups and composed salads in summer, but I am careful to serve small portions, and to follow up with something of a different nature.

Dinners I prepare at home are easy, quick, and, while not "instant," not elaborate either. Too elaborate a fuss, I have learned, is not only extremely time-consuming, but showy and self-conscious, and in the end may even detract from the food. The desired effect—an interesting meal, in which things taste like wonderful examples of what they are—can be achieved without undue art or artifice. The depth of interest necessary for a memorable meal can be attained with an unusual sauce accompaniment, a different vegetable treatment, or a frothy dessert. I almost always make *real* desserts, as opposed to a dish of strawberries or a slice of melon, for a handful of reasons: (1) I like desserts, (2) it is fun to make desserts, (3) desserts can be made in advance, (4) desserts make an impressive finale that is in fact a statement of caring.

The spontaneous dinner party of course eliminates the possibilities of even having a dessert ready, yet there are kinds of food that work as elegantly in impromptu gatherings as when they have been planned for weeks in advance. Lobsters, for example, can be thrown in a pot, a salad assembled, a French bread bought or removed from the freezer, and some rich sinful dessert like a chocolate or Grand Marnier soufflé prepared while the main course cooks. A fresh chicken, stuffed with a handful of pungent herbs like tarragon or rosemary, can be roasted on a bed of potatoes, carrots, leeks, and turnips, and the same principle applies to dessert. If you have a well-stocked

Dinner parties at home are my favorite form of entertaining.

larder, last-minute social events become even easier. With some of the lesser staples in the cupboard or freezer, capers to garnish smoked salmon, tart shells to fill with custard and berries, homemade pesto or marinara sauce to add to pasta or vegetables, you can elevate an ordinary meal to the extraordinary in a matter of minutes.

To a certain extent, I am seasonal with menus. The first asparagus or lamb or suckling pig in spring, apples and pears in October, are irresistible. I usually amble through the local markets as the first step of a dinner party. But I look too for the unusual and out-of-season—New Zealand black currants in February, Black Forest mushrooms, a new sweet seedless tangerine that might go into a tart—which could provide a great treat for guests. When I am having six or eight people (our usual) to dinner, I try to compress all the work into a day, or even a half day, because, like other working women, I have limited time. For a large formal affair, however, several days' preparation is unavoidable.

Serving a meal graciously is a matter of planning, too. First there is the question of seating arrangements. Above all be *kind* to guests: think about who would be comfortable with whom, who should get to know whom; match the extroverts with the introverts; and, unless they are inseparable, separate spouses. Place cards (store-bought or handmade, inscribed with your best writing) are necessary at a dinner of more than twelve, for a host cannot direct that many people to their places gracefully. If it pleases you to take extra care with the place cards, insert them in a shiny apple before each setting, or prop them against miniature vases of flowers.

Then there are the mechanics of serving, of which there are three basic styles. These days, *plate serving,* for which a guest's plate is composed in the kitchen or at a sideboard before presentation, is the popular way to serve in restaurants and at large dinners, because it is not only efficient but also affords an opportunity to arrange the entree decoratively. With the so-called *French method,* each guest is served from platters that are passed, usually by a servant. This is more formal, and although it may suit a large dinner, it is unnecessary and rather pretentious with a small group. For dinners of up to eight or ten people, most of us serve in the convivial *family style,* with the host carving the meat and the hostess distributing vegetables from dishes put directly on the table. As well as the number of guests, the specifics of your menu will determine how you will serve it. A complicated dish, like a boned stuffed duck, which you might have to rearrange to make beautiful, would suggest plate service. Most of the dishes included in the following dinners are suitable for any method of serving. If you choose to serve family style, organize all your plates in advance—dinner plates in the kitchen, ready to be warmed and brought to the host; salad and dessert plates on a sideboard, so that you can move gracefully from course to course without undue fuss or clatter. Plan, too, for a second serving of the entree and salad. Appetites vary, and it is nicest to offer everyone at least a little bit more. Then clear plates, two by two or with the aid of a tray, but as inconspicuously as possible, enlisting the help of your spouse, or a chosen friend (but *not* all the women at the table).

A dinner party can be very rewarding for a hostess. She has an opportunity to set a fabulous table and show off more than usual with her meal. And while this may require more effort, guests will respond more appreciatively. In fact, they may be seduced into staying at the table too long. To find that time has flown by and friends have been sitting together for three and a half hours may be complimentary, but nevertheless it is better if a hostess moves her guests into another room before they become comatose. Adjourning to the living room (or to a patio in summer) to serve coffee and liqueurs refreshes people, opens up a group, and prevents a party from going on too late into the night.

A plump Cornish hen looks wonderful set on a drabware plate and surrounded by braised carrots, Brussels sprouts, and shallots.

A Spring Dinner for Six to Eight

I BEGIN WITH THIS DELIGHTFUL spring dinner because it is elegantly simple.

Simple here means both unfussy and easy. Except for the chickens, which are boned, stuffed, and ready for a quick 30 minutes in the oven, everything is made in advance. The rolls and the vegetables need heating; other dishes have only to be arranged and presented.

The time for this dinner is May or June, when the first bounty of a new growing season is appearing in markets: sweet melons, those wonderful early strawberries and blueberries. The colors in this meal are full—golden-roasted hens, bright vegetables, red and blueberries—and the flavors delightfully honest and fresh.

MENU

Fresh Melon with Prosciutto
Boned Cornish Hen Stuffed with Wild Rice
Whole Braised Shallots
Whole Braised Brussels Sprouts
Braised Carrots   Watercress Endive Salad
Fromage St. André   Pistolets aux Noix
Strawberries and Blueberries with Raspberry Grand Marnier Sauce
Madeleines
Blanc de Blanc Wine, Demitasse

Fresh Melon with Prosciutto

SERVES 6

1   melon
½   pound prosciutto, sliced
    paper thin
1   lime

Cut the melon in half lengthwise, and cut each half into 10 to 12 thin wedges. Seed and peel.

Arrange 3 or 4 melon wedges on each plate, and cover with 2 or 3 slices of prosciutto. Serve with a wedge or slice of lime.

VARIATION: Use mango, papaya, or fresh figs instead of melon.

Below: *Peking ducks and amethyst glasses complement a first course of succulent Israeli melon and thinly sliced prosciutto, garnished with lime.*

Boned Cornish Hen Stuffed with Wild Rice

The boning process takes some practice, but with a sharp knife and patience you should master the technique after a couple of tries. Boning makes this popular little bird an elegant alternative to chicken. In this recipe the Cornish hens are stuffed with wild rice, roasted for 30 minutes, and glazed with crab apple jelly cooked with white wine vinegar.

1 ¾-pound Cornish hen serves one person.

WILD RICE STUFFING 4 CUPS

2 small onions, finely minced
2 carrots, finely diced
2 small stalks celery, finely diced
4 tablespoons butter
  Sprig of thyme
1 bay leaf
2 cups wild rice
3 to 3½ cups boiling water or stock
  Salt and pepper

GLAZE

1 cup crab apple jelly melted with 1 tablespoon white wine vinegar

To make the stuffing, sauté the vegetables in the butter for 10 minutes. Add the herbs, the wild rice, and the boiling water. Cover, and cook for approximately 30 minutes. Stir occasionally to avoid sticking. Test for seasoning. When rice is cooked, drain off any liquid and fluff with a fork. Cool before stuffing the hens.

Allow ½ cup cooked stuffing per bird. Loosen the skin and push the cooked rice under the skin. Skewer and truss as shown in the pictures.

Roast hen in a 350° oven for approximately 30 minutes. Brush with glaze during final 15 minutes and again after removing hens from oven. Let stand for 5 minutes before serving.

NOTE: Cornish hens larger than ¾ pound can be cut in half to make two servings.

Turn hen breast-side down on cutting board. Cut down both sides of backbone.

Remove meat from rib cage, cutting as close to the bone as possible.

Remove whole carcass from the meat.

Remove thigh bones from each leg.

Lay bird skin side up.

Loosen skin from the meat.

Insert ½ cup stuffing under skin.

Turn hen over and "sew" skin closed with a bamboo skewer.

Tuck wing tips under breast and tie drumsticks together tightly.

Place breast side up in a buttered baking dish and roast as directed.

Whole Braised Shallots
SERVES 8

Shallots are becoming popular not only as an ingredient in recipes, but also as an independent vegetable. They are pretty, delicately flavored, and an excellent accompaniment to roasted fowl and meats. To serve as a vegetable, you should allow 4 medium shallots per person.

32 medium shallots
8 tablespoons (1 stick) butter
Salt and pepper to taste

Peel the shallots. To help them cook faster, cut a small cross in the root end.

Put shallots in a heavy covered casserole with butter and salt and pepper. Add water to cover shallots halfway.

Bring to a boil, then reduce heat so liquid simmers. Cook 20 to 30 minutes, or until shallots are tender. Uncover, and raise heat to reduce liquid to one-third. Serve hot.

Whole Braised Brussels Sprouts
SERVES 6 TO 8

1 pound Brussels sprouts
4 tablespoons (½ stick) butter
Salt and pepper to taste

Preheat oven to 350°.

Wash and trim Brussels sprouts. Cook for 5 minutes in a large kettle of boiling, salted water. Drain and put in a heavy covered casserole with butter and salt and pepper. Top Brussels sprouts with a round of buttered brown or waxed paper and cover casserole. Bake 20 to 30 minutes until fork tender.

Braised Carrots
SERVES 6 TO 8

1 pound carrots, finger size if possible
4 tablespoons (½ stick) butter
½ cup water
Salt, pepper, nutmeg to taste
Pinch of sugar

Peel and wash carrots. If using large carrots, cut into 2-inch pieces and round off cut edges with a paring knife; leave carrots whole if using finger-size carrots. Cook for 3 to 5 minutes in a pot of boiling, salted water. Drain and place in a casserole with the butter, salt, pepper, nutmeg, and sugar. Add water and cover. Cook over low heat about 25 to 30 minutes until liquid has evaporated and carrots are tender.

Watercress Endive Salad
SERVES 10

VINAIGRETTE
½ cup light olive oil
3 tablespoons almond oil
4 to 5 tablespoons Balsamic vinegar
2 tablespoons Dijon mustard
Freshly ground pepper
Salt to taste

3 bunches watercress
½ pound endive, cut into thin, lengthwise strips
2 bunches rugola, if available
2 packages enok mushrooms, trimmed

To make the vinaigrette, shake all ingredients vigorously in a jar. Refrigerate if not to be used within a few hours.

Wash, dry, and gently trim the salad greens. Toss in a large salad bowl with ¾ cup vinaigrette. Arrange on the salad plates and decorate with bunches of trimmed enok mushrooms.

Pistolets aux Noix
36 ROLLS

These small round rolls are a perfect accompaniment to cheese and salad. The walnuts lend an unusual texture and taste to French bread. Provide plenty of these rolls even if you have to make the recipe twice or three times—they are very popular.

1 recipe Homemade French Bread (page 106)
1½ cups coarsely chopped walnuts

Make the bread according to directions. After the second rising, add the walnuts and knead well. Divide the dough into ⅓-cup-size pieces. Shape into smooth round balls and flour well.

Set in buttered rounded French bread pans or on baking sheets. Cover loosely and let rise until double in bulk.

Preheat oven to 400°. Slash tops of rolls with a sharp knife or razor. Spray lightly with water and bake for about 20 minutes, or until golden. Cool on racks.

Raspberry Grand Marnier Sauce
APPROXIMATELY 2 CUPS SAUCE

An excellent topping for iced lemon mousse, fresh berries, or ice cream.

2 12-ounce packages frozen raspberries, thawed, or 1 quart fresh raspberries
¾ cup sugar
3 tablespoons Grand Marnier

Press the berries through a fine sieve. Add the sugar and stir until completely dissolved. Add the liqueur and chill until ready to use.

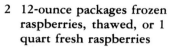

Madeleines
36 MADELEINES

Scalloped shell-shaped madeleine pans are essential for this recipe.

¼ pound (1 stick) unsalted butter
4 eggs
¼ teaspoon salt
⅔ cup sugar
1 teaspoon vanilla
1 cup sifted flour

Preheat oven to 375°. Butter and flour madeleine pans carefully.

Melt butter and let it cool.

Beat eggs, salt, and sugar together until thick, about 8 minutes. Add vanilla. Fold in flour, rapidly but gently. Fold in butter gently, but make sure it does not settle to bottom. Quickly spoon mixture into madeleine pans. Bake until golden, about 10 minutes. Remove from pans. Cool on racks.

NOTE: Madeleines may be dusted with confectioners' sugar after baking.

Opposite: Madeleines were made famous by Marcel Proust. Light and delicately flavored, they are baked in special pans of various sizes. Madeleines add a perfect touch to almost any dinner menu and combine particularly well with fruit.

A Light Summer Dinner for Four to Six

ONE DAY WHEN I HAD MANY pounds of fish to poach, few pans, and little time until an assigned dinner, I devised a new rapid-fire method for oven-poaching fillets on a jelly-roll pan. The fish dish in the menu below, a thin cross-grain slice of salmon I call a scallop, is typical of this whole menu: light, colorful, quick to execute, yet full of delicate and distinctive flavors. Its accompaniments, an herb-scented risotto and julienned carrots and string beans, cook while you poach the scallops and prepare beurre blanc. The dessert is prepared a day in advance.

❧ MENU ❧

Asparagus with Beurre Blanc
Salmon Scallops with Sorrel Sauce
Julienned Carrots and String Beans   Risotto
Iced Lemon Mousse Tartlets
Meursault Wine

Meissen china, antique English silver, Victorian crystal, and parrot tulips display this light summer dinner to its best advantage.

170

Asparagus with Beurre Blanc

SERVES 6

Beurre blanc *is a light, delicious sauce for vegetables, meats, and seafood. A chiffonade of sorrel leaves can be stirred in at the last moment for color and a slightly different flavor. You can also use vinegars flavored with herbs other than tarragon (sage complements breast of chicken) or raspberries (delicious with sautéed paper-thin pork chops).*

For a dinner party of any size, decide how many stalks to serve each person and buy by count rather than weight. I prefer medium or very fat asparagus to accompany the main course; 4 fat stalks per person are plenty. As a first course, you may want 6 stalks for each person; if you choose the skinny variety, allow 10.

BEURRE BLANC

6   shallots, peeled and finely minced
¾   cup tarragon or white wine vinegar
¾   pound (3 sticks) unsalted butter, cut into 1-inch pieces
    Salt and pepper to taste

24 fat asparagus stalks, peeled and trimmed

To make the sauce, simmer shallots in vinegar for 10 minutes. Remove from heat and cool slightly. Strain.

Whisk the butter, 1 tablespoon at a time, into vinegar until smooth. The mixture should have the same consistency as thin mayonnaise. Season to taste. Use immediately, or keep warm over warm water. Do not reheat, or the butter will melt and the mixture will separate.

To prepare asparagus, steam stalks on a rack over boiling water until tender, about 3 to 4 minutes. Serve immediately with beurre blanc.

NOTE: It is important when cooking asparagus to have all one size. For appearance as well as tenderness, peel almost to tips with a carrot peeler. Cut the asparagus so all stalks are the same length.

Salmon Scallops with Sorrel Sauce

SERVES 6

3   tablespoons butter
3   tablespoons shallots, finely minced
1   to 1½ pounds salmon fillets
1   cup fish stock or dry white wine
    Salt and white pepper

SORREL SAUCE
    Fish poaching liquid
½   cup dry white wine
1   cup heavy cream
2   cups sorrel leaves
2   egg yolks
    Salt and pepper
    Lemon juice

Put the fish in the freezer for 10 minutes. Holding a very sharp knife at a 60° angle, cut the fish into thin (⅛-inch) slices, 3 × 4 inches.
Cut the sorrel leaves in thin strips, or chiffonade.

Preheat oven to 375°. Butter a jelly roll pan. Sprinkle minced shallots on the sheet. Put the pan in the oven for 4 to 5 minutes.

Put salmon scallops on top of the shallots in a single layer. Sprinkle with stock and salt and pepper. Cover with buttered parchment or waxed paper and return pan to oven. Bake 4 to 5 minutes. Do not overcook or the fish will dry out. Remove the fish from the oven and transfer to a heated platter. Keep warm while making the sauce.

Strain any liquid from the pan into a saucepan. Add the wine and bring to a boil. Add the cream and boil 5 minutes.

Beat the egg yolks in a bowl. Add ½ cup of the hot cream mixture drop by drop, whisking continuously. Add the yolk mixture to the remaining cream mixture. Do not boil. Season with salt and pepper and lemon juice. Just before serving heat to below boiling point and add the sorrel. Cook without boiling for 2 minutes.

Pour sauce over and around the salmon. Serve hot.

NOTE: If sorrel is not available, substitute watercress leaves and the juice of ½ lemon.

Asparagus with beurre blanc.

Julienned Carrots and String Beans
SERVES 6

Julienned vegetables are cut into thin strips of equal length. The result is a tender, very attractive presentation.

1 pound carrots, peeled
1 pound string beans
4 tablespoons (½ stick) unsalted butter
Salt and pepper to taste

To prepare vegetables, cut carrots into 2- to 2½-inch pieces. Cut each piece in half lengthwise, and cut the halves into strips about ⅛ inch thick. String beans should be cut into equal lengths, then cut lengthwise into thin strips.

Steam the vegetables separately over boiling water until just tender, only 2 to 3 minutes. Toss with butter, season lightly, and serve hot.

VARIATION: This method can be used for beets, parsnips, turnips, and squash.

NOTE: Julienned vegetables can be cooked in advance, cooled immediately in ice water, and drained. To serve, toss with hot butter until heated through.

Risotto
SERVES 6

2 tablespoons butter
1 medium onion, very finely minced
1½ cups short-grain Japanese-style rice
3 cups thin Fish Stock (page 115)
Herb bouquet

1 teaspoon salt
Pepper
¼ cup chopped fresh parsley

Preheat oven to 350°. Melt butter in a heavy, covered casserole.

Sauté onion for 5 minutes. Add the rice, and cook over high heat 2 to 3 minutes to braise. Add the stock. Bring to a boil. Add herb bouquet, salt, and sprinkling of pepper. Cover and bake in oven for 18 to 20 minutes.

NOTE: Water, chicken stock, or meat stock can be substituted for fish stock.

An herb bouquet consists of a sprig of thyme, a bay leaf, and 2 or 3 parsley sprigs tied loosely with a string.

Iced Lemon Mousse Tartlets
TWELVE 3-INCH TARTLETS

1 recipe Perfect Plain Tart and Tartlet Crust (page 236)
½ recipe Iced Lemon Mousse (page 98)

GARNISH
Whipped cream, candied pink violets, lemon peel

Prepare pastry according to master recipe.

Prepare mousse according to directions, and spoon into prepared tartlet shells. Refrigerate until serving time.

Garnish with whipped cream and candied violets or lemon peel.

Dessert, mints, and tea served in the library after dinner. Pink lusterware teacups and pink double tulips add a delicate touch.

A Neoclassic Dinner for Eight to Ten

*O*N A PUBLISHING TOUR IN Peking, Andy and I had been very warmly received by our Chinese hosts, and when they made a reciprocal trip, we were particularly anxious to please them. I wanted to show them the workings of an American home and to serve them a typical but not ordinary dinner. I thought of lamb, for it had been wonderful that spring, and it was not common in China. In the morning I went on a market foray with only that idea on my list. I returned with tomatoes, carrots (for a purée), and, as the pièce de résistance, gigantic globe artichokes. I extracted a few rarities from my cupboard, including guava jelly, which I knew would make a nice glaze for the meat, and some gooseberry juice, which I folded into whipped cream to make a distinctly non-Oriental instant mousse.

Dinner lasted four hours, of which at least one was devoted to the artichokes. I watched as our guests discarded the leaves one by one and placed them in artistic patterns on their plates, each arrangement different, each at least as beautiful as the original artichoke. Everyone ate intently, and at the end of the meal one of the delegates said the gooseberry mousse made him smile.

❧ MENU ❧

Artichokes Smothered with Tomatoes and Herbs
Roast Leg of Lamb with Garlic-Guava Glaze
Homemade French Bread   Broiled Tomatoes   Carrot Purée
Gooseberry Mousse   Bordeaux Wine

Giant globe artichokes.

American blue green goblets and a handmade tablecloth set off a neoclassic dinner of roast lamb, carrot purée, and broiled tomatoes with herbs—a simple yet elegant meal combining old and new.

tichokes are very resilient and will take a lot of punishment.) Be careful not to tear off outer leaves. Stand artichokes upright in a deep, covered casserole.

Combine all topping ingredients. Spoon some of the mixture into center cavity of artichoke, and sprinkle rest over tops and between outer leaves. Add enough water to cover bottom third of artichokes. Bring to a boil, and reduce heat so that artichokes simmer. Cover and cook until tender but not mushy, about 30 to 45 minutes. Serve hot, warm, or at room temperature.

Roast Leg of Lamb with Garlic-Guava Glaze
8 TO 10 SERVINGS

1 leg of lamb (about 6 pounds)
  Salt and pepper to taste
3 cloves garlic, peeled and slivered
  Fresh rosemary sprigs
1 10-ounce jar guava jelly, melted over low heat

Rub lamb with salt and pepper. With point of sharp knife, cut slits in skin; stuff with garlic slivers and rosemary.

Place on rack in pan and roast at 350° about 1½ hours, basting occasionally with jelly. Internal temperature of lamb should be 130° (rare) to 145° (medium) on a meat thermometer. Let lamb rest about 15 minutes before carving.

Artichokes Smothered with Tomatoes and Herbs

This is an unusual alternative to the plain boiled artichoke we are used to. The tomatoes and herbs create their own delicious sauce, so additional dressings are unnecessary.

Allow 1 artichoke per person and multiply the topping accordingly.

Juice of 2 lemons

TOPPING FOR EACH ARTICHOKE

1 shallot, finely minced
1 small onion, thinly sliced
1 tablespoon olive oil
1 medium tomato, peeled, seeded, and coarsely chopped
1 tablespoon chopped parsley
¼ teaspoon salt
  Freshly ground pepper
½ teaspoon tiny capers (optional)

GARNISH
  Chopped fresh basil, oregano, or marjoram

To prepare artichoke, cut off stem and pointed top. Trim the prickly points off leaves with scissors. Soak trimmed artichokes for 30 minutes in a bowl of water and the lemon juice. This softens the artichokes and prevents discoloration. Remove from water and pry apart the center of the artichoke and scoop out the hairy core with a sharp teaspoon. (This takes a little practice, but ar-

Homemade French Breads
SEE RECIPE, PAGE 106

174

Broiled Tomatoes

One medium-size tomato will serve 1 guest. If tomatoes are large, however, they can be cut in half crosswise to serve 2. You can also use cherry tomatoes, allowing 4 per person.

TOPPING FOR EACH
TOMATO
1 tablespoon fresh white
   bread crumbs
1 teaspoon chopped parsley
1 teaspoon olive oil
   Pinch crushed garlic
   Tiny sprig fresh rosemary or
   thyme, finely chopped
   Salt and pepper to taste
½ teaspoon grated Parmesan
   cheese (optional)

Combine topping ingredients. Cut off stem of tomato and mound topping on cut side. Broil under low heat until topping is slightly browned and tomato heated through, about 3 to 4 minutes.

NOTE: Tomatoes can be cooked in a preheated 400° oven for 10 to 12 minutes until hot but not mushy.

Carrot Purée
SERVES 8 TO 10

1½ pounds carrots
4 tablespoons butter
1 teaspoon sugar
   Salt, pepper, freshly grated
   nutmeg
   Pinch dried thyme

Peel carrots and cut into 2-inch pieces. Put into heavy saucepan, barely cover with water, and add butter and sugar. Cook over medium heat until very tender, about 30 to 40 minutes. Drain and purée in blender or food processor until smooth. Season with salt, pepper, nutmeg, and thyme. Serve hot.

Gooseberry Mousse
8 SERVINGS

I grow a large number of gooseberry bushes, and each year I have so much gooseberry juice that I am forced to find new uses for it. This mousse is delightfully light and extremely delicious, as well as being very, very simple. I also use the juice for glazes and berry sauces. However, you can substitute juice made of black currants, red currants, or raspberries if you don't have gooseberries.

1 quart gooseberries
1 quart heavy cream
½ cup sugar

Cook berries in 2 cups water until they are tender and very soft. Strain the gooseberries through several layers of cheesecloth and reserve the juice. This can be refrigerated for several days, or frozen until ready to use.

Whip the cream until stiff. Add 1 cup gooseberry juice and the sugar and mix well. Spoon into chilled glasses and refrigerate until ready to serve.

Gooseberry mousse, a simple concoction of gooseberry juice (raspberry would do just as well) and whipped cream, should be served in goblets with a light-weight silver or bone spoon.

175

Bouillabaisse for Twelve to Sixteen

IN SUMMER OR EARLY FALL, when the variety of fish available is impressive and tempting, a bouillabaisse is an entertainment in itself. It is such a highly visual meal that I like to have all of its elements displayed on great platters when guests arrive—lobsters, clams, mussels, red snapper. . . . A single entree containing such a plentitude of good ingredients is festive, important. And while bouillabaisse is not the most economical stew to make, it goes a long way. Saffron is expensive, but it is key to enhancing the wonderful taste that results from a varied combination of fish and shellfish, the specifics of which will depend on your local fishmonger.

Once you have done the shopping, this whole meal can be put together in one hour. I begin by presenting everyone with a small, deep bowl of homemade pasta with a sauce of tomatoes, basil, anchovies, and capers. All I serve with the main course, which owes its extraordinary flavor to fast cooking, is a basket of hot buttered French bread and a simple green salad vinaigrette. For dessert: a crème caramel, made the day before.

❧ MENU ❧

Fettucini with Tomato-Anchovy-Caper Sauce
Salade Vinaigrette   Homemade French Bread
Bouillabaisse
Crème Caramel
Cold White Wine, Icy Beer

Fettucine with Tomato-Anchovy-Caper Sauce

12 TO 16 SMALL PORTIONS

SAUCE

- 6 green onions, chopped
- 2 cloves garlic, finely minced
- 10 plum tomatoes (or 1 large can peeled plum tomatoes), coarsely chopped

- 1 2-ounce tin of flat anchovies
- 12 ounces tiny capers, drained (use half a 24-ounce jar)
- ¼ cup chopped parsley

- 2 pounds fettucine
- 10 Sicilian olives
- 10 cherry tomatoes, sliced
  Basil leaves
  Grated Parmesan cheese

In a heavy skillet, sauté the green onions and garlic in oil for 3 minutes. Add the plum tomatoes, anchovies, and capers and sauté for 10 minutes. Add the parsley (you may also add chopped fresh basil or oregano).

Cook for 3 minutes longer. The sauce is very good used immediately, but it will keep 1 or 2 days in the refrigerator.

To cook the fettucine, put it into a kettle of rapidly boiling, salted water. Cook 3 to 4 minutes, or until the pasta is al dente (barely tender). Drain. Toss with a little butter.

To serve, put the cooked vermicelli on a large platter. Spoon the sauce over the top. Decorate with the olives, sliced cherry tomatoes, and basil leaves. Season with salt and pepper and grated Parmesan cheese.

A small portion of pasta with tomato sauce is a perfect first course for a bouillabaisse dinner.

Salade Vinaigrette

SERVES 16

Salad greens should be purchased no more than a day before serving. The freshness of the ingredients is of utmost importance in creating a delicious salad.

For this salad, choose either several types of greens or just one perfect lettuce. When bibb or ruby lettuce is at its best in my garden, I often choose 1 small head per person, wash it without tearing it apart, and serve it whole as an individual salad.

- 2 pounds assorted salad greens (bibb, ruby, endive, chicory, romaine, Boston, radicchio, watercress, arugula, or escarole lettuce)
- 1½ cups French Vinaigrette (page 104)

Wash and spin dry the salad greens. Tear into pieces.

Prepare vinaigrette according to directions. Immediately before serving, toss with greens. Salad will become soggy if tossed too early.

NOTE: Endive can be served as whole spears or cut crosswise on an angle and tossed in the salad.

Homemade French Breads

SEE RECIPE, PAGE 106

Bouillabaisse

SERVES 12 TO 16

I like to serve bouillabaisse on the porch on a cloth-covered table. When guests arrive they see their dinner in its uncooked state, arranged on huge platters. I then cut up the fish and lobster and proceed to cook the stew before the guests. We sit down to a small first course of pasta, or sometimes to a salade composée in which case I don't serve salad after the bouillabaisse.

Piping hot from the stove, the bouillabaisse is brought to the table, usually in 2 heavy cast iron Japanese pots (heavy, large frying pans will do equally well). I serve this dinner to at least 8 guests (the more guests, the more varieties of fish you can include). Allow approximately ½ pound of fish per person, excluding shellfish.

Choose a large variety of fish to make a lavish display. Use at least 8 varieties from the following list:

- 3 pounds striped bass (firm), cut into 2-inch pieces
- 2 pounds red snapper (firm), cut into 2-inch pieces
- 1 pound halibut (firm), cut into chunks
- 1 pound haddock (firm), cut into chunks
- 1 pound cod (firm), cut into chunks
- ½ pound scrod (firm), cut into chunks
- 1 pound weakfish (firm), cut into 2-inch pieces
- ½ pound sole (delicate), cut into 2-inch pieces
- 1 lobster, cut into pieces

Opposite: *Bouillabaisse makes an impressive display in an informal setting.*

- 4 soft-shelled crabs (if available), left whole
- 1 pound sea scallops (delicate), served whole
- 12 clams
- 16 mussels

- ½ cup olive oil
- 3 yellow onions, sliced
- 4 cloves garlic, crushed
- 4 tomatoes, chopped
- ½ head fresh fennel, thinly sliced
  Branch of thyme
- 1 bay leaf
- ⅛ teaspoon dried fennel
  Piece of orange peel
  Salt and pepper to taste
- 2 big pinches saffron
  Fish stock, leek poaching liquid, or water

  French bread slices, crisply toasted

In a large heavy-bottomed frying pan cook the onions in the olive oil for 5 minutes. Do not brown. Add the garlic, tomatoes, fennel, and remaining flavorings.

Arrange the firm fish chunks over the sautéed vegetables and add enough liquid to come halfway up but not covering the fish. Bring the stock to a rapid boil. Cook over very high heat 3 minutes, spooning

hot liquid over fish. Add the remaining delicate fish and shellfish and cook an additional 5 minutes, covered.

Remove from the heat. Check that the clams and mussels have opened. If not, cover pan and return to high heat for a minute or two longer.

Serve immediately by spooning the liquid into deep bowls over toasted French bread slices. Serve the fish right from the pan, or arrange on a large heated platter and allow guests to help themselves.

Crème Caramel

TWO 1-QUART DESSERTS

This crème caramel is so smooth and creamy that guests invariably leave none for a breakfast snack.

- 2 cups sugar
- 2½ cups heavy cream
- 2½ cups milk
- 1 vanilla bean, or 1 teaspoon vanilla extract
- 6 eggs
- 6 egg yolks

Line two 1-quart tin charlotte molds with caramel: Dissolve ½

cup sugar with 2 tablespoons water in each mold by swirling the water into the sugar. *Do not stir.* Cover mold and place on low heat until sugar is completely dissolved. Uncover and raise heat. Boil syrup until it begins to turn a golden color. Swirl pan over heat, and when desired caramel color is reached, remove from heat and plunge bottom of mold into cold water for a few seconds to stop the cooking. Swirl the caramel around the sides of the mold and invert on a plate to cool.

Preheat oven to 325°.

Simmer the cream and milk with the vanilla for 5 minutes.

Beat the remaining 1 cup sugar into the eggs and yolks and continue beating until mixture is light and fluffy. Gradually, add the hot milk and cream, beating continually. Strain the mixture into the prepared molds. Put the molds in a pan and pour boiling water into the pan to come halfway up the molds. Bake for about 45 minutes, or until custard is firm. Cool.

To unmold, run a sharp knife around the edge of the custard. Put the serving dish over the mold and quickly invert. Pour the remaining caramel around the custard.

A creamy, incredibly smooth crème caramel ends the feast.

A Formal Dinner for Twenty-four

When I lived in a six-room apartment on Riverside Drive, I used to have sit-down dinners for eighteen as a monthly matter of course. I'd scurry around, borrowing tables, chairs, and dishes, run to Mother's in New Jersey for silver, and stay up late ironing napkins. Then I'd squash everyone into our dining room, and Andy and I would serve, as efficiently as

humanly possible, some complex entree like parsleyed ham en croûte with Madeira sauce. Noise and a wonderful young confusion always reigned.

Planning for a large group means coping with space problems, probably renting tables and chairs, shopping carefully for wines, as well as organizing a meal on a grand scale. Nonetheless, there are times of celebration and festivity when twenty-four is the right number, and a sit-down dinner the right context. With a clear timetable, expert organization, and several people to help serve and clean up, it need not be either an arduous or an anxiety-producing task.

This dinner begins simply with a mélange of sautéed mushrooms, enriched with a little heavy cream and made quite exotic by the addition of whatever wild or forest mushrooms are available for purchase in local Oriental greengrocers or specialty food shops: cepes and morels, with their musty wood fragrance; shitake, meaty in taste; porcini, or dried European mushrooms. Once, after having read some nineteenth-century European novel, I served this creation under glass (individual glasses I had unearthed at a tag sale). My affectation turned out to be not only amusing but efficacious, for, as those great old hotel chefs obviously knew, the mushrooms stayed hot and retained all their fragrance. When we lifted the little domes, we were virtually assaulted with the wonderful aroma. The pork roast, which cooks quite happily for an hour without any attention, is accompanied by three light and unusual purées, which complement and contrast with the meat. The napoleon, which is made in steps and assembled the afternoon of the party, is sumptuous but light, a composition of puff pastry, custard cream, and tangy black currant sauce.

Sautéed Wild Mushrooms
SERVES 24

There is no substitute for wild mushrooms. The pungent yet delicate flavors make this a most elegant first course. An unusual presentation is to serve each mound of mushrooms under glass—domes, if you happen to have some, or upside-down goblets.

Allow 1 pound fresh wild mushrooms for every 6 to 8 persons. These mushrooms are very light and because they are strongly flavored go a long way. (Dried mushrooms can also be used; they are sold by the ounce. Check with the grocer about quantities.)

4 pounds fresh wild mushrooms (Black Forest, shitake, cepes, chanterelles, morels, porcini)
1 pound unsalted butter
1 quart heavy cream
   Salt and pepper
1 cup finely chopped parsley

Wash the mushrooms. Pat dry. Slice Black Forest or shitake mushrooms ¼ inch thick. Others may be left whole, if small. Heat the butter until hot in a large skillet. Sauté the mushrooms for 3 to 4 minutes. Add the cream, season lightly, and cook 2 to 3 minutes longer. Sprinkle with chopped parsley and serve immediately.

N O T E : There are 4 or 5 varieties of dried mushrooms available in some stores: cepes, porcini, chanterelles, morels. These must be plumped for 10 minutes in warm water or Madeira before being drained and sautéed as above. A mixture of the various mushrooms is very good.

Wild mushrooms "sous cloches" and wild mushrooms uncovered. A little glass dome holds in all the perfume, and when removed the fragrance is incredible.

❧ MENU ❧

Sautéed Wild Mushrooms
Boneless Loin of Pork with Prunes
Purée of Fennel
Purée of Celeriac and Potato
Napoleon with Black Currant Sauce
Burgundy or Bordeaux Wine

Roast pork with prunes is the basis for the perfect dinner for a large group.

Boneless Loin of Pork with Prunes
SERVES 24

Have your butcher bone a loin section of pork for you. A 6-rib portion will serve six people easily. He should remove all fat except for ⅛ inch on the outside and form it into as neat a round roast as possible. It should be covered with a thin layer of fatback and tied to keep its shape during roasting.

  2 12-rib sections pork roast, boned and wrapped with thin layer of fatback
  3 tablespoons vegetable oil
 12 medium onions, finely chopped
  8 tablespoons butter
 1½ pounds pitted prunes, soaked for 1 or more hours in 2 cups Madeira
  1 cup balsamic vinegar
  8 cups rich beef or veal stock
     Salt and pepper

Preheat oven to 350°. Brown the roasts in hot oil in a heavy casserole.

Sauté the onions in the butter until soft, in a roasting pan large enough to hold the pork. Put the pork on top of the onions and cover the casserole tightly. Bake for approximately 1½ hours, until the meat is tender and cooked through.

Put the meat on a heated platter; remove strings and fatback. Strain the juices into a heavy saucepan. Drain the prunes. Add to the pan juices the Madeira, vinegar, and stock, and bring to a rapid boil. Reduce the liquid to 4 cups. Add the drained prunes to the sauce and cook for 3 to 4 minutes. Taste for seasoning.

Cut the meat into slices ½ inch thick and serve with a few spoonfuls of the sauce and 2 or 3 prunes per person.

Purée of Fennel
SERVES 24

This is an unusual and exciting taste to most people and complements meat in an extraordinary fashion.

  6 large bulbs of fennel
 ½ pound (2 sticks) unsalted butter
 ½ teaspoon salt
  6 tablespoons rice
  1 cup heavy cream
     Salt and freshly ground pepper

Trim the fennel, removing the stems, the root end, and hard center core. Chop into pieces and rinse in cold water.

Melt the butter in a heavy skillet. Add the fennel and salt, cover, and cook over low heat until fennel is tender (approximately 25 to 30 minutes).

Cook the rice in ½ cup boiling water until soft.

Combine the fennel, butter, and rice in a food processor and purée, adding the cream. Season with salt and pepper. Reheat in a double boiler over moderate heat.

Purée of Celeriac and Potato
24 SERVINGS

  4 pounds celeriac (knobby celery root)
  2 pounds potatoes, peeled
  1 pound (4 sticks) unsalted butter
  1 quart heavy cream
     Salt and freshly ground pepper

Scrub the celeriac and cook it in water to cover until tender. Cool, then peel and purée it in a food processor.

Boil the potatoes until tender. Mash potatoes or put through a ricer.

Mix the celeriac with the potatoes; add the butter and cream and season highly. Serve hot.

Napoleon with Black Currant Sauce
SERVES 24

One day I was given a large quantity of black currants that had been imported from New Zealand. They were perfectly ripe, so I boiled them with water, strained the juice, and sweetened it with a bit of sugar. It was such a thick, rich sauce I served it with homemade napoleons—with great success.

Napoleons are made of puff pastry layers filled with a pastry cream made especially light by the addition of unsweetened whipped cream, folded in at the last moment.

  1 pound **Perfect Puff Pastry** (page 237), preferably made with cream

PASTRY CREAM (2½ CUPS)
  1 cup milk
 ½ vanilla bean
 ¼ cup plus 1 tablespoon sugar
  3 egg yolks
  1 tablespoon flour (preferably rice flour for lightness)
  1 tablespoon cornstarch
  1 teaspoon unsalted butter
  1 cup heavy cream, softly whipped

BLACK CURRANT SAUCE
  2 cups black currant juice
 ½ to ¾ cup sugar
  2 tablespoons black currant liqueur or juice of 1 lemon

To make pastry, prepare according to master recipe. Roll out into a rectangle and cut into thirds. Roll out each third to 1/16 inch thick, keeping rectangles equal sized. For easy handling, cut each strip into 2 rectangles, each approximately 6×8 inches. Water-spray baking sheets and place the pastry rectangles on them. Prick all over with fork tines. In a preheated 425° oven, bake until evenly browned, about 20 minutes. Cool completely on racks.

To make pastry cream, scald the milk, vanilla bean, and ¼ cup sugar. Beat egg yolks with remaining sugar until thick. Sprinkle in flour and cornstarch and continue beating until well mixed.

Remove vanilla bean from milk. Beat half the hot milk into yolk mixture. Return this to remaining hot milk and bring to a boil quickly, whisking very fast to prevent scorching. Remove from heat and pour into a bowl to cool. Rub top of pastry cream with butter to prevent a skin from forming. Cover with plastic wrap and cool completely. Immediately before using, fold in softly whipped cream with a wooden spoon.

To make sauce, stir juice, sugar, and liqueur over low flame until completely blended. Chill until ready to use.

To assemble, place a pastry strip on serving plate. Spread a ½-inch layer of pastry cream on strip and top with another piece of pastry. Repeat process. Sprinkle top layer with confectioners' sugar, and cut into 4 serving pieces, each approximately 2×6 inches. Repeat with remaining pastry strips.

To serve napoleons, spoon black currant sauce on individual plates. Place finished pastry on top of sauce.

VARIATION: Red raspberry juice or purée can be substituted for black currant to make the sauce.

CHAPTER EIGHT

The Holiday Party

HOLIDAYS AND ENTERTAINing go together, for a holiday by its nature is a communal celebration. A holiday is also simple, for it has a built-in spirit, and a built-in style. Respecting and celebrating that spirit is what holidays are about. If ever I find myself straying from that premise, or my enthusiasm waning with modern-day commercial sell or sophisticated fuss, I go back to childhood memories—the sight of a fat turkey, a Christmas cookie tree, or a Valentine box—for they are reminders of what is basic. The uncomplicated, romantic things that are part of a child's holiday can correct and inspire my adult thinking.

An earthenware bowl filled with fragrant hot-mulled cider.

Our Farmhouse Thanksgiving for Eight

THANKSGIVING IS A TIME FOR family, real or adopted. It has always been my favorite holiday.

Early on Thanksgiving morning, when I walk out into our garden and pick vegetables from the frozen soil to grace our table, I feel proud, productive, and grateful. Our family dinner, like Thanksgivings of old, is truly a celebration of the harvest. Although the ingredients are strictly time-honored native produce—turkey, cranberry, pumpkin, squash—little surprises make tradition more interesting. The pumpkin makes its appearance in a soup served in its natural shell; the cranberries in a crunchy nut sauce for the turkey. I add raisins soaked in cognac to the standard bread dressing, and for yams I substitute parsnips, a less familiar colonial root vegetable. These surprises are fun, and to me they make an eloquent point about the continuing life of a tradition.

❧ MENU ❧

Roast Turkey with Herbed Corn Bread Dressing
Pumpkin Soup in a Pumpkin Shell
Pickled Beets   Assorted Relishes
Oven-Braised Parsnips with Brussels Sprouts
Oven-Braised White Onions
Laura's Maple-Nut Hubbard Squash Purée
Cranberry-Currant-Walnut Sauce
Buttermilk Chive Biscuits   Herb Butter
Applesauce Spice Cake   Lemon Curd Tartlets

Roast Turkey
with
Herbed Corn Bread Dressing
SERVES 8 TO 10

This savory stuffing is a favorite in our house.

DRESSING
1 recipe Corn Bread (next page)
½ cup dark raisins
½ cup cognac
2 cups chopped onions
2 cloves garlic, minced
½ cup butter
1 pound bulk pork sausage
½ cup chopped shallots
1½ cups chopped tart apples
1 cup chopped celery
1 15-ounce can chestnuts, drained and chopped, or 2 pounds freshly roasted and peeled chestnuts
½ cup snipped fresh parsley
1 tablespoon dried sage leaves

2 teaspoons dried marjoram leaves
1 teaspoon dried thyme leaves
¼ teaspoon ground cloves
⅛ teaspoon cayenne pepper
2 teaspoons salt
1 teaspoon pepper
2 eggs, beaten

1 16-pound turkey

Make corn bread a day in advance. Cut into cubes; reserve.

Soak raisins in cognac overnight.

In large skillet, sauté onions and garlic in butter over medium heat until soft, about 5 minutes. Add sausage and shallots; cook until sausage is brown, about 10 minutes. Stir in apples and celery; cook until soft, about 10 minutes. Drain.

Combine corn bread cubes, raisin mixture, sausage mixture, and remaining ingredients except for eggs. Toss; stir in eggs.

Follow the directions on page 192 for preparing, stuffing, and roasting the turkey.

Above: *Turkey and chicken molds line the mantel shelves.*

Left: *Our Thanksgiving dinner is traditional, with a few surprises.*

Corn Bread

1 LOAF OR 36 TINY
MUFFINS

1½ cups yellow cornmeal
1 cup sifted all-purpose flour
⅓ cup sugar
1 tablespoon baking powder
1 teaspoon salt
1½ cups milk
¾ cup melted butter, cooled
2 eggs, slightly beaten

Heat oven to 400°.

Combine cornmeal, flour, sugar, baking powder, and salt in a large bowl. Mix milk, butter, and eggs in medium-size bowl. Stir milk mixture into cornmeal mixture just until moistened.

Pour batter into greased 9 × 5 × 3-inch loaf pan or spoon into tiny muffin pans. Bake until golden, 35 to 40 minutes for loaf, 18 to 20 minutes for muffins. Cool on a wire rack 5 minutes. Remove from pan; cool completely on rack.

Pumpkin Soup
in a Pumpkin
SERVES 8

A novel way to serve soup. Choose a fresh, hard, sugar pumpkin for your tureen, or substitute a hollowed-out Hubbard or French poitiron.

6 cups chicken broth
2 to 3 cups pared pumpkin, cut into ½-inch cubes
1 cup thinly sliced onion
1 clove minced garlic
1½ teaspoons salt
½ teaspoon dried thyme leaves
5 peppercorns
½ cup whipping cream, warmed
1 teaspoon snipped fresh parsley

In a covered saucepan, heat all ingredients except cream and parsley to boiling. Reduce heat; simmer, uncovered, 20 minutes.

Remove ½ cup of the pumpkin with slotted spoon; reserve. Simmer remaining pumpkin mixture, uncovered, 20 minutes longer; transfer to large bowl.

Purée 2 cups of the pumpkin mixture in blender or food processor; return puréed mixture to pot. Repeat with remaining pumpkin mixture. Heat puréed mixture to boiling; reduce heat. Simmer uncovered for 10 minutes.

Stir warm cream and reserved pumpkin into soup; garnish with parsley. Serve hot in a hollowed-out sugar pumpkin which has been warmed 20 minutes in a 350° oven.

Pickled Beets
4 CUPS

2 pounds small beets
½ cup Japanese vinegar or white vinegar
2 tablespoons brown sugar
1 tablespoon caraway seeds
Salt and freshly ground black pepper to taste

Cut off beet greens, leaving 3 inches of stem. Wrap beets in foil and bake in 350° oven for 1 hour, or until tender. Cool beets and slip off the skins.

Mix together the remaining ingredients. Toss beets in the dressing and chill until ready to serve.

Oven-Braised Parsnips
with Brussels Sprouts
SERVES 8

4 large parsnips, pared, cut into quarters
1 teaspoon salt

¼ cup packed brown sugar
3 tablespoons unsalted butter
Salt and pepper
2 pints Brussels sprouts, trimmed and rinsed
2 tablespoons butter
Rosemary sprigs (optional)

In medium-size saucepan, heat parsnips and 1 teaspoon salt in water to cover, to boiling. Cook until tender, 10 to 15 minutes; drain. Arrange in well-buttered shallow baking dish; sprinkle with sugar; dot with butter; season to taste with salt and pepper. Bake parsnips in 350° oven until sugar and butter are melted and parsnips are glazed, about 20 minutes.

Meanwhile, cook Brussels sprouts in 3 cups boiling salted water until tender, 8 to 10 minutes; drain. Toss with butter and season with salt and pepper. Arrange on serving platter with parsnips. Garnish with rosemary sprigs, if desired.

N O T E : Some of the Brussels sprouts can be arranged on the serving platter with turkey.

Oven-Braised
White Onions
SERVES 24

4 pounds (about 64) small white boiling onions
1½ teaspoons salt
¼ pound (1 stick) unsalted butter
½ teaspoon white pepper

GARNISH
2 teaspoons snipped fresh parsley

Heat oven to 350°. In medium-size saucepan, boil onions and 1 teaspoon salt in water to cover for 1½ minutes; drain. Peel while warm. Cut an X in root end of each onion; put in a single layer in 13 × 9 × 2-inch baking dishes. Dot with butter; sprinkle with remaining salt and pepper. Cover with buttered

parchment paper or aluminum foil. Bake until onions are tender, about 30 minutes. Remove paper. Bake until light brown, about 10 minutes more.

Serve hot, garnished with parsley.

Laura's Maple-Nut
Hubbard Squash Purée
10 SERVINGS

6 cups squash meat (Hubbard or Butternut)
½ cup butter
½ cup heavy cream
⅔ cup maple syrup
¼ teaspoon cinnamon
⅛ teaspoon freshly grated nutmeg
1 teaspoon salt
Freshly ground black pepper
¾ cup chopped pecans or walnuts

Cut the peeled and seeded squash into small pieces and cook in boiling water until very soft (about 20 minutes). Drain.

Purée squash in food processor or blender, or mash by hand, 2 cups at a time. Return to saucepan and stir in remaining ingredients. Blend well. Turn into warm serving dish. Serve very hot.

Cranberry-Currant-Walnut
Sauce
MAKES 6 CUPS

1 pound fresh cranberries, or 1 package (16 ounces) frozen cranberries
1¼ cups sugar
1 cup red currant preserves
1 cup water
1 cup coarsely chopped walnuts
2 tablespoons grated orange peel

Combine cranberries, sugar, preserves, and water in large saucepan; heat to boiling; reduce heat. Simmer uncovered 20 minutes; skim foam; remove from heat. Stir in walnuts and orange peel. Refrigerate, covered, overnight.

Buttermilk Chive Biscuits

SEE VARIATION, PAGE 132

Below: *Roast turkey with corn bread stuffing virtually glistens on the table.*

Herb Butter

SEE RECIPE, PAGE 92

Applesauce Spice Cake

SERVES 10 TO 12

½ cup unsalted butter
1 cup firmly packed brown sugar
1 egg
1¾ cups cake flour
1 cup raisins
1 cup currants
1 cup coarsely chopped walnuts
½ teaspoon salt
½ teaspoon ground cloves
1 teaspoon baking soda
1 teaspoon cinnamon
½ teaspoon freshly grated nutmeg
1 cup thick applesauce, heated

Preheat oven to 350°. Butter and flour a tube pan (I like to use a gugelhupf mold).

Cream butter with sugar. Add egg and beat well.

Sift a bit of flour over the raisins, currants, and walnuts. (This prevents sinkage during baking.) Sift remaining flour with other dry ingredients. Beat into butter mixture, then stir in applesauce, and finally raisins, currants, and nuts. Pour batter into prepared pan and bake for approximately 40 minutes.

Remove from oven, cool in pan 5 minutes, and turn out onto rack to cool completely.

Lemon Curd Tartlets

SEE RECIPE, PAGE 92

Thanksgiving Medley for Twenty-four

THANKSGIVING CAN ALSO BE A melting pot kind of holiday in which traditional and nontraditional elements can come together harmoniously. If guests have traveled a long distance, I serve hors d'oeuvres informally, as a predinner refreshment; here, slivers of country ham sandwiched between tiny triangles of blueberry scones, and crispy gingerbread snaps: both interesting mouthfuls that won't diminish a holiday appetite. I love purées, and here let predictable squash, carrot, and chestnut take that form. The cranberry turns up in the stuffing and in one of the desserts; pumpkin and butternut squash in rich pies. And the turkey holds its own, bedded on a platter of fresh rosemary, which scents the whole table. Last come turkey-shaped cookies, made with an oversized cutter designed by a sculptor friend of ours and decorated by my daughter with royal icing.

MENU

Gingersnaps with Chutney Cream Cheese

Baked Ham on Blueberry Scones   Mother's Mushroom Soup

Roast Turkey with Fruit and Nut Stuffing   Chestnut Purée

Carrot and Squash Purée   Onions Stuffed with Swiss Chard

Honey Squash Pie   Grateful Pudding with Sour Lemon Sauce

Turkey-shaped Sugar Cookies   Pumpkin Molasses Pie

Mincemeat Tartlets   Chocolate-Pecan Tartlets   Cranberry Tartlets

Unusual flavors and textures mingle in fruit and nut stuffing.

Gingersnaps with Chutney Cream Cheese

APPROXIMATELY 70 HORS
D'OEUVRES

¼ cup dark brown sugar
⅓ cup molasses
¼ cup (½ stick) unsalted butter, softened to room temperature
1 egg
1 teaspoon baking soda
¼ teaspoon salt
¼ teaspoon ground allspice
½ teaspoon ground cinnamon
¼ teaspoon ground cloves
½ teaspoon ground ginger
2¼ cups flour

CHUTNEY CREAM CHEESE

1 8-ounce package cream cheese, softened to room temperature, blended with ¼ cup finely chopped mango chutney

To make gingersnaps, cream the sugar, molasses, and butter in a large mixing bowl. Add the egg and beat until fluffy.

Sift into another bowl the baking soda, salt, allspice, cinnamon, cloves, ginger, and ¾ cup of the flour. Add this mixture all at once to the molasses mixture and beat until the ingredients are just mixed. Stir in the remaining 1½ cups flour and then beat to form a stiff dough.

Divide the dough into 1-cup amounts, flatten the portions, and wrap each in plastic wrap. Refrigerate for at least 2 hours, preferably overnight.

Preheat the oven to 350°. Lightly butter 2 large baking sheets. On a lightly floured surface, roll out the dough to about ⅛ inch thick. With a crimped pastry wheel, cut the dough into 1 × 2-inch rectangles. Put them on the baking sheets and then, with a fork, prick them in an even pattern. Bake the cookies until crisp, about 10 minutes. Transfer them to wire racks and allow to cool completely.

Serve with a bowl of chutney cream cheese.

Baked Ham on Blueberry Scones

SEE VARIATION, PAGE 58

Below: *Silverware, crystal, plates, and a big turkey platter are set out on the table in our kitchen, ready for the feast.*

Mother's Mushroom Soup
SERVES 8 TO 12

My mother has been making this traditional Thanksgiving soup for as long as I can remember.

4 to 6 large dried Polish mushrooms (or cepes or porcini, available in specialty food shops)

12 large dried shitake mushrooms (available in Oriental food shops)

3 quarts homemade or canned beef broth

5 medium carrots, peeled, trimmed, and finely diced

5 ribs celery with leafy tops, trimmed and finely diced

2 large onions, peeled and finely chopped

2 tablespoons finely chopped fresh parsley leaves

1 pound fresh domestic mushrooms, wiped, trimmed, and sliced

3 tablespoons chopped fresh dill, or 2 teaspoons dried dill

1 tablespoon coarse (kosher) salt (omit if using canned beef broth)

½ teaspoon freshly ground black pepper

½ cup very small dried macaroni (bows, squares, alphabet, orzo)

2 tablespoons butter

2 tablespoons flour

1 cup sour cream

Soak the Polish and shitake mushrooms for 4 hours in 2 cups cold water.

In a large pot, bring the broth to a simmer. Add the carrots, celery, onions, and parsley to the broth and cook, uncovered, over low heat for 20 minutes, stirring occasionally.

Drain the mushrooms that have been soaking; strain and reserve the mushroom-flavored liquid. Cut the mushrooms into pieces slightly larger than the diced vegetables. Add the mushrooms and liquid to the soup. Simmer for 15 minutes.

Add the sliced fresh mushrooms, dill, salt (if using homemade beef broth), and pepper to the soup. Simmer 15 minutes. Bring the soup to a full boil. Stirring constantly, add the macaroni. Reduce the heat to a gentle boil and, stirring occasionally with a slotted spoon to prevent the macaroni from sticking, cook the soup another 4 to 7 minutes, or until the macaroni is done to taste.

Meanwhile, melt the butter in a saucepan and blend in the flour, stirring until the mixture is smooth. Add 2 tablespoons of the sour cream and stir until it is well blended. Combine this mixture with the rest of the sour cream.

When the macaroni tests done, add the thickened sour cream to the soup, and stirring constantly, simmer gently until it is completely incorporated, about 3 minutes. This soup is delicious served very hot.

Roast Turkey with Fruit and Nut Stuffing
SERVES 12 TO 14

1 18- to 20-pound turkey

1 recipe Fruit and Nut Stuffing

GIBLET BROTH

2 medium onions, peeled and sliced

1 carrot, peeled and sliced

3 parsley sprigs

1 bay leaf
Salt

4 tablespoons softened butter

2 tablespoons snipped fresh rosemary leaves, or 2 teaspoons dried rosemary

2 tablespoons snipped fresh thyme leaves, or 2 teaspoons dried thyme

1 cup dry vermouth

GARNISH

Rosemary and thyme sprigs

Preheat oven to 375°. Remove the neck and giblets from the turkey and put them in a medium-size saucepan with 1 quart water. Add the onions, carrot, parsley, and bay leaf and simmer, partially covered, over very low heat for 3½ to 4 hours, checking occasionally to make certain that the liquid has not evaporated.

Rinse the turkey inside and out with cold running water, and pat it dry with paper towels. Lightly sprinkle the main cavity and neck cavity with salt.

Turn the turkey breast side down and loosely stuff the neck cavity with about 2 cups of stuffing. Pull the neck skin over the cavity and fasten it to the back of the turkey with skewers or wooden picks. Turn the turkey breast side up and fold the wing tips underneath the turkey so that the tips are almost touching. Lightly stuff the main cavity with about 6 to 7 cups of stuffing. Place a double layer of aluminum foil over the exposed stuffing to prevent its charring as the bird roasts. Tie the drumsticks together with kitchen twine, or if your turkey has a metal clamp, arrange the drumsticks so that the clamp will hold them in place. Rub the softened butter over the skin.

Put the turkey, breast side up, on a metal rack in a roasting pan and roast it in the lower half of the oven for 2½ hours. Then add the herbs and vermouth to the pan drippings. Continue roasting the turkey until done, about 1 to 1½ hours. If the turkey begins to brown too much, cover it loosely with aluminum foil. To test for doneness, insert a fork into the thickest part of the thigh; the juices will run clear when the turkey is done. To test with a meat thermometer, insert the thermometer into the thickest part of the thigh, without touching a bone; the turkey is done when the temperature reaches 180° on the thermometer. Remove the rack containing the turkey from the pan and allow the turkey to rest for 20 minutes before carving.

To make gravy, skim off fat in pan, strain giblet broth into drippings in pan, stir over high heat, taste for seasoning, and strain into a gravy boat.

Transfer the turkey to a heated platter and garnish with sprigs of rosemary and thyme.

Fruit and Nut Stuffing
FOR A 20-POUND TURKEY—APPROXIMATELY 9 CUPS

18 whole pitted prunes

½ cup dried currants

1 cup dark raisins

24 dried apricot halves

¼ cup bourbon

3 tart cooking apples, unpeeled, cored, chopped

3 large onions, peeled and diced

2 celery ribs, diced

4 tablespoons melted butter

⅔ cup whole macadamia nuts

⅔ cup whole cashews

1 cup unsalted walnut pieces

2 cups whole raw cranberries

1 teaspoon ground cloves

¼ teaspoon cayenne pepper

1 teaspoon ground ginger

1 teaspoon ground cinnamon

1 teaspoon dried chervil leaves

1 teaspoon finely minced fresh parsley leaves

2 teaspoons salt

½ teaspoon freshly ground black pepper

2 eggs, slightly beaten

If you are using salted macadamia nuts and salted cashews, put them in a strainer and remove the salt by holding them under cold running water; dry them on paper towels. Heat 2 teaspoons vegetable oil in a skillet and add the nuts. Toast them, stirring constantly, until golden.

Put the prunes, currants, raisins, and apricot halves in a bowl and pour the bourbon over the fruit. Cover bowl and soak overnight.

Combine the apples, onions, and celery in a large skillet along with the butter. Cook the mixture over moderate heat, stirring occasionally, until the onions are soft and the celery is tender, about 10 minutes.

Transfer the sautéed onion mixture to a large mixing bowl. Add the macerated fruit and all remaining ingredients. Gently mix the stuffing with 2 large spoons or your hands until evenly blended. Set the stuffing aside while you prepare the turkey for roasting.

Chestnut Purée
SERVES 12

You should use fresh chestnuts for this purée. To remove the chestnuts'
shell and bitter skin, cut off a small strip of the shell and cook chestnuts in boiling water for 1 minute. Remove from heat and peel with a sharp knife. Drop any "difficult" chestnuts back into boiling water and repeat the process.

8   cups peeled chestnuts
3   stalks celery
    Large herb bouquet (parsley, bay leaf, and fresh or dried thyme)
3½ cups beef or veal stock
5   tablespoons butter
    Salt, pepper, sugar to taste

Simmer chestnuts, celery, and herb bouquet in stock until chestnuts are tender but not mushy, about 20 minutes. Drain chestnuts and reserve cooking liquid. Discard celery and bouquet.

Purée chestnuts in food processor, or food mill if possible. Add butter, and season with salt and pepper. Add a pinch or two of sugar if necessary. Serve hot.

NOTE: To reheat, thin purée with reserved cooking liquid if too thick, and heat over boiling water, stirring occasionally.

Roast turkey, purées, stuffed onions, mushroom soup, fruit and nut stuffing, and bite-size hors d'oeuvres– an unusual Thanksgiving meal.

Carrot and Squash Purée
SERVES 24

4 pounds carrots
2 medium butternut squash
2 cups water
1 cup light cream or half-and-half
½ pound (2 sticks) unsalted butter
2 teaspoons salt
1 teaspoon freshly grated nutmeg
½ teaspoon freshly ground white pepper

Peel the carrots and cut into 1-inch chunks. Peel the squash. Halve and remove the seeds. Cut into 1-inch chunks. Put the carrots and squash in separate saucepans. Add one cup of water to each. Cover the pans and bring to a boil. Reduce the heat and simmer, partially covered, over low heat until the vegetables are fork-tender, 15 to 20 minutes for the squash, 25 to 30 minutes for the carrots. Drain off and discard the liquid, or reserve it for use in soups or stocks.

Purée the cooked vegetables in a food mill, food processor, or blender. Transfer the purée to a large mixing bowl and beat in the cream, butter, salt, nutmeg, and pepper. Serve hot.

Onions Stuffed with Swiss Chard
SERVES 24

24 medium yellow onions, each about 2½ inches in diameter
6 tablespoons unsalted butter
1 teaspoon freshly ground black pepper
1 cup homemade or canned chicken broth
2 pounds fresh Swiss chard or spinach

2 tablespoons olive oil
2 large cloves garlic, peeled and finely chopped
2 tablespoons finely chopped fresh parsley leaves
⅓ teaspoon freshly grated nutmeg
2 teaspoons salt

Partially fill a large saucepan with water and bring to a boil. Add the unpeeled onions and boil, uncovered, for 10 minutes. Drain the onions and cool them by running cold water over them. Trim off the root ends and peel off the outer skins. Cut off the top third of each onion and hollow out the centers, reserving the removed portions. The onion shells should be about ⅓ inch thick.

Preheat the oven to 350°. Put the onion shells in a large shallow baking dish, dot them with 2 tablespoons of the butter, sprinkle them with ¼ teaspoon of the pepper, and add the chicken broth to the dish. Cover the dish and braise the onions for 30 minutes, basting occasionally.

Meanwhile, trim away and discard the stems of the Swiss chard; wash the leaves well. Put the leaves, still wet, in a pot, cover, and steam over low heat for 5 to 10 minutes for Swiss chard (3 to 5 minutes for spinach). Drain the leaves well and then gently squeeze out the excess moisture.

Heat the olive oil in a skillet, add the garlic, and sauté briefly over low heat. Chop the reserved onion portions and add them to the skillet along with the Swiss chard, parsley, nutmeg, salt, and remaining butter and pepper. Cook over low heat, stirring constantly, for about 5 minutes. Remove from the heat and purée in a food mill, blender, or food processor.

Remove the onions from the oven when done and fill the hollows with the hot purée. Serve with the braising juices.

Top: *A rich honey squash pie, garnished with a maple leaf.*
Bottom: *Mincemeat tartlets and chocolate pecan tartlets.*

Honey Squash Pie
ONE 9- OR 10-INCH PIE

1 recipe Perfect Pie Crust (page 234)

FILLING
1 butternut squash, about 2 pounds
½ teaspoon ground cinnamon
1 teaspoon ground ginger
1 teaspoon salt
¼ cup honey
½ cup molasses
5 eggs
¾ cup heavy cream

Make the pastry according to master recipe and line a 9- or 10-inch pie dish.

To make the filling, cut the squash in half and remove the seeds. Put a rack in a saucepan, add water to within 1 inch of the rack, set the squash halves on the rack, cut sides up, and bring the water to a boil. Cover the pan and steam the squash for 20 to 25 minutes, or until it is fork-tender. If necessary, add more boiling water to the pan as the squash steams.

Remove the squash from the pan, and when it is cool enough to handle, scoop out the flesh with a spoon; discard the shells. Using a food processor, blender, or food mill, or by pressing it through a metal sieve, purée the squash. You should have about 2½ cups.

Put the purée in a large bowl and, using a wooden spoon, beat the cinnamon, ginger, salt, honey, and molasses into it. In a separate bowl, whisk together the eggs and cream, and blend into the squash mixture.

Preheat the oven to 450°. Put the pie dish on a baking sheet and pour ¾ of the filling into it. Pour the remaining filling into a small pitcher. Put the pie on the center shelf of the oven and pour the remaining filling into it. (This method avoids the possibility of spilling the pie while you are transferring it to the oven.)

Bake the pie for 10 minutes. Then reduce the temperature to 325° and bake for an additional 45 minutes, or until the center of the filling is firm when the baking sheet is moved gently back and forth. Serve warm, at room temperature, or chilled.

Grateful Pudding with Sour Lemon Sauce
SERVES 24

An old-fashioned steamed bread pudding flavored with mace, lemon, and cognac.

¼ cup golden raisins
¼ cup muscat raisins
¼ cup cognac
  Grated rind of 1 lemon
6 cups white bread, crusts removed, cut into ½-inch squares
3 cups whipping cream
1 vanilla bean, 2 inches long
6 eggs
1 cup sugar
½ teaspoon mace

SOUR LEMON SAUCE
¾ cup sugar
1½ tablespoons cornstarch
⅙ teaspoon salt
1¼ cups hot water
3½ tablespoons unsalted butter
4 tablespoons lemon juice
3 teaspoons grated lemon rind

Soak raisins in cognac with lemon rind overnight. Drain.

Butter and sprinkle with sugar a 2-quart covered metal pudding mold, including inside of lid. Layer the bread alternately with the plumped raisins in the mold.

Scald the cream with the vanilla bean. Cool slightly. Remove vanilla bean, split it open, and scrape the seeds into the cream.

Beat the eggs with the sugar until light. Gradually pour in the cream. Add the mace. Pour over the bread.

Secure lid and steam for 1 hour on a rack in a covered kettle with enough water to come ⅔ up the side of mold. The water should simmer gently.

To make sauce, combine sugar,

Turkey-shaped sugar cookies.

cornstarch, and salt in top of double boiler. Add hot water and cook 3 to 5 minutes, until thick. Add the butter, lemon juice, and rind and continue cooking until smooth.

To serve, unmold warm pudding onto a serving plate and serve with a bowl of sour lemon sauce.

Turkey-shaped Sugar Cookies
SEE RECIPE, PAGE 209

A tempting array of Thanksgiving desserts—pies, tartlets, sugar cookies, and grateful pudding with sour lemon sauce.

Pumpkin Molasses Pie
ONE 9-INCH PIE

1 recipe Perfect Pie Crust (page 234)

1 large pumpkin, approximately 3 pounds
½ cup water
4 eggs, lightly beaten
½ cup honey
½ cup milk
½ cup heavy cream
¼ cup molasses
½ teaspoon ground ginger

½ teaspoon cinnamon
1 teaspoon salt

Prepare pie crust according to master recipe, and line a 9-inch pie dish. Freeze any remaining pastry.

Preheat oven to 375°.

To prepare filling, peel, seed, and cube pumpkin and place in covered saucepan with water. Cook slowly over low heat until pumpkin is very tender. Drain well, and purée in blender or food processor, adding a little liquid to thin if necessary.

Combine remaining ingredients, mixing completely, and stir in 3

cups of puréed pumpkin. Mix together and pour into prepared crust. Bake approximately 1 hour, or until custard is firm and top is a glossy golden brown. Cool completely before serving.

NOTE: Canned pumpkin can be substituted for homemade purée.

Mincemeat Tartlets
12 TARTLETS

1 recipe Perfect Plain Tart and Tartlet Crust (page 236)

MINCEMEAT
2½ pounds tart red apples, unpeeled, cored, seeded, chopped
1 pound ground beef chuck
1 pound dark raisins
¾ pound packed dark brown sugar
¾ pound dried currants
½ pound ground beef suet
¼ pound candied citron, chopped
2 cups apple cider
2 cups brandy

2 cups pitted tart cherries
(optional)
½ cup dark molasses
2 quinces, pared, seeded,
chopped (optional)
1½ teaspoons ground cloves
1½ teaspoons ground cinnamon
1½ teaspoons ground mace
1½ teaspoons ground nutmeg
1½ teaspoon salt

GARNISH
Walnut halves

Combine all ingredients for mincemeat in a heavy casserole. Heat to boiling. Reduce heat and simmer, uncovered, 2 hours; skim fat; refrigerate.

Follow directions for making twelve 3-inch unbaked tartlet shells. Fill pastry shells with mincemeat. Garnish with walnut halves. Bake for 20 minutes in 350° oven. Cool.

NOTE: Remaining mincemeat can be refrigerated up to 3 weeks, or frozen.

Chocolate Pecan Tartlets
12 TARTS

1 recipe Perfect Plain Tart
and Tartlet Crust (page 236)

FILLING
3 ounces bittersweet chocolate
3 tablespoons unsalted butter
¾ cup sugar
1 cup light corn syrup
3 eggs
1 teaspoon vanilla extract
1 cup pecans, coarsely
chopped

GARNISH
Pecan halves

Make the pastry according to master recipe, lining 3-inch tart pans. Put the shells in the refrigerator while preparing the filling.

Preheat the oven to 300°.

Melt the chocolate and butter in a small bowl in the oven. When the mixture is melted remove from the oven and stir. Set aside.

Heat the sugar and corn syrup in a saucepan and stir until the sugar is partially dissolved. Bring the mixture to a boil. Reduce heat and simmer 2 minutes, stirring constantly with a wooden spoon.

Beat the eggs in a bowl and stir in the chocolate and butter mixture. Mix well. Add the syrup, whisking hard. Add the vanilla and pecans, stirring well to blend. Allow the mixture to cool slightly.

Increase the oven temperature to 350°. Remove the tart shells from the refrigerator and put on a baking sheet. Fill the shells with the chocolate filling, making sure that the nuts are evenly distributed. Decorate the tops with pecan halves. Bake for 45 minutes or until the filling has set. Cool before serving.

Cranberry Tartlets
24 TARTLETS

2 recipes Perfect Nut Crust
(page 236)

CRANBERRY FILLING
2 envelopes (2 tablespoons)
unflavored gelatin
6 cups fresh or dry-frozen
cranberries
2 cups sugar
1 cup red currant jelly

GARNISH
1 cup heavy cream, whipped

Prepare the crust and, using your fingers, press the dough firmly against the bottoms and sides of 3-inch tart pans so that it is about ⅛

Brilliant red cranberries are combined with red currant jelly in a crunchy nut crust to make these beautiful looking tartlets.

inch thick. Chill the shells for 1 hour.

Preheat the oven to 350°. Put the shells on a baking sheet and bake until slightly golden and firm, about 12 to 15 minutes. Remove the baking sheet from the oven and set the tart pans on a rack to cool. Then carefully remove the shells from the pans.

To prepare the filling, stir the gelatin into ½ cup cold water until dissolved. Wash and pick over the cranberries. In a saucepan, combine the cranberries with the sugar and jelly. Gently boil the mixture, uncovered, over moderate heat, stirring occasionally, for 15 minutes. Remove the pan from the heat, cool the mixture slightly, and stir in the softened gelatin.

When the mixture is cool, divide it evenly among the tart shells. Chill the tarts and serve topped with the whipped cream.

Christmas Presents and Decorations

*C*HRISTMAS IS, FOR ME, A TIME OF intense domestic involvement. Many of the visible tokens of celebration—the decoration of the house and the presents for friends—are in fact family projects that are relaxing and pleasurable.

My daughter, Alexis, sixteen, now undertakes her own preparations, and they are wonderfully elaborate. For weeks she wears a secret smile and putters about, making fruitcakes and spice cakes for her friends, and concocting new versions of cookies. Last year, inspired by a magazine picture, she baked huge gingerbread suns, and posted them in our kitchen windows. They may become a family tradition.

A Chocolate Chip Cookie Tree: This was our first edible tree. The cookies are a large, crunchy, irresistible variation on Tollhouse, developed and made famous locally by Alexis (see page 93 for recipe). While the cookies are still warm, they are pierced with a needle, to create holes through which lengths of red ribbon can be drawn. When cool, they are hung from the boughs of a small tree in profusion.

A Tree for the Birds: This tree belongs in a corner of the garden, where it will provide a midwinter treat for the birds. It is so colorful, however, that you may want to keep it inside until after the holidays. Let the children mastermind the decoration or make it a family project for an intimate at-home evening. String popcorn, string cranberries, and drape a tree, large or small, with these garlands. Add lady apples, tied with ribbon. Just before you dispatch the tree to the out-of-doors, hang suet balls and small mesh bags of birdseed from the outside branches.

Fruitcake garnished with holly and nestled in a grapevine wreath.

A Gingerbread House: A gingerbread house is a dramatic example of the great pleasure of the ephemeral. Planning its design; hand-crafting its many components; adding bits of personal fancy; and then, when it is complete and properly displayed, eating it—this is the sort of act that thrills cooks again and again. See the pages that follow for directions for a gingerbread mansion.

Edible Presents: Making edible presents for friends and neighbors is one of the nicest ways to get in the mood for Christmas. My favorites include traditional fruitcakes and plum puddings, as well as bourbon cakes, bourbon balls, jellies (crab apple, red pepper), jams, herb vinegars, and bottles of crystal red cranberry liqueur.

Alexis's brown sugar chocolate chip cookies hang from this tree, making an unusual, edible Christmas decoration for our house.

Red Pepper Jelly
FOUR 8-OUNCE JARS

Red pepper jelly is made in late September, when the bell peppers are turning red in the garden. It is a clear, rosy-hued jelly that is both piquant and sweet. I love to eat it with cream cheese on dark bread, or on a slice of toasted pain de mie *(white French loaf bread). It is also a fine companion to, or glaze for, roast pork.*

- 3 cups of chopped and seeded sweet red peppers
- ½ cup chopped, seeded hot peppers (red or green)
- 2 cups cider vinegar
- ½ teaspoon salt
- 5½ cups granulated sugar
- 1 bottle pectin

Combine peppers with vinegar in a heavy saucepan. Simmer for 15 minutes. Strain juice through a jelly bag. Do not squeeze.

Bring juice to a boil. Add salt and sugar; bring to a full rolling boil and boil for 1 minute. Remove from heat, stir in the pectin and skim off the foam. Ladle into hot, sterilized jelly jars and seal with screw-on tops or melted paraffin.

Crab Apple Rosemary Jelly
2 TO 2½ PINTS

A fragrant, clear jelly delicately flavored with rosemary—made even more interesting with a sprig of fresh rosemary suspended in each jar.

- 5 cups ripe, unblemished crab apples, stems and seeds removed
- 2 cups water
- Sugar to measure
- Sprigs of fresh rosemary

Cut the apples into chunks. Add water and simmer until soft.

Strain the juice through 3 layers of cheesecloth or through a jelly bag.

For each cup of juice, add ¾ cup sugar. Bring syrup to a boil and cook quickly until a temperature of 220° is reached. While syrup boils, swirl a large sprig of rosemary through the liquid.

Remove from heat, skim, and pour into ½-pint jars. Add 1 sprig of rosemary to each jar and seal with paraffin.

A dazzling array of fruits preserved in different liqueurs.

Fruits in Liqueurs

Make these when fruits are at the height of their season, and save until Christmas.

Strawberries in Rum
Cherries in Brandy
Raspberries in Kirsch
Peaches in Grand Marnier or Brandy
Apricots in Amaretto

Raspberries in Cognac
Grapes in Sambuca
Plums in Brandy
Orange Slices in Cointreau

Make a sugar syrup of 2 cups granulated sugar and 1 cup water. Heat syrup to 230°. Add appropriate liqueur, using 1 part liqueur to 1 part syrup, and pour over fruit that has been packed into clean glass jars. Seal and store for at least 2 months in very cool place or in the refrigerator until ready to use.

Bourbon Bread
3 SMALL LOAVES

These currant-studded, bourbon-flavored tea breads make wonderful holiday gifts. They are light, sponge-cakey, and flavorful.

    2   cups confectioners' sugar
    ½   pound (2 sticks) unsalted
        butter, at room temperature
    5   eggs, separated
    2   tablespoons bourbon
    4   teaspoons grated orange rind
    2¼ cups sifted cake flour
    1   teaspoon baking powder
    ½   teaspoon grated nutmeg
    ¼   teaspoon salt
    ½   cup currants plumped in 3
        tablespoons bourbon
        Confectioners' sugar

Preheat oven to 350°. Butter 3 small (7¼×3¾-inch) loaf pans and line bottoms with waxed paper.

Cream sugar with butter until light and fluffy. Add egg yolks, lightly beaten, to sugar and butter. Beat

well. Add bourbon and orange rind.

Sift flour with baking powder, nutmeg, and salt. Fold the dry ingredients into the egg mixture alternately with the 3 tablespoons of bourbon in which the currants were plumped. Fold in the currants.

Beat the egg whites until stiff. Fold them into the batter carefully.

Spoon the batter into loaf pans. Bake for 45 minutes, or until toothpick inserted in center comes out clean.

Cool 10 minutes in the pans, then turn out onto racks to cool completely.

Before wrapping, dust tops of breads with confectioners' sugar.

Bourbon Balls
40 TO 48 BALLS

    2½ cups vanilla wafers
    1   cup pecans
    ⅔   cup good bourbon

Left: *Ruby red raspberries in a brandy syrup make a wonderful gift for friends.* **Below left:** *Chocolate chip cookies arranged like a wreath on an old sifter.* **Below right:** *One of my special gift baskets—tea breads, fruitcake, homemade jellies, and maple syrup.*

1 cup confectioners' sugar
plus confectioners' sugar for
coating
3 tablespoons cocoa
2 tablespoons white corn
syrup

Pulverize the wafers in a food processor and put in a bowl. Grind the pecans and add to the wafer crumbs. Blend the remaining ingredients (except coating sugar) 10 seconds and add to the mixture. Mix well.

Roll into balls 1 inch in diameter and roll in confectioners' sugar.

Store, airtight, at least 24 hours before serving.

Mrs. Maus's Fruitcake
2 CAKES

This is the traditional fruit cake of our family. It is a dense, heavy, very rich cake which gets better and better as it ages.

1 pound (4 sticks) butter, at
room temperature
2 cups sugar

12 eggs
6 pounds candied fruits and
fresh nuts (choose from the
following: citron, lemon
peel, orange peel, cherries,
apricots, walnuts, pecans)
½ cup molasses
2½ cups all-purpose flour
2 tablespoons allspice

GLAZE
1 cup apricot jam
⅓ cup brandy

GARNISH
Whole dried apricots, pecan
halves

Preheat oven to 275°. Butter two 9-inch cake pans or 2 loaf pans. Line with waxed paper, butter again, and flour.

Cream butter and sugar until creamy and light. Add the eggs one at a time, beating batter until fluffy. Stir in the fruits, nuts, and molasses, blending well.

Sift the flour with the allspice and stir into the batter cup by cup until well mixed.

Spoon into the prepared cake pans. Set pans in a shallow pan with 1½ to 2 inches hot water. Bake for 3 to

3½ hours, until done. Test with toothpick. Cool in pans on a cake rack.

Remove from pans, pull off waxed paper, and glaze with strained apricot jam heated with brandy. Decorate with dried apricots and nut halves and glaze again. Let glaze harden before wrapping in cellophane. Keep in cool place. To serve, slice very thinly.

Herb Vinegars

It is both easy and practical to make your own vinegars, which you can flavor with herbs, garlic, or berries, for there is almost always some wine left over after dinner—if not in the bottle, then in glasses.

I keep two giant mason jars in a dark, cool cupboard in the kitchen, one for red wine and one for white, each containing a "mother of vinegar," the amoebalike mass that ferments vinegar, to which I simply add the respective leftovers.

Several months are necessary for full fermentation. When enough

vinegar has accumulated, fill interesting old bottles, or just recycled wine or vinegar bottles, and add several sprigs of tarragon, thyme, mint, or basil, shallots, or cloves of garlic, or raspberries, blueberries, or blackberries.

NOTE: You can obtain a "mother" from an old jar of good vinegar, or take a piece from a friend who has nurtured his own.

Cranberry Cordial
6 CUPS

This simple-to-make cordial is a perfect Christmas or Thanksgiving gift. Three ingredients, little preparation, and 22 days result in a colorful tart-sweet drink for after-dinner imbibing.

2 cups crushed cranberries
2 cups sugar
2 cups vodka

Combine ingredients and store in a covered jar in a cool place for at least 22 days. Strain and serve as an after-dinner drink.

Left: *Herb-flavored vinegars.* **Right:** *Apricots and cinnamon.*

Homemade edible gifts for friends displayed in our front hall.

Gingerbread Mansion

Making a gingerbread mansion can be the perfect occasion for a small holiday party, because at the crucial moments of assembling walls and mounting the roof you will need extra hands. Except for the exterior shaping, a memorable gingerbread house calls for last-minute decisions and spontaneous invention.

The perfection of a gingerbread house is the least important of its aspects. In fact with gingerbread all flaws are reparable, for another coat of frosting covers all.

For the large gingerbread mansion pictured, make 5 batches of dough. A strong electric mixer is necessary.

½ pound (2 sticks) margarine
1 cup brown sugar
1¼ cups unsulfured molasses
3 eggs
8 to 9 cups sifted all-purpose flour
1 tablespoon baking soda
1 teaspoon salt
1 teaspoon allspice
1 teaspoon cinnamon
1 teaspoon ground cloves
1 teaspoon ground ginger

Cream margarine and sugar until smooth. Add molasses and eggs. Beat until smooth.

Sift 3 cups of flour with the baking soda, salt, and spices. Gradually beat into the sugar mixture. Add 5 to 6 cups more flour, beating until just mixed. Dough will be heavy and stiff. Form into 2 balls, wrap in plastic wrap, and chill at least 2 hours.

Preheat oven to 350°. Butter or vegetable-spray baking sheets (the sheets should be flat, with no edges, large enough to hold the largest shape).

Roll out ball of dough directly on the baking sheet to ⅛ inch thick. Place the largest pattern piece on rolled dough and with a sharp, small knife, cut neatly around edges. Carefully remove scraps and press together into a ball. Reserve scraps for small pieces. Continue rolling and cutting until all pieces are done.

Bake pieces 10 to 15 minutes, until done but not browned. Remove baked pieces carefully from baking sheet onto rack to cool. (If pieces are very large, use rack larger than baking sheet. Put rack over baked gingerbread and, holding carefully, turn pan, gingerbread, and rack upside down. Allow to cool, then reverse gingerbread. The upper side of the baked gingerbread should be the outside of the house.)

ROYAL-ICING "GLUE"
3 cups sifted confectioners' sugar
2 egg whites

Beat sugar with egg whites until thick and smooth. Correct consistency with additional sugar or egg whites if necessary.

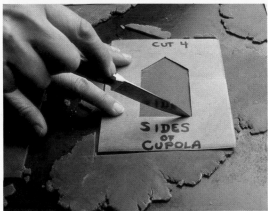

Cut large pieces of mansion from rolled-out dough. For smaller pieces, roll scraps right on buttered baking pans and cut out shapes with a sharp knife. Remove trimmings.

Cool all baked pieces on racks and store in a dry place until ready to assemble. Any cracked pieces can be mended with the royal-icing "glue."

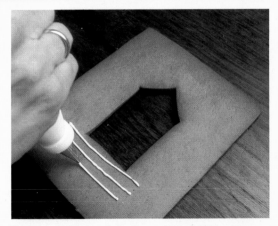

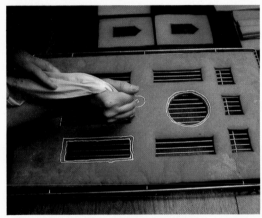

Decorate each piece before assembling. This takes a lot of time and can be done over a period of several days. Use a small round pastry tip (Ateco #1) for

piping royal icing (see recipe, page 209). Whimsical detail and architectural outlines can be ornáte or simple as your mood dictates.

On the front of the mansion, outlines around openings of windows and doors create the feeling of architectural surfaces.

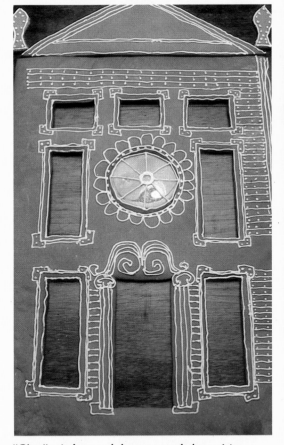

"Glass" windows and doors are made by melting sugar with a little bit of water to hard-ball stage (250°–265°) and pouring the mixture onto an oiled surface to harden. The "glass" is then affixed with royal-icing "glue" from the inside of the mansion.

To assemble the mansion, hold two sides upright and apply the royal-icing "glue" liberally on the inside angle. Hold in place until dry while you repeat the process with the remaining sides. (Several pairs of hands are useful here.) Affix roof, pediment, finials, and cupola in the same way, gluing from the inside. Finish trimming and seal outer edges with royal icing piped through a star tip (Ateco #30). Decorate with tiny lights and evergreen.

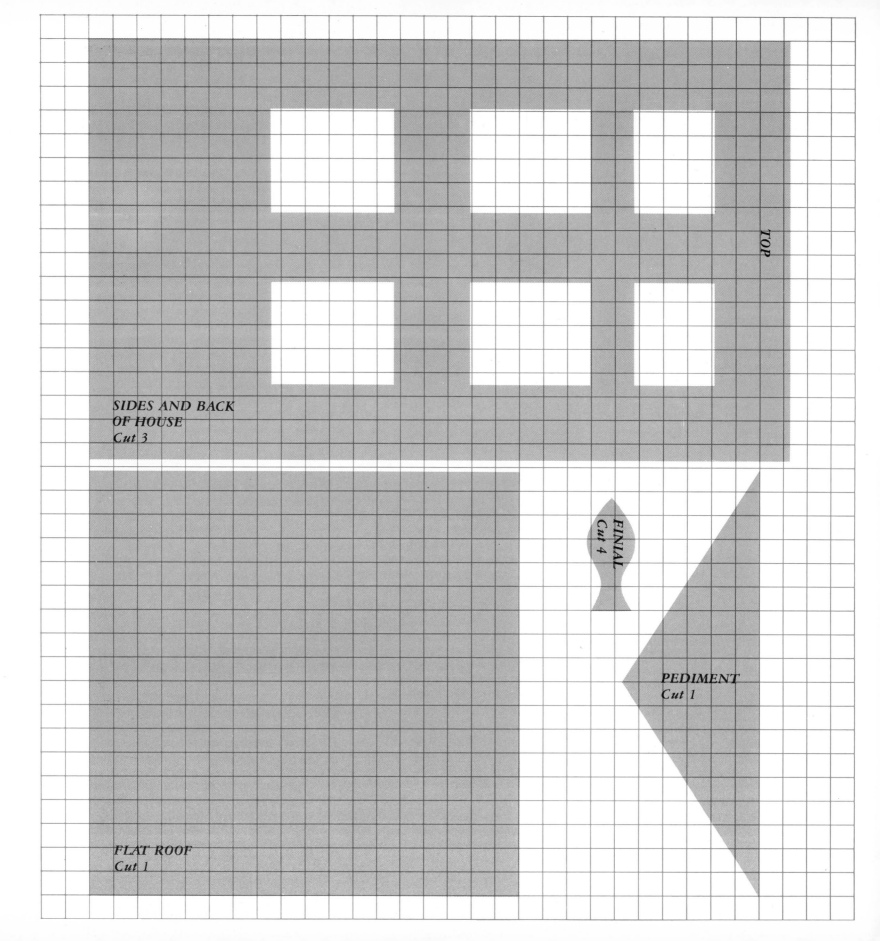

SIDES AND BACK
OF HOUSE
Cut 3

TOP

FINIAL
Cut 4

PEDIMENT
Cut 1

FLAT ROOF
Cut 1

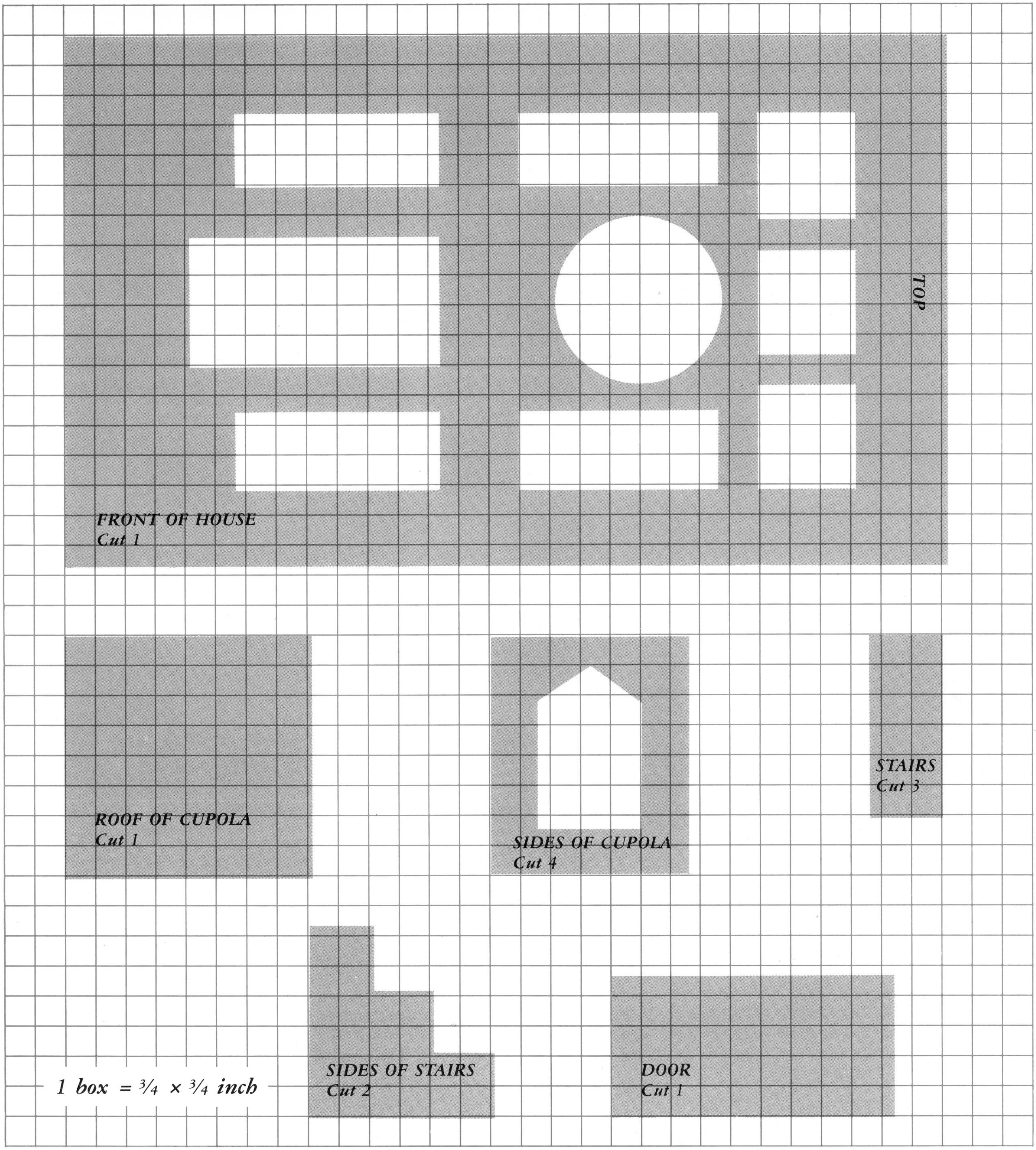

TOP

FRONT OF HOUSE
Cut 1

ROOF OF CUPOLA
Cut 1

SIDES OF CUPOLA
Cut 4

STAIRS
Cut 3

1 box = ³/₄ × ³/₄ inch

SIDES OF STAIRS
Cut 2

DOOR
Cut 1

A Children's Christmas Party

WHEN OUR DAUGHTER, ALEXIS, was small, we used to usher in her school vacation with a children's party to bake sugar cookies for a cookie tree. When the cookies were decorated, the children set aside their favorites to take home for presents or decoration, and with the rest decked out a little pine tree in our kitchen.

The place is the kitchen, where beforehand you set up a comfortable work space—a generous table or two laid with cookie cutters, rolling pins, flour shakers, spatulas, paring knives, and a great mound of dough, made the day before and chilled overnight. The shapes a cookie might take need not even be limited to cookie cutters, for with mother's supervision tracings and freehand creations are possibilities, too. While the cookies are baking, children can busy themselves poking cloves into oranges and lady apples to make pomander balls for presents or ornaments.

The icing of the cookies is a matter of pure whimsy. The primitive touch of a young child is as decorative as the patient application of a sophisticate. Have ready a generous supply of pastry bags, Number 1 tips, and a lineup of little bowls of colored frosting, and the children will work in their own inspiring style. (Past-

Neighborhood children make Christmas gifts at our house.

ry bags are not nearly as cumbersome as they look, and children love them.) The most spectacular cookies result from using spectacular shades of frosting. These are made by introducing a few drops of food coloring into bowls of white royal icing. Specialty stores stock a palette of food colorings that goes far beyond primaries into rusts, roses, vermilions, and jades. Even more refined shades can be mixed yourself. Have fun with the decoration, as you might with a painting, or a doodle.

While the cookies are drying is the perfect time for refreshments before a fire or under the small pine tree upon which the cookies will soon be hung. A big bowl of fresh popcorn, imperfect cookies, and hot cider swizzled with cinnamon sticks will make everyone happy. Then it is time to thread the cookies with nearly invisible milliner's wire and deck out the tree.

❧ MENU ❧

Iced Sugar Cookies   Fresh Popcorn
Apples   Oranges
Cold Milk
Hot Cider with Cinnamon Sticks

Sugar cookies in the shape of turkeys, horses, fish, and hearts decorated with icing in unusual shades look wonderful on the mantel at holiday time.

Above left: *Our artist friend Naiad Einsel crafted a giant cookie cutter using our cat "New Kitty" as a model.*

Right: *More iced sugar cookies in a variety of shapes and sizes.*

Iced Sugar Cookies

APPROXIMATELY 2 DOZEN

2 cups flour
¼ teaspoon salt
½ teaspoon baking powder
½ cup butter

1 cup sugar
1 egg
2 tablespoons brandy
½ teaspoon vanilla

ICING
1 cup confectioners' sugar
1 egg white
Few drops of lemon juice

Sift together dry ingredients. In an electric mixer, cream butter and sugar; add egg, brandy, and vanilla and beat well. Add dry ingredients a little at a time and mix until well blended. Wrap and chill dough for at least 30 minutes before rolling.

Preheat oven to 400°. On a lightly floured board, roll out ⅓ of the dough at a time. Roll to about ⅛ inch thick and cut out with cookie cutters. Put shapes on buttered baking sheets and bake for 10 minutes. Do not allow to brown. Cool on racks.

Mix icing ingredients until smooth. Spread on cooled cookies and sprinkle with colored sugars, or pipe designs in various colors onto cookies with pastry bag.

Sugar Cookie Cutouts

Each year my friend Naiad Einsel creates new and whimsical shapes for cookie cutouts. Some of my favorites are reproduced here for you to copy and use. First, enlarge the shapes by tracing the outline of the pattern onto graph paper, square by square. Cut out and transfer to cardboard for actual use. (Since the cardboard is sturdier, it will withstand many cutout sessions.) I like to make the cookies quite large. A suggested scale is shown; however you can make them larger or smaller as you wish. Roll the iced sugar cookie dough directly on a buttered cookie sheet and cut out the shape with a pointed knife. Remove the scraps carefully and bake until lightly browned around the edges. Remove to a cooling rack and decorate with a pastry bag and #1 tip using royal icing tinted with your choice of colors. Let the icing dry completely and store cookies in tightly covered tins or boxes until ready to use. If you wish to hang the cookies from a tree or mantel, make a small hole in the top of the cookie with a heavy needle or metal cake tester while still hot. I use milliner's wire drawn through the hole for hanging.

Royal icing is simply confectioners' sugar mixed with egg whites. Make a smooth, creamy icing that is not runny but thin enough to press through the pastry-bag tip. Put small amounts of icing into bowls and color with baker's paste vegetable dye, available at culinary specialty stores. These dyes come in many unusual shades: purples, bright blues, pinks, greens, browns, and many more.

The lines on these cookie shapes are merely decorating guides. The real fun in icing cookies is letting your imagination take over. The "New Kitty" cookie is actually Birdi Kins's interpretation of a real cat's face. Our kitty actually posed while the decorations were being done.

Of course, it is necessary to supervise young children while making and decorating cookies. Guide them carefully in the use of sharp knives and hot ovens.

1 **box** = ½ × ½ **inch**

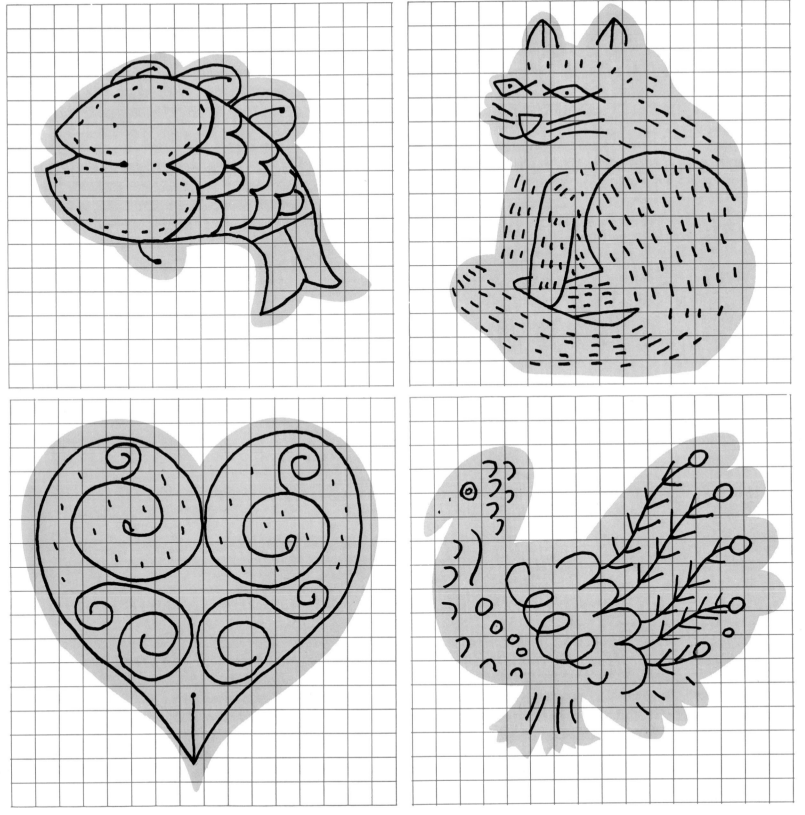

Christmas Open House for Fifty

*W*HEN OUR HALLS ARE DECKED out, our presents made and arrayed, and a fire has been lit, we invite friends to an afternoon open "all over the house" party, to enjoy it all with us. This party is fluid and friendly, festive but informal, as any open house must be.

The dining-room table is decked with holiday desserts: an old-fashioned fruit kuchen, a Lane cake (named for its source, my sister-in-law's family in South Carolina), and a platter of glacéed grapes and strawberries; on the sideboard sits a bowl of hot mulled red wine. Down the hall in the parlor, eggnog froths in a silver bowl, so rich it needs no accompaniment. Next door, the library table is set for tea, around a centerpiece of croquembouche. And the kitchen is ready for children: mulled cider on the stove, sugar cookies and chocolate chip cookies mounded on platters.

Opposite page: *An antique star quilt is the background for the children's buffet set in front of the hearth.* Above: *Baskets filled with cookies for the children to take home.* Right: *Gingerbread gnomes, with just their pointed hats frosted bright red.*

❧ MENU ❧

Lane Cake   Croquembouche
Alexis's Brown Sugar Chocolate Chip Cookies
Sugar Cookies   Fruit Kuchen
Strawberry and Green Grape Tarts in Nut Crusts
Glacéed Green Grapes and Red Strawberries
The Original Eggnog
Mulled Cider, Tea, Mulled Wine

Lane Cake

SERVES 10 TO 12

1 cup (2 sticks) unsalted butter
2 cups sugar
1 teaspoon vanilla
3¾ cups sifted cake flour
3½ teaspoons baking powder
¾ teaspoon salt
1 cup milk
8 egg whites

ICING
12 egg yolks
1½ cups sugar
½ teaspoon salt
¾ cup (1½ sticks) unsalted butter
¾ cup bourbon
1½ cups muscat raisins

½ cup bourbon
1½ cups shredded coconut, preferably unsweetened
1½ cups pecan halves
1½ cups candied kumquats or cherries

OPTIONAL GARNISH
Fresh kumquats

Preheat oven to 375°. Butter and flour four 9-inch cake pans.

To make cake, cream butter, sugar, and vanilla. Sift dry ingredients to-gether and add to butter mixture alternately with milk.

Beat egg whites until glossy but not dry. Fold into cake batter. Divide mixture evenly and pour into prepared pans. Bake 15 minutes. Remove from oven and cool layers on racks.

To make icing, cook egg yolks, sugar, salt, and butter in double boiler until thick and translucent. This may take as long as 30 minutes. Add bourbon and whisk until fluffy and creamy. Mix in raisins and allow to cool.

To assemble the cake, dribble ½ cup bourbon evenly over four layers. Spoon a bit of icing over tops of each layer, and sprinkle with coconut. Stack layers on top of one another. Spread remaining icing over entire top and sides. Arrange pecans and candied fruit in a decorative pattern. Wrap cake in foil to set icing and chill until serving time.

To serve, place on platter and surround with fresh kumquats, if desired.

NOTE: This cake improves as it ages, and can be made up to 3 weeks in advance. Keep well wrapped in the refrigerator.

Shirley Lane's Lane cake.

Croquembouche

Croquembouche means "crunch in the mouth" and is a mound of pastry cream-filled puffs stuck together with shiny caramel. Nougat cut into decorative shapes adorns the croquembouche. Guests pluck off the puffs with their fingers. This recipe makes about 70 puffs, enough for a small pyramid. Repeat the recipe for a larger dessert.

PUFFS (PÂTE À CHOUX)
1½ sticks unsalted butter
2 cups water
¼ teaspoon salt
1 tablespoon sugar
1½ cups flour
6 large eggs
GLAZE
1 egg beaten with 1 teaspoon water
PASTRY CREAM (CRÈME PÂTISSIÈRE)
6 egg yolks
½ cup sugar
½ cup sifted flour
2 cups milk, scalded
3 tablespoons butter
1 teaspoon vanilla
2 tablespoons cognac
Pinch salt
NOUGAT
2 cups sugar
Juice of ½ lemon
1½ cups toasted finely ground almonds
CARAMEL
2 cups sugar
⅔ cup water
2 tablespoons corn syrup

Preheat oven to 425°. To make the puffs, melt the butter in the water with salt and sugar over low heat. Remove from heat and beat in flour with a wooden spoon until completely mixed. Return to heat and stir vigorously for 2 to 3 minutes. Mixture will form a mass, and a film will form on bottom of pan.

Remove from heat and, one by one, add eggs, beating vigorously after each addition.

Using a pastry tube with ½-inch opening, form puffs on a buttered baking sheet. Glaze each puff with the beaten egg and water, using a pastry brush. Smooth the top of each puff. Put in the oven for 20 minutes. Remove from oven and pierce each puff with a sharp knife. (This allows the steam to escape so that the interior of the puff is not soggy.) Return to the oven for 10 minutes more. Cool puffs on a rack. While cooling, prepare pastry cream.

To make the cream, beat the egg yolks, gradually adding the sugar, until mixture is thick and pale yellow. Beat in the flour. Add the hot milk in dribbles, reserving ½ cup for thinning. Return to pot in which milk was scalded, and stir mixture over high heat until it comes to a boil. It will become lumpy first and then will smooth out with vigorous stirring. Be careful not to scorch the bottom of the pot. The cream should be thick, but add milk if too thick to pipe.

Add the butter, 1 tablespoon at a time. Flavor with vanilla, cognac, and salt. Cool completely. Inject the pastry cream into the puffs with a ¼-inch pastry tip.

To make nougat, melt the sugar with the lemon juice in a heavy pot. Do not stir. Boil together until a thick amber syrup is formed. Stir in the almonds and spread the mixture on an oiled marble slab while warm. Cut with a sharp knife into a round for the base, and into small triangles for decoration. Keep nougat warm in a 250° oven. (It cannot be cut or shaped if it hardens.)

To make the caramel, bring the ingredients to a boil over high heat. Do not stir. Cover pan (allowing steam to dissolve any crystals that might form). Uncover pan and boil several more minutes, until syrup is amber. Reduce heat to keep syrup from hardening.

Dip the filled cream puffs, one by one, into the caramel syrup and arrange on the nougat base, forming a cone resembling a pyramid. The caramel holds the cream puffs together.

NOTE: Assemble the croquembouche the day of the party, as it cannot be refrigerated. However, the cream puffs, pastry cream, and nougat can be prepared in advance.

A dramatic croquembouche surrounded by fresh flowers makes a spectacular centerpiece on the table in the library.

Alexis's Brown Sugar Chocolate Chip Cookies
SEE RECIPE, PAGE 93

Sugar Cookies
SEE RECIPE, PAGE 89

Fruit Kuchen
SERVES 12 TO 16

PASTRY
- 1 cup (2 sticks) unsalted butter
- 3 cups sifted unbleached flour
- ¼ cup sugar
  Grated rind of 1 lemon
- 2 egg yolks
- ¼ cup ice water

FRUIT FILLING
- 6 dried apricots or prunes
- 5 large dried figs
- 6 dates
- ½ cup raisins
- ½ cup rum
- 6 tablespoons unsalted butter
- ¼ cup honey
- ½ teaspoon cinnamon
- ½ teaspoon nutmeg
  Grated rind and juice of 1 orange
- 4 large tart apples

GARNISH
  Softly whipped cream

To prepare pastry, cut butter into flour (you can use a food processor to do this, but be careful not to overwork). Add sugar and lemon rind. Mix egg yolks into iced water, and quickly mix this into flour.

Press dough together with fingers and chill 15 minutes.

Butter a 10½ × 15-inch baking sheet with sides, or a 12-inch pizza pan. Press chilled dough into pan, bringing dough up the sides. Chill at least 1 hour. Bake in 350° oven until pastry is light golden color, about 25 minutes.

To make fruit filling, soak dried fruits in rum 3 hours or overnight. (If figs are very dry, simmer first in water 5 to 10 minutes.) Melt 4 tablespoons butter in heavy skillet and add honey, spices, and orange rind and juice. Peel, core, and slice apples ¼ inch thick and add to but-

ter mixture. Sauté over medium heat until just soft.

Drain dried fruits and arrange apricots, figs, and dates in the center of the tart. Encircle with apple slices, overlapping or placing them close together. Arrange the raisins around the apples at the edge of the tart.

Melt remaining 2 tablespoons butter into mixture left from cooking apples. Pour over fruits in tart. Refrigerate.

To serve, warm kuchen 10 minutes in a 325° oven. Garnish with softly whipped cream.

Strawberry and Green Grape Tarts in Nut Crusts

SEE RECIPE, PAGE 241

Glacéed Green Grapes and Red Strawberries

Glacéed fruits can be prepared several hours before the party. They must be kept in a dry, cool place.

SUGAR GLAZE

2 cups sugar
½ cup water

Small clusters of seedless grapes
Perfect large strawberries

Dissolve the sugar in the water in a very heavy 1-quart saucepan, swirling the pan. (Do not use a spoon.) Set pan over medium heat and continue to swirl liquid until it becomes clear. Raise heat, cover, and bring to a rapid boil. (The steam that condenses on the lid falls back into the syrup and keeps crystals from forming and prevents the glaze from becoming cloudy.) Boil for about 3 minutes, uncover, and insert candy thermometer in the syrup. When the hard ball stage (265°) is reached, reduce flame to keep the syrup at that temperature.

Dip the grape clusters and then the strawberries in the syrup for just a second (to cover) and put on a baking sheet which has been lightly oiled or sprayed with vegetable oil.

The Original Eggnog

SERVES 16

12 eggs, separated
1½ cups superfine sugar
1 quart whole milk
1½ quarts heavy cream
1 quart bourbon

½ cup dark rum
2 cups cognac
Freshly grated nutmeg

Beat egg yolks until thick and pale yellow. Gradually add sugar to yolks. With a wire whisk, beat in milk and 1 quart cream. Add bourbon, rum, and cognac, stirring constantly.

Just before serving, beat egg whites until stiff. Fold into mixture. Whip remaining heavy cream until stiff and fold in. Sprinkle with nutmeg.

Mulled Cider

APPROXIMATELY 32 SERVINGS

1 gallon cider, freshly pressed if possible
8 3-inch cinnamon sticks
4 apples, studded with cloves
10 whole allspice

Combine ingredients and simmer for 30 minutes. Serve hot from a large earthenware bowl and ladle into cups.

VARIATION: For spiked cider, add ½ cup light rum.

Mulled Wine

APPROXIMATELY 32 SERVINGS

4 bottles Burgundy wine
1 teaspoon allspice
1 2-inch cinnamon stick
12 whole cloves
½ cup sugar
½ teaspoon angostura bitters

Combine all ingredients and heat, but do not boil. Let sit, hot, until ready to serve. Strain into a heated punch bowl and serve.

Top: *Glacéed grapes and strawberries.* **Middle:** *Strawberry and grape tarts in nut crusts.* **Bottom:** *Fluffy eggnog in a silver bowl.*

Christmas Day Dinner

AFTER THE MERRIMENT OF THE open house, we are always content to settle back into the simple shape of our family to celebrate Christmas Eve and Day. For the past ten years, we have had the same small traditional Christmas Eve dinner for the three of us—champignons under glass (for the fun of those ritualistic domes), parsleyed baby rack of lamb, a gratin of potatoes, an endive and watercress salad, and a baby croquembouche for dessert. We have a small amount of wonderful caviar first, drink champagne, and play a favorite recording of Handel's *Messiah*. After dinner, we decorate our large tree, and make a few quick trips to neighbors to distribute the presents.

Christmas Day dinner is a dinner of surprises: the mussel soup (billi bi), a roast pork rather than ham or turkey, a spicy quince preserve, and cranberries in unusual forms—a tart and a liqueur. When the gingerbread house is lit with candles, we bring out the plum pudding and set it aflame.

❦ MENU ❦

Billi Bi

Crown Roast of Pork

Wild Rice Stuffing with Prunes

Spicy Quince Preserve   Baby Carrots   String Beans

Whole Braised Brussels Sprouts   Watercress Endive Salad

Cranberry Nut Tart   Applesauce Spice Cake

Cranberry Cordial

Plum Pudding with Hard Sauce

Billi Bi

SERVES 10

Billi Bi is an elegant mussel-flavored cream soup. Serve it garnished with cooked mussels.

4 pounds mussels
4 yellow onions, sliced
4 shallots, chopped
2 stalks celery, diced
2 bay leaves
4 sprigs parsley
1 teaspoon thyme
    Pinch cayenne pepper
    Salt and freshly ground
    pepper to taste
4 tablespoons butter
2 cups dry white wine
4 cups heavy cream
2 egg yolks, slightly beaten

Rinse and scrub mussels. Put them in a large stockpot with the onions, shallots, celery, bay leaves, parsley, spices, butter, and wine. Bring to a boil and simmer, covered, for 5 to 10 minutes, shaking the pot to move the mussels around. Strain the liquid through 2 layers of cheesecloth. Remove the mussels from the shells, discard, and reserve

Opposite: Crown roast of pork with paper frills.

mussels for a garnish or use in a rémoulade or vinaigrette.

Bring the liquid to a boil. Add the cream and boil. Remove from the heat and add the egg yolks slowly, whisking briskly. After this step, do not boil or yolks will curdle. Serve hot or cold, with the shelled mussels as a garnish.

Crown Roast of Pork

In this recipe the pork is tenderized and its flavor heightened by the use of a dry marinade. It is then filled with a wild rice stuffing and roasted until just done. The presentation with the rib bones bedecked with paper frills is a very festive way to serve pork. Give your butcher a little warning to prepare the crown roast. Allow 2 ribs per person.

SALT MARINADE (PER
POUND OF MEAT)

2 teaspoons kosher salt
½ teaspoon freshly ground
    black pepper
½ teaspoon each sage, thyme,
    and bay leaf

Pinch allspice
1 clove garlic, mashed
1 recipe Wild Rice Stuffing
   (page 167)
12 whole pitted prunes, soaked
    in cognac
4 tablespoons lard, vegetable
   oil, or butter
1 yellow onion, thinly sliced
1 carrot, thinly sliced
4 cloves garlic, minced
   Herb bouquet

GRAVY

1 cup white wine
4 tablespoons chopped shallots
3 tablespoons butter
½ cup heavy cream
   Salt and pepper

The day before serving, rub the salt marinade well into the meat and put it in a large covered bowl in the refrigerator. Turn every 3 hours.

The next day, prepare the stuffing according to directions.

Preheat oven to 350°.

Rub all the marinade off the meat and pat dry with paper towels. Add the lard, onions, carrots, and garlic to the roasting pan. Sauté vegetables until soft, about 10 minutes. Put the roast in the pan, fill the center with the stuffing, and top with prunes. Add the herb bouquet to pan. Cover and roast 15 minutes. Reduce the heat to 325° and continue roasting, allowing 30 minutes per pound. A meat thermometer should register 180°. To brown the roast, remove the cover ½ hour before completion time. If bone tips brown too quickly, cover each one with a piece of raw potato or aluminum foil. Transfer the roast to a heated platter.

To make the gravy, add the wine, shallots, and butter to the pan juices. Boil the mixture down to ⅓ its original quantity, stirring with a fork to incorporate the drippings. Add the cream and heat without boiling. Season to taste. Strain into a gravy bowl.

Spicy Quince Preserve

5 TO 6 HALF-PINTS

If you are fortunate enough to grow quinces or know someone who does, this is a special way to preserve them. This spicy concoction is delicious with roast pork or ham. Jars of these preserves are a wonderful, coveted gift, so make enough to give to special friends.

2 pounds quinces, peeled and
   cored
2 cups cider vinegar
1 cup water
2½ cups sugar
2 cinnamon sticks
1 tablespoon whole cloves
¼ cup sliced, peeled ginger

Cut quinces into slices. Cover with water, bring to a boil, and cook until almost tender. Drain. (Reserve the liquid for poaching other fruits or making apple jelly.)

Boil the vinegar, 1 cup water, sugar, spices, and ginger for 5 minutes. Add the quinces and cook just until the quinces are clear and tender.

Spoon the quinces into hot sterile jars and cover with the boiling syrup. Seal immediately.

Baby Carrots

SERVES 10

30 to 40 baby carrots
4 tablespoons butter, melted
   Salt and pepper to taste
   Freshly grated nutmeg

Peel and trim carrots. Steam over boiling water until just tender, about 5 minutes. Remove from heat.

To serve, toss in hot butter. Season with salt, pepper, and a pinch of nutmeg.

String Beans
SERVES 6

Choose young string beans with no blemishes for this. They must be unwrinkled, and should snap when broken in half.

- 2 tablespoons butter
- 1 small garlic clove, peeled and crushed
- 1½ pounds tender green beans
  Salt and pepper to taste

Melt butter with garlic.

Snap stem end off the beans. Steam, covered, over boiling water or cook in a large pot of boiling water until just tender, about 3 to 5 minutes, depending on size of beans. Drain, toss with garlic butter and seasonings, and serve immediately.

NOTE: String beans can be cooked ahead, cooled immediately in ice water, drained, covered, and set aside. To serve, toss with hot butter until heated through.

Whole
Braised Brussels Sprouts
DOUBLE RECIPE, PAGE 168

Watercress Endive Salad
SEE RECIPE, PAGE 168

Cranberry Nut Tart
ONE 10-INCH TART

- 1 baked Perfect Nut Crust (page 236)

CRANBERRY FILLING
- 1 envelope softened gelatin
- 3 cups fresh cranberries

220

- 1 cup sugar
- ½ cup red currant jelly

GARNISH
- 1 cup heavy cream, whipped

Soften gelatin in ¼ cup cold water. In a saucepan, combine the cranberries, sugar, and jelly. Cook for 10 minutes over low heat. Cool slightly and stir in the gelatin. Cool thoroughly; pour into crust. Chill. Serve with whipped cream.

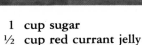

Applesauce Spice Cake
SEE RECIPE, PAGE 189

Cranberry Cordial
SEE RECIPE, PAGE 201

Plum Pudding
SERVES 10 TO 15

Plum pudding can be made anywhere from a few weeks to a year in advance and allowed to ripen in a cool place. It must be steamed 2 hours before serving. Leave it in hot water until ready to serve with hard sauce.

- ½ pound dried currants, plumped with 2 tablespoons cognac and enough hot water to cover
- ½ pound dark raisins, finely cut
- ¼ pound candied kumquats, finely diced
- ¼ pound glazed orange peel, finely diced
- ¼ pound glazed lemon peel, finely diced
- ¼ pound citron, finely diced
- ½ pound walnuts, finely chopped
- 1 cup flour
- 1 teaspoon baking soda

1 teaspoon salt
1 teaspoon cinnamon
¼ teaspoon nutmeg
¾ teaspoon mace
½ pound ground suet
3 slices thin-sliced bread soaked in ½ cup apple juice
1 cup dark brown sugar
3 eggs, beaten
⅓ cup black currant jam or preserves
¼ cup brandy or cognac
1 teaspoon sugar
½ cup cognac

Oil a 2-quart steamer mold or pottery bowl very well with vegetable oil and let it stand as you make pudding.

Combine the fruits and nuts in a large bowl. Sift flour, baking soda, salt, and spices into the fruit and nuts. Add the suet, bread, brown sugar, eggs, and jam and blend well. Beat with a wooden spoon to lighten the mixture. Pour into mold. Cover with a circle of parchment paper and put on a rack in a large kettle with enough water to come halfway up the sides. Cover and keep water boiling, replenishing as necessary. Steam for 6 hours.

Uncover pudding and pour brandy over it; put a piece of waxed paper over it; put a piece of waxed paper over pudding; replace parchment and set in a cool place or on low shelf of refrigerator to ripen.

To serve, steam for 2 more hours and invert on a serving platter. Add the 1 teaspoon sugar to the cognac, heat, pour over warm pudding, and flame with a match. Serve with hard sauce.

Hard Sauce
1½ CUPS

8 ounces whipped unsalted butter, softened

Plum pudding, hard sauce, and spice cake—traditional Christmas desserts.

Pinch salt
2 cups sifted confectioners' sugar
1 egg yolk
4 tablespoons heavy cream
4 tablespoons cognac

Put ingredients in a food processor and mix until smooth and creamy. Put sauce in tightly covered jar. Refrigerate.

Remove from refrigerator at least 1 hour before serving.

Valentine's Day Dinner for Two

IF THANKSGIVING IS COLONIAL, and Christmas medieval, then the tradition of Valentine's Day is Victorian. The custom of sending love tokens is much older historically (St. Valentine, the martyred saint whose name is honored, lived in the third century), but it seemed to find perfect expression in Victoriana. Hearts and flowers, misty poetry, cupids, doilies, ceremony, Flaubert, Chopin, Poe. "For love's sake" had a mysterious, forbidden drama then. Although I don't seem to receive lace-edged handkerchiefs, hand-dipped chocolates, or unsigned cards anymore, I have clear memories of my own Valentine's Days, mostly from my childhood. I loved the ritual of making a box covered in red velvet, trimmed with cherub cutouts and doilies, that I hoped would be filled with valentines. I made one again for my daughter, and now she makes them herself, with girlish anticipation. For the sake of romance, it still pleases me to make special cards, with bits and pieces of fussy materials, that can be used as place cards at a special Valentine's dinner.

Valentine's Day is a whimsical event and, if only for sentiment, deserves an elegant dinner for two. While it is fun to collect heart-shaped dishes and create a nostalgic table, romance can be conveyed simply, too—with paper doilies and red napkins, red roses and baby's breath. A special fancy can come as a finale—perhaps heart-shaped sugar cookies or coeur à la crème—desserts conceived, it seems, for this very day.

❧ MENU ❧

Cream of Watercress Soup
Julienne of Zucchini

Rack of Lamb   Potatoes Dauphinoise with Wild Mushrooms

Coeur à la Crème Fraîche   Heart-shaped Sugar Cookies

Champagne

Cream of Watercress Soup
SERVES 2 TO 4

A delicate, lovely soup which is excellent all year round. Spinach can be substituted for watercress.

¼ cup minced onions
2 tablespoons butter
2 bunches watercress
¼ teaspoon salt
2 tablespoons flour
4 cups chicken stock, boiling
2 egg yolks
1 cup heavy cream
  Salt and pepper to taste

In a heavy 2- to 3-quart saucepan, cook the onion in butter for 10 minutes, or until tender. Trim, wash, and dry the watercress, saving a few leaves for garnish. Add the leaves and tender stems to the onion. Sprinkle with salt. Cover and cook over medium-low heat for 5 to 10 minutes. Stir in the flour, cook for 5 minutes, add the boiling stock, and cook 5 minutes longer.

Purée mixture in a food processor or force through a food mill. Set aside, uncovered, until ready to serve.

To serve, reheat the soup to a simmer. Beat the egg yolks into the cream. Add the soup very slowly to the egg-cream mixture, whisking vigorously. Return the soup to the stove to heat but do not allow to simmer or the yolks will curdle. Season with salt and pepper. Garnish with reserved watercress leaves, which have been immersed in boiling water for 30 seconds and then freshened in ice water.

Julienne of Zucchini
SERVES 2

2 small zucchini
  Butter
  Salt and pepper to taste

Cut each zucchini into ⅛-inch-thick matchsticks of equal length. Steam over boiling water until just tender, about 2 minutes. Toss with butter and salt and pepper.

❧ Rack of Lamb
SERVES 2

Buy the smallest, youngest rack of lamb you can find. There are usually 7 rib chops to a rack. Have your butcher trim the rack very well, leaving the bones as long as possible. One rack is ample for 2 people. Rack of lamb should be served on the rare side; be careful not to overcook.

    Unsalted butter, softened
2 cloves garlic, finely minced
4 tablespoons Dijon-type mustard
4 tablespoons finely chopped parsley
2 tablespoons olive oil
  Salt and freshly ground pepper to taste
1 2-pound rack of lamb

Preheat oven to 500°. Butter a heavy baking pan (large enough to hold the lamb).

Combine the garlic, mustard, parsley, olive oil, and salt and pepper. Stir into a paste. Coat the meaty side of the rack with the paste. Put the rack of lamb in the baking pan, coated side up. Roast in the hot oven for 20 to 25 minutes, until golden brown outside but pink and rare inside. If the rib bones begin to brown too much, cover with aluminum foil.

To serve, carve into individual chops and put 2 on each plate. Spoon the carving juices over the meat.

Above: Coating rack of lamb.

Below: Wrapping rib bones with foil to prevent burning.

Potatoes Dauphinoise with Wild Mushrooms

SERVES 2

1 clove garlic, peeled
2 tablespoons butter
¾ pound potatoes, peeled and thinly sliced
½ teaspoon salt
Pepper to taste
1 ounce fresh wild mushrooms (cepes or porcini) sautéed in 2 tablespoons butter
½ cup heavy cream

Preheat oven to 325°.

Rub a shallow 8-inch au gratin dish with garlic, and butter generously. Arrange the sliced potatoes in concentric circles sprinkling with salt, pepper and sautéed mushrooms. Pour in the cream and bake approximately 30 to 45 minutes, or until the cream has been absorbed and the tops of potatoes are a deep golden color.

NOTE: If fresh wild mushrooms are not available, you can use dried wild mushrooms plumped in 2 tablespoons warm water and drain before layering.

Coeur à la Crème Fraîche

SERVES 4 TO 6

Known as cheese heart, the coeur à la crème is a fitting end to the Valentine Dinner. Porcelain or straw baskets in the shape of hearts are made especially for this dessert. The porcelain has little holes in the bottom so that the whey can seep from the cheese mixture, leaving a dense, rich concoction.

Traditionally, the coeur is served with whole strawberries and a strawberry sauce. This recipe serves more than required, but it is just as good the next day.

¾ pound cottage cheese
8 ounces cream cheese
½ cup Crème Fraîche (page 104), or sour cream
1 tablespoon confectioners' sugar
½ cup heavy cream

STRAWBERRY SAUCE

1 quart strawberries or two 10-ounce packages frozen berries
1 cup sugar (½ cup if using frozen berries)
2 tablespoons kirsch

GARNISH
Whole strawberries

In the bowl of an electric mixer, combine the cottage cheese, cream cheese, and crème fraîche. Beat until smooth. Add the confectioners' sugar. Whip the cream and fold it into the cheese mixture.

Line a 3-cup heart mold with cheesecloth, letting the cloth hang over the edges. Spoon the mixture

Left: *Coeur à la crème fraîche with strawberry sauce.*

into the lined mold; fold the cheesecloth over the top and put the mold on a tray in the refrigerator overnight.

To make strawberry sauce, mash the berries. Cook over low flame with sugar until soft. Press through a fine sieve, add kirsch, and chill.

To serve, unfold cheesecloth and invert mold on a serving plate. Remove cheesecloth. Garnish with strawberries and pour some sauce around coeur. Serve additional sauce in a bowl or pitcher.

Heart-shaped Sugar Cookies

SEE RECIPE, PAGE 209

For Valentine's Day, sugar cookies can be cut out in heart shapes (see page 211) and whimsically decorated with royal icing of different hues, or inscribed with a special message.

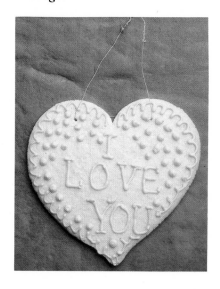

Easter Lunch for Fourteen to Twenty

I*N MY CHILDHOOD HOME, A RELI-*gious tradition influenced the rhythm of our holiday. It is a custom in the Polish Catholic church for the priest to visit each parishioner to bless the Easter food. So on Friday night, we would set the din-ner table with starchy linens and baskets, and lay out all the ingre-dients, cooked and uncooked, that would make our weekend meals: raw eggs and hard-boiled eggs; kielbasa, which would be roasted until crispy; schaun, the beet horseradish eaten with the

kielbasa; a Polish ham; potatoes; pierogi; raisin- and almond-stuffed babkas; and a sweet kulich. In the midst of this bounty we displayed the eggs we had decorated in the way my grandmother had taught us. It is a simple method, using a wrapping of red and yellow onion skins, secured with cheesecloth, to color the eggs while they hard-boil, and produces beautifully marbled creations.

At our house now, we open Easter morning hunting for the eggs Andy has hidden all over our four acres at dawn. To the onion-skin eggs we add eggs dyed a blue distilled from lavender flowers, and a yellow from tansies, as well as our Araucana chicken's own eggs, naturally pale speckled blue. We have invited neighborhood children and any available cousins, and when they return we give them baskets that I have laid with fresh hay and filled with chocolate bunnies and chicks. Lunch follows in the afternoon.

This is our family's traditional Polish Easter feast. The table is set off with white linens and all the flowers of spring—grape hyacinths, irises, tulips, and daffodils.

🍃 MENU 🍃

Marbleized Hard-Boiled Eggs *Cabbage Pierogi*

Roasted Kielbasa *Sorrel Soup* *Baked Easter Ham*

Purée of Fresh Peas *Garlic-Scalloped Potatoes*

Brandied Peaches *Babka*

Chocolate-Glazed Easter Bunnies, Lambs, and Turkeys

Marbleized Hard-Boiled Eggs

Everyone will admire these colored eggs. They resemble the Italian marble eggs sold as paperweights. All you need are lots of onion skins (yellow, white, and red), cheesecloth, eggs (brown, white, and Araucana blue if you can get them), some string, and lots of patience. The colored skins dye the eggs beautiful shades of mottled brown.

Cut cheesecloth into 7-inch squares. Put a piece on the palm of your left hand. Put 1 layer of onion skins on top of the cheesecloth. Overlap skins so no cheesecloth shows.

Put the uncooked egg in the center of the onion skins. Gather the edges of the cheesecloth and twist the cheesecloth tightly around the egg so that the egg is completely covered with onion skins. Secure with a small piece of string.

Do as many eggs as desired, then put the eggs in the large kettle, cover with cold water, and bring to a slow boil. Boil for 12 minutes, stirring gently. Allow eggs to cool in the liquid and then unwrap.

Cabbage Pierogi
APPROXIMATELY 8 DOZEN DUMPLINGS

Of all the Polish dishes I love, my very favorite is cabbage pierogi. I have consumed up to 20 of these delectable dumplings at one sitting, to the amazement of my family. The sweet cabbage filling is time-consuming to make, but well worth the effort.

FILLING

10 pounds green cabbage, trimmed and cored

2 8-ounce packages cream cheese

½ stick unsalted butter, at room temperature
   Salt and freshly ground pepper

DOUGH

1 egg, slightly beaten

1 cup milk

1 cup water

3 tablespoons sour cream

4½ to 5 cups flour

Cut the cabbages into quarters. Steam until very tender, approximately 20 to 30 minutes. Drain and cool. In a strong but thin linen towel, squeeze as much of the liquid from the steamed cabbage as possible. Squeeze only a small handful at a time. Discard the juice.

Grind the squeezed cabbage with the fine blade of a meat grinder. Add the cream cheese and softened butter and season highly with salt and pepper. Set aside.

To make the dough, whisk the egg, milk, water, and sour cream together. Add the flour, 1 cup at a time, mixing well after each addition. Turn out onto a floured board and knead until smooth and elastic. This may take 10 minutes. Add as little additional flour as possible.

Put ball of dough under an inverted bowl until ready to use.

To make the pierogi, cut the dough into 4 pieces. On a floured board roll one piece of dough into a round ¹⁄₁₆ inch thick. Keep rest of dough covered. With a cookie cutter or glass tumbler (2½ to 3 inches in diameter), cut the dough into rounds. For each pierogi take 1 round of dough, stretch it a bit with your fingers, and spoon about 2 tablespoons of the cabbage onto the center.

Fold the circle in half and press the edges together. I crimp the edges with my fingertips into a decorative pattern. Be sure to seal the edges well or the filling may fall out during cooking. Put finished dumplings on a towel or tray that has been lightly sprinkled with cornmeal. Continue rolling dough until all the filling has been used up.

Bring a very large kettle of water to the boil. Add 1 tablespoon salt to the water and cook about 20 perogi at one time in simmering water until they are tender and float (about 5 to 6 minutes). Remove to a serving dish with a slotted spoon and dribble with butter. Leftover pierogi can be reheated in the oven, or on top of the stove in a heavy skillet.

STEP-BY-STEP DIRECTIONS

1. Mixing the dough.

2. Turning dough onto floured board.

3. Kneading dough until smooth and elastic.

4. Rolling dough for cutting.

5. Using a glass to cut dough into rounds.

6. Placing filling in the center of each dough round.

7. Pinching edges together with thumb and forefinger.

8. The finished pierogi set on a tray sprinkled with cornmeal. ▶

Roasted Kielbasa
SERVES 14 TO 20

The traditional Polish Easter breakfast consists of oven-roasted smoked kielbasa and lots of hard-boiled eggs. I like to extend breakfast into an early Sunday dinner and serve the kielbasa and eggs as an hors d'oeuvre.

2 rings of kielbasa, approximately 2 pounds each, preferably freshly smoked

Preheat oven to 350°. Gently poach the sausage rings in simmering water for 15 minutes. Then put the rings on baking sheets and roast for 20 minutes, or until skin is crackling and just beginning to brown.

Cut into ½-inch slices, on the diagonal, and serve with rye bread and strong horseradish with beets.

Sorrel Soup
SERVES 20

In Eastern Europe sorrel is known as sour grass. It makes a delicious soup at Easter because sorrel is one of the first vegetables to appear in the spring garden. Sorrel is very easily grown as a perennial and each garden should have 5 or 6 plants, which will last for years and provide the family with plenty of sour grass for soups and sauces.

⅔ cup finely minced yellow onions
6 tablespoons butter
6 cups sorrel leaves, washed and dried, cut into thin strips
1 teaspoon salt
5 tablespoons flour
12 cups homemade chicken stock, boiling

Salt and pepper to taste
4 egg yolks
1½ cups heavy cream
3 tablespoons butter, softened to room temperature

In a covered pan, cook the onions in 6 tablespoons butter for 10 minutes; do not brown. Add the sorrel and salt, and stir over low heat for about 5 minutes.

Sprinkle on the flour and stir, cooking over moderate heat for 5 minutes. Stir in the boiling stock. Simmer the soup for 10 minutes. Season with salt and pepper.

Beat yolks lightly with the cream. Pour 1 cup of hot soup into the egg mixture, then add it to the soup. Do not let the soup boil after the egg yolks have been added or the yolks will curdle.

Serve the soup hot, enriched at the last minute with the softened butter. (If serving cold, omit the butter.)

Baked Easter Ham
SERVES 20

I always buy a smoked, uncooked whole ham for Easter from a wonderful Polish butcher named Kurowycky. He makes the very best leanest kielbasa and other Polish sausages, and he mail-orders (see note).

1 12-pound uncooked smoked ham, bone in
1 jar Dijon mustard with whole seeds
2 cups apricot jam
½ cup dry sherry

Preheat oven to 275°. Line a baking pan with foil. Put the ham on the foil, fat side up. Wrap well with another piece of foil. Bake for 3½ hours. Remove from oven, unwrap, and with a large, sharp knife cut off the rind and all but ¼ inch of fat. Make a glaze by combining the remaining ingredients.

Score the fat in a diamond pattern, making the lines ¾ inch apart. Pour out any pan juices and lightly coat the ham with the glaze and return it to the oven. Every 15 minutes spoon more of the glaze over ham. The ham should be done in 1 hour. Remove to a serving platter until ready to carve. (Do not refrigerate before serving.)

VARIATION: The ham can be studded with whole cloves in a decorative pattern, and then glazed.

NOTE: Kurowycky and Sons is located at 124 First Avenue, New York City, NY 10003. Telephone number: (212) 477-0344.

Brandied Peaches

Rub the fuzz from ripe, firm peaches with a towel. Weigh peaches.

For each pound of fruit make a thick sugar syrup of 1 cup sugar and 1 cup water. Boil 2 minutes. Boil the peaches in the syrup for 5 minutes.

Pack the fruit in sterilized wide-mouthed mason jars. Pour hot syrup over peaches, filling jars ¾ full. Add brandy to ¼ inch of top of jar. Seal at once. Store in a dark cool place to ripen, at least 2 months.

Kielbasa, Easter eggs, babka.

Garlic Scalloped Potatoes
SERVES 14 TO 20

The French call this dish gratin dauphinois and it has many, many versions. I prefer this one, without cheese or eggs.

3 pounds yellow potatoes, peeled and sliced very thin
2 cloves garlic
6 tablespoons unsalted butter
Salt and pepper
1½ pints heavy cream

Preheat oven to 325°.

Rinse the sliced potatoes in cold water. Pat dry in a towel. Rub a shallow earthenware dish with the garlic cloves and butter well. Arrange the sliced potatoes in layers in the dish and season with salt and pepper. Dot with remaining butter and pour the cream over the potatoes. Bake about 1½ hours; it is very important that the temperature be low enough so that the cream does not curdle as it is absorbed slowly into the potatoes.

During the last 10 minutes, turn the heat up to 400° to brown the top. Serve directly from the dish.

Purée of Fresh Peas

SERVES 14 TO 20

An excellent way to use mature peas.

- 3 pounds shelled peas
- 3 tablespoons unsalted butter
  Pinch sugar
- 2 mint leaves, finely chopped
- 6 tablespoons heavy cream

Cook peas in salted water until tender. Drain and purée in a food processor. Add the remaining ingredients and mix thoroughly. Reheat over simmering water. Thin with more cream if necessary.

N O T E : If you wish, use frozen petits pois. Cook briefly in boiling water before puréeing.

Babka

3 CAKES

This is our family's traditional Easter cake. The recipe makes three 8-inch cakes. I bake them in decorative copper and tin pans, but they are just as delicious baked in tube pans.

- 2 cups milk, scalded
- ½ pound (2 sticks) unsalted butter
- ⅔ of a 2-ounce yeast cake
- ¼ cup warm water
- 4 eggs
- 4 egg yolks
- 1 cup sugar
- 1 teaspoon salt
  Grated rind of 2 oranges
  Grated rind of 1 lemon
- 1 teaspoon vanilla
- 1 tablespoon Grand Marnier
- 8 to 9 cups sifted unbleached flour
- 1 cup slivered almonds, chopped

- 1 cup muscat raisins
- 1 cup golden raisins

Heat the milk; stir in the butter until melted; cool to lukewarm. Proof the yeast in the warm water.

Beat the eggs, egg yolks, and sugar until thick. Add the salt, grated rinds, vanilla, and Grand Marnier. Add the milk-butter mixture to the egg mixture. Stir in the yeast.

Add the flour, a cupful at a time, mixing with a wooden spoon. The dough should not be dry, but it should not be sticky. Too much flour will make a dry, crumbly cake. Add the almonds and raisins.

Turn the dough onto a floured board and knead for about 5 minutes, until dough comes away from your hand. Butter a very large bowl and put dough in bowl. Cover and let rise until doubled in bulk. Punch down and let rise a second time until almost doubled.

Preheat oven to 350°. Butter the pans generously. (You can sprinkle pans with a tablespoon of sugar if you wish.) Divide the dough into 3 portions. Arrange evenly in the pans and cover loosely. Let rise to tops of pans.

Bake cakes in oven for 30 to 45 minutes, until golden brown. There should be a hollow sound when you tap the top with your knuckles. Cool for 5 minutes in the pans, then turn out onto racks to cool.

Chocolate-Glazed Easter Bunnies, Lambs, and Turkeys

I have a collection of molds of various birds, beasts, shells, and hearts, and not long ago I began baking cakes in them. I use my madeleine batter as the cake and either dust them with confectioners' sugar or glaze them with chocolate icing.

Butter the molds very well, taking care not to leave any lumps of butter in the fine indentations of the mold. Sprinkle flour into the molds and shake out very well. This combination of butter and flour should insure that the baked cakes come out of the molds easily.

Make 1 batch of the Madeleine batter (page 168) at a time. Fill the molds ¾ full. If there are details such as the lamb's face, be sure to spread some of the batter carefully into the indentations. Prop the

molds in and on other metal baking pans so that they are level and bake on baking sheets in a preheated 350° oven. I sometimes use crumpled-up aluminum foil to support the molds. Test for doneness with a toothpick

Turn out of the molds onto racks to cool. Sprinkle with confectioners' sugar, as you would a madeleine, or glaze, using a soft brush, with an icing made of 8 ounces semisweet chocolate melted with 1½ cups heavy cream.

Whimsical madeleine cakes in the shape of hens, lambs, and shells, glazed with chocolate and set in straw with real eggs.

CHAPTER NINE

Just Desserts

*I*N ENGLAND, A PROPER DES-
sert consists of fruit and nuts; in France, fruit and cheese.
But in America, dessert is a grand finale, a reward for
good behavior, and, above all, a fanciful sweet.

America's sweet tooth is as famous as its hamburg-
er. Judging from colonial behavior, it is not a current
phenomenon. In eighteenth-century cookbooks, desserts
were sumptuous and multitudinous. Miss Eliza Leslie
listed 10 kinds of pie, 24 puddings, 64 cakes, 16 flavors
of ice cream (including almond orange ice), and uncount-
able cookies, dumplings, and fritters. George Washing-

Clementine tart—glazed fruits cover an orange-flavored nut filling.

ton, in a single summer, consumed $200 worth of ice cream, and Martha was largely responsible for the development of the dessert table, groaning with confections, which became the truly stylish way to serve refreshments after an entertainment of music or dancing. There is something rather endearing about a nation with a penchant for sweets; it speaks of whimsy, a sense of fun, and a youthful belief in the value of treats.

Today, with our national quest for slimness, a dessert party is perhaps even more of a treat—a stylish debauchery. It is also a graceful way to entertain large groups of people, because one dessert goes a long way, several even further. Because a tableful of confections is not only extravagant but beautiful to look at, it has a natural elegance. And best of all, perhaps, it is easy to execute, because desserts can be prepared entirely in advance. You don't even need any service, for there is nothing to do after you have set up the table.

I suggest larger parties here for several reasons: first, because one or two desserts will suffice for a small gathering of, say, six to ten, and no special planning is required. It is easy some evening when you have made a soufflé, or tried a recipe for crêpes, to call up friends and ask them to share the impromptu indulgence. Second, because much of the attraction of a dessert party comes from a wealth of offerings, which, given the fact that one cake or one tart feeds eight to twelve people, naturally accommodates a crowd.

Desserts look elegant with virtually any setting—crystal chandeliers and white linens or country roughhewn. I do think it is important to garnish most desserts in some imaginative way, however, because it complements them and personalizes them. With very few exceptions, I find an enormous difference of appeal between a bakery cake and a home creation. The bakery creation may be quite perfect—glossy, symmetrical, even wonderful tasting—but it is as embalmed and sterile-looking as a store mannequin. There is no sense of when it was made or who made it. In a way, I prefer a lopsided cake, for it says something. Consequently, I give a lot of thought to presentation, to finding a complementary odd-shaped or odd-sized dish. I place a white coconut cake, for example, on a bed of golden-toasted coconut on a large tray, which looks interesting, gives you a taste clue, and can be nibbled at. Instead of glazing a cheesecake with the traditional strawberry topping, I now substitute a half dozen crystallized strawberries, for a different look. I surround a strawberry tart, which is a brilliant glossy red, with a wreath of nasturtiums, which are brilliant flat orange. And I stand a gathering of redwine-poached pears on end in a long glass boatlike dish, crowning each with a single tiny crystallized violet.

Perfect Pastry

IF YOU PLAN TO TAKE THE time and care to make a special pie or tart for your guests, a light, flaky homemade crust is essential: One crust, two crusts, lattice top, plain flaky, and buttery—the possibilities in pastry are as vast as the possibilities in fillings. With a little step-by-step guidance (provided on the next four pages) and practice, you will discover making pastry is quite easy and well worth the effort. I've found that everything from miniature quiches for a cocktail party to elaborate dessert pies can be created successfully from only a few "perfect" recipes: the old-fashioned pie crust; the plain tart and tartlet crust (which is the one I prefer for most tarts, because the pastry shell is unbelievably thin yet does not crumble); the sweet tart and tartlet crust, much like a delicate cookie dough; a special nut crust; and buttery puff pastry.

A bowl of iced lemon mousse and raspberry Grand Marnier sauce, trays holding chocolate-glazed strawberries, and a heart-shaped double diablo cake surrounded by bright red and purple pansies are ready to be set on the dessert table.

Perfect Pie Crust
ONE DOUBLE-CRUST 9-INCH PIE

2 cups all-purpose flour
½ teaspoon salt
1½ sticks (¾ cup) unsalted butter
3 tablespoons margarine or chilled vegetable shortening
¼ cup ice water

Hand Method: In a large bowl, sift the flour and salt. Cut the chilled butter and margarine into 1-tablespoon bits and add to the flour. With a pastry cutter, work flour and shortening together until mixture resembles coarse meal. Add the ice water little by little, pressing the pastry together into a ball. Wrap and chill for at least 1 hour.

It is very important to work the pastry as little as possible. Don't overhandle. A secret to light, flaky pastry is to keep the mixture cool, add as little water as possible, and mix only as much as necessary.

Food Processor Method: Put flour and salt in bowl of machine. Cut butter and margarine into the flour. Process a few seconds until mixture resembles coarse meal. Drop by drop add the water, processing very briefly. The whole process should take 20 to 30 seconds. Wrap and chill the pastry for at least 1 hour.

If pastry has been chilled for a long time, let it sit at room temperature for at least 15 minutes before rolling.

Lightly flour a pastry board, marble counter, or kitchen counter. Divide the pastry in half. Pat each piece of pastry into a flat round. Lightly flour the rolling pin. Roll pastry in one direction only, turning pastry continually to prevent it from sticking to the surface.

Using pie plate as a guide, measure rolled-out pastry—it should be slightly larger than the pie plate and ⅛ inch thick. Fold rolled pastry circle in half so you can lift it more easily. Unfold, gently fitting the pastry into the pie plate, allowing pastry to hang evenly over the edges. Do not trim the pastry yet.

Fill the pie with filling. Then roll out the second crust in same manner as for bottom. Fold circle in half and with a sharp, pointed knife cut little vents in a decorative pattern. Place folded pastry on one half the pie. Unfold, pressing top and bottom pastry together. Trim edges with scissors, leaving a ½-inch overhang. Fold bottom pastry overhang over top and press firmly to seal. Crimp rim, using fingers or the tines of a fork.

The perfect old-fashioned double-crust apple pie (see recipe page 247).

Cut butter into dry ingredients.

Work butter and shortening into flour until . . .

. . . mixture resembles coarse meal.

Add ice water drop by drop and work in.

After chilling, divide in half and press into flat round.

Flour board and rolling pin.

Roll each flattened half into a round ⅛ inch thick.

Fold in half and lift into pan.

Press into pan and smooth bottom.

Place sliced apples (or other filling) on bottom crust.

Fold remaining pastry in half and cut decorative slits.

Place pastry on top of filling and press edges together.

Cut excess pastry.

Crimp edges with fingers or tines of fork.

Brush with milk for simple glazed finish.

Perfect Plain Tart and Tartlet Crust

ONE 10-INCH TART
(PLAIN OR LATTICE),
TWO 9-INCH TARTS,
TWELVE 3-INCH TARTS,
OR TWENTY-FOUR TINY
TARTLETS

2 cups all-purpose flour
¼ teaspoon salt
4 tablespoons unsalted margarine
¼ pound (1 stick) unsalted butter
Approximately 4 tablespoons ice water

Put flour and salt in bowl of food processor. Cut the butter and margarine into small bits and add to the flour. Process 10 seconds, or until mixture resembles coarse meal. Add the water little by little, processing as little as possible (10 to 15 seconds). Dough should just hold together in the bowl, but not be wet or sticky. Turn out onto plastic wrap, press into a ball, and chill at least 1 hour before using.

To form tart or tartlet shells, use twice as many pans as projected number of tarts or tartlets. Lightly butter or spray with vegetable oil the insides of half the pans.

Roll half the pastry on a lightly floured board to slightly less than ⅛ inch thick. Cut the pastry slightly larger than the pans, press into the pans, and cut away excess with your thumb. Repeat process with rest of pastry. In the case of a large tart, cut the pastry large enough so that there will be a ½-inch overhang.

Press the unbuttered pans on top of each of the pastry-filled pans.

These act as weights and will prevent shrinkage and puffing while baking. Line large tarts with aluminum foil and weight with beans or rice.

Chill tart or tartlets on baking sheets until ready to bake. This may be done the day before. Do not leave unbaked pastry in the tart shells longer than this or discoloration may occur. Any unused pastry can be tightly wrapped and chilled (up to 2 days) or frozen.

Preheat oven to 375°. Bake the shells for 15 to 17 minutes. Press down any pans that puff up. When pastry seems to be coloring very slightly around edges, remove top pans and return pastry to oven to dry out. Do not brown. Cool the shells on racks. If not to be used immediately, store in a tightly covered plastic container in the freezer.

Thaw before using.

Perfect Nut Crust

TWO 9-INCH TARTS OR
TWELVE 3-INCH TARTS

10 ounces finely chopped walnuts or almonds
½ pound (2 sticks) unsalted butter, softened
⅓ cup sugar
3 cups flour
1 egg, beaten
1 teaspoon vanilla or almond extract

Preheat oven to 350°.

Mix together all the ingredients until well blended, using an electric mixer or wooden spoon.

Divide the mixture in half and press into 9-inch buttered springform tart pans; or press into twelve 3-inch tartlet pans. Chill for 30 minutes before baking for 15 to 20 minutes, or until golden brown.

Place rolled-out pastry in pan and press to sides.

Use rolling pin to cut off excess pastry.

Line tart with aluminum foil and weight with beans.

Trim excess pastry from tartlet pans with thumb.

Use extra tartlet pans as weights instead of beans.

Baked tart and tartlet crusts.

Perfect Sweet Tart and Tartlet Crust

ONE 10-INCH TART,
TWO 9-INCH TARTS, OR
TWELVE 3-INCH TARTLETS

14 tablespoons (1¾ sticks) unsalted butter
2⅓ cups flour
Pinch salt
3 tablespoons sugar
2 egg yolks beaten with 4 to 5 tablespoons ice water

In the food processor, cut the butter into the flour. Add the salt and sugar. Do not overwork. Little by little add the egg yolks and water. Process 15 to 20 seconds. Turn pastry onto a floured board, and blend the pastry by pressing it into a ball and then kneading it quickly with the heel of your hand until no lumps remain. As with all pastry, work as quickly as possible, and use as little additional flour as possible to avoid toughening the dough.

Chill dough at least 20 minutes.

After chilling, roll ⅛ inch thick and cut into shapes slightly larger than the tart or tartlet pans. Press pastry into the tartlet (or tart) pans and cut off excess with your thumb. Chill in pans before baking. Any unused pastry can be tightly wrapped and chilled or frozen for future use.

Red currant tart in almond nut crust (see variation page 241).

Perfect Puff Pastry

APPROXIMATELY 2
POUNDS

I have experimented with all types of recipes for puff pastry—best results come from using no shortcuts and the very best ingredients.

1 pound all-purpose flour
1 pound (4 sticks) unsalted butter
1¼ cups heavy cream (or 1 cup water)
1 teaspoon salt

Weigh the flour accurately. With an electric mixer beat the butter smooth. Add ½ cup of the flour. Mix until smooth. Scrape this "dough" onto a piece of waxed paper, form into a square cake, wrap, and chill. (Square should be 5 × 5 inches.)

Put the remaining flour in a mixing bowl and add the cream and the salt. Mix carefully into a smooth dough, but be careful not to overmix. Press dough into a ball and chill, wrapped, for a few minutes.

Roll the dough ball into a rectangle approximately 6 inches wide and 12 inches long. Place the butter square in the center of the rectangle, and fold over the dough to completely encase the butter. Press the edges of the dough together, sealing as well as possible. Chill so that the dough and butter get to the same temperature.

Roll the dough on a lightly floured board into a long rectangle about ⅜ inch thick. Fold into thirds and roll again into a long rectangle ⅜ inch thick. Roll the dough carefully, matching edges as well as possible and folding into as neat rectangles as possible. It is important that the butter be distributed evenly between the layers of dough so that the pastry will puff evenly.

Chill the dough at this point. After 1 hour, repeat the rolling and folding 2 times. Chill again for 1 hour and repeat the process 2 more times. By the sixth fold, the dough should be extremely smooth and silky, with no lumps of butter visible. Use as little flour as possible for the rolling, and brush off any excess before folding the dough.

Classic puff pastry gets 6 turns. If the dough becomes too elastic, let it rest in a cool place for 15 or 20 minutes before rolling. Wrap the dough in plastic wrap and refrigerate until ready to use. Freeze after 2 days.

A Small Dessert Buffet for Twenty

SEVEN GLORIOUS DESSERTS WILL fill a dining-room tabletop after dinner and provide amply for twenty people. In the following selection, there is an interesting range of tastes and textures: pastry crusts of various kinds, fruits, nuts, and a chocolate cake–chocolate mousse confection. Figuring eight or ten full servings per dessert, a guest may choose two or three, or, with half portions, indulge in a dainty taste of everything.

❧ MENU ❧

Le Marquise au Chocolat

Italian Plum Tartlets   *Pear Frangipane Tart*

Iced Lemon Mousse with Raspberry Grand Marnier Sauce

Apple Tart Normande

Strawberry and Grape Tarts in Nut Crusts

Open Bar, Coffee, Demitasse

A red-checked cloth covered with asparagus ferns and colorful flowers provides the perfect setting for an informal buffet of special desserts. Granny Smith apples and a plate of homemade cookies add to the display.

Le Marquise au Chocolat
SERVES 12

A 6-cup bowl is lined with strips of génoise and filled with a rich chocolate mousse, chilled, turned out, and glazed with chocolate for this dessert that resembles a chocolate ball. Make the cake and mousse a day in advance and glaze it the day you serve it.

GÉNOISE
4 tablespoons butter
⅔ cup plus 2 tablespoons sugar
4 eggs, separated
1 teaspoon vanilla extract
    Pinch of salt
1¼ cups sifted cake flour

MOUSSE
4 eggs, separated
¾ cup superfine sugar
¼ cup Grand Marnier
6 ounces semisweet chocolate
4 tablespoons espresso coffee
1½ sticks unsalted butter, at
    room temperature
    Pinch salt
1 tablespoon sugar

CHOCOLATE GLAZE
6 ounces semisweet chocolate
¾ cup heavy cream
1 to 2 tablespoons water

To make the génoise, butter a 9-inch cake pan, line with waxed paper, and butter and flour the paper. Melt the 4 tablespoons butter and let it cool. Preheat the oven to 350°.

Beat the ⅔ cup sugar into the egg yolks for 8 to 10 minutes, or until thick and pale yellow. Add the vanilla.

Beat the egg whites and salt until stiff but not dry. Add the remaining 2 tablespoons sugar and beat until whites are glossy. Fold ⅓ of the egg whites into the yolk mixture. Blend in ⅓ of the flour, then ⅓ more of the egg whites, then ⅓

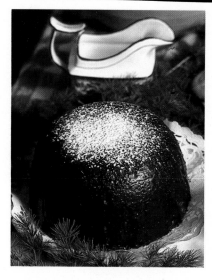

Le marquise au chocolat.

more of the flour. Complete the process, then gently fold in the melted butter. Do not overmix. Keep the batter light and fluffy.

Spoon into pan and bake until cake has puffed and pulled slightly from the edges of the pan (25 to 30 minutes). Cool on a rack.

To make the mousse, beat the egg yolks and superfine sugar until thick and pale yellow. Add the Grand Marnier and put mixture in top of double boiler over simmering water, beating constantly until mixture is almost too hot for your finger (4 to 5 minutes). Immediately cool over a bowl of ice, stirring until it is the consistency of thin mayonnaise.

Melt the chocolate with the coffee in a 300° oven. Add the butter bit by bit and stir until smooth and creamy. Beat chocolate mixture into the yolk mixture.

Beat the egg whites and salt until stiff. Sprinkle on the sugar and beat until glossy. Fold ⅓ of the whites into the chocolate to lighten the mixture. Gently fold in the rest.

To form the marquise, butter a 6-cup stainless steel mixing bowl. Cut the génoise cake into 3 thin

layers and cut 2 layers into wedges that will completely line the bowl. Press the cake to the sides of the bowl. Spoon the mousse into the lined bowl. Fill to the very top. Cover the top with the uncut layer of cake. Cover with plastic wrap and refrigerate, preferably overnight. Turn out onto a serving plate for glazing.

To make the glaze, melt the chocolate in a heavy saucepan with the cream. Cool to lukewarm. If too oily or too thick (depending on the chocolate) thin with boiling water. Spread the entire surface of the marquise with the glaze, using a brush or spatula. Sprinkle with powdered sugar.

Italian Plum Tartlets
8 TARTLETS

1 recipe Perfect Sweet Tart and Tartlet Crust (page 237)
½ cup brown sugar
20 Italian prune plums
    Grated rind and juice of 2 lemons
    Freshly grated nutmeg
3 tablespoons unsalted butter

Prepare pastry according to master recipe.

Roll pastry ¼ inch thick and line eight 3-inch tartlet pans. Sprinkle a little brown sugar in each shell.

Preheat oven to 375°.

Pit the plums and cut into quarters. Arrange plum pieces in each shell. Sprinkle with lemon rind, a bit of lemon juice, and the remaining sugar. Grate a little nutmeg on top of each tartlet. Dot with small bits of butter.

Bake about 20 to 25 minutes.

Pear Frangipane Tart
ONE 9-INCH TART

A rich pâte sucrée is the base for

this tart filled with frangipane and topped with pears. As with most tarts and pies, this one must cool and set for several hours before being sampled.

PÂTE SUCRÉE
6 tablespoons unsalted butter
2 cups unbleached flour
½ cup sugar
1 egg

FRANGIPANE
½ cup unsalted butter
½ cup sugar
1 egg
1 cup finely ground blanched almonds
3 tablespoons dark rum
1 tablespoon flour
1 teaspoon almond extract

POACHED PEARS
½ cup sugar
1 cup water
3 to 4 pears

Apricot Glaze (variation, page 241)

Cut the butter into the flour by hand or by using a food processor. Add the sugar and then the egg. Turn onto a floured board and knead lightly until completely mixed. Press into a ball. Wrap and refrigerate at least 1 hour.

Roll dough on a floured board into an 11-inch circle. Line a 9-inch tart pan. If dough cracks, press it together with your hands. Trim edges. Chill the crust.

Preheat oven to 425°.

To make the frangipane, cream the butter and sugar in an electric mixer. Add the egg, almonds, rum, flour, and extract. Beat until smooth. Spread evenly in chilled tart shell. Refrigerate until pears are ready.

To poach pears, bring the sugar and water to a boil and simmer for 2 minutes. Peel the pears and cook in the syrup just until tender. Cool. Cut in half, core, and slice crosswise. Place on top of the frangipane in a decorative fashion.

Bake the tart for 45 minutes. If top browns too quickly, cover with foil. Remove from oven and brush the top with glaze.

Iced Lemon Mousse

SEE RECIPE, PAGE 98

Apple Tart Normande

SEE RECIPE, PAGE 106

Strawberry Tart in Nut Crust

ONE 9-INCH TART

The crunchiness of the crust is a surprise when one tastes this sensational-looking dessert. The strawberries must be handpicked, from either the garden or the fruit store. Use only the most perfect, uniform berries. An interesting variation for this tart is to use tiny fraises des bois rather than giant berries. The tart is best assembled the day of the party and refrigerated for at least 4 hours before being cut.

1 **Perfect Nut Crust (page 236)**
  whole strawberries (approximately 3 pints per tart)

GLAZE

1 **6-ounce jar red currant jelly**
1 **tablespoon plain gelatin**
¼ **cup Grand Marnier or cognac**
½ **pint heavy cream, whipped**

Make and bake the crust according to master recipe. Cool.

Arrange hulled strawberries upside down on the crust.

To prepare glaze, heat the jelly in a saucepan. Dissolve gelatin in the Grand Marnier and add to jelly. Stir over low heat until mixture is clear. Spoon or brush over the strawberries. Serve with the cream.

VARIATIONS: Instead of strawberries, use 1 quart blueberries or seedless grapes, sliced in half, or ⅛-inch slices of 10 peeled kiwi fruit. Substitute apricot jam for the red currant jelly and strain before glazing.

You can also substitute 2½ cups fresh red currants for strawberries; use the red currant glaze.

A strawberry tart in nut crust.

A Country Pie Party for Fifty

WITH THE ADVENT OF THE FOOD processor, it is possible to whip up a half-dozen pie shells easily in the course of a morning and, as pastry freezes exceptionally well, stock the freezer for the future.

A pie party becomes easy with more than one set of hands to help. It is a natural for a large club meeting or a country get-together, when each person can bring his favorite example. A hostess must then only organize the contributions, lay a festive table with plaid or gingham linens, and set up the beverages.

❧ MENU ❧

Mile-High Lemon Meringue Pie   Mincemeat Lattice Tart

Pecan Pie   Coconut Cream Pie   Pear Almond Tart

Peach Cranberry Tart   Old-Fashioned Double-Crust Apple Pie

Black Bottom Pie   Sour Cream Raisin Pie

Pumpkin Molasses Pie

Cold Apple Cider, Iced Tea, Coffee

Far left: *A dazzling array of homemade country pies: one crust, two crust, lattice top, and plain.*

Left: *Mile-high lemon meringue pie—one of my personal favorites. My mother and I baked it when we had extra egg whites on hand and made a meringue as high as the oven would allow.*

Mile-High
Lemon Meringue Pie
ONE 9-INCH PIE

Cool the pie for at least 3 hours before cutting, but don't hasten the cooling in the refrigerator or the meringue will start to melt.

1 recipe Perfect Pie Crust (page 234)

FILLING
1¼ cups sugar
½ cup flour
Pinch salt
1½ cups water
5 egg yolks, beaten
2 tablespoons grated lemon peel
½ cup lemon juice
4 tablespoons unsalted butter

MERINGUE
8 to 12 egg whites
6 tablespoons sugar
½ teaspoon cream of tartar
½ teaspoon vanilla extract
Pinch salt

Prepare pastry according to master recipe. Divide in half and bake pastry bottom in 9-inch pie plate as directed. Refrigerate or freeze remaining pastry for future use.

Preheat oven to 350°.

In top of double boiler over simmering water, combine sugar, flour, salt, and water. Cook 10 minutes, or until mixture thickens.

Remove from heat and beat in egg yolks, 1 at a time. Return to heat and cook 6 to 7 minutes, stirring constantly, until thick and smooth. Add grated peel. Remove from heat; stir in lemon juice and butter. Set aside and cool.

To make meringue, beat egg whites until fluffy. Add cream of tartar, vanilla, and salt. Continue beating, adding 1 tablespoon of sugar every minute. Beat until stiff peaks are formed, 7 to 8 minutes.

Pour filling into the baked pie shell. Spoon meringue over filling. Mound in peaks, covering filling completely. Bake 15 minutes, or until peaks are golden brown.

Mincemeat Lattice Tart
ONE 10-INCH TART

The filling for this traditional winter holiday pie is also excellent in small tartlets or in a double-crust pie.

1 recipe Perfect Plain Tart and Tartlet Crust (page 236)

FILLING
1 pound apples, peeled, cored, and chopped
½ pound walnuts or almonds, chopped
½ pound brown sugar
½ pound raisins
½ pound suet, chopped fine
½ pound currants
¼ pound chopped citron
1 cup apple cider
¼ teaspoon each mace, cinnamon, cloves, and nutmeg
½ cup brandy

EGG GLAZE
1 egg beaten with 1 tablespoon water

At least one day before serving, combine all the filling ingredients, stirring well. Refrigerate or freeze until ready to use.

Prepare pastry following directions in master recipe. Roll out half of the pastry and line a 10-inch tart pan with a removable bottom. Leave ½-inch pastry overhang. Spoon filling into pie shell.

Preheat oven to 350°.

Prepare egg glaze.

Roll out remaining pastry into rectangle ⅛ inch thick. With pastry wheel or knife, cut in ½-inch strips. Weave pastry strips in lattice pattern over filling. Secure ends of strips to rim of pie with glaze. Brush lattice with glaze. Turn up edge of overhanging crust to cover ends and crimp. Bake 40 to 50 minutes, or until golden brown. Remove and cool on rack.

Before serving, remove tart from pan.

Pecan Pie
9-INCH PIE

1 recipe Perfect Pie Crust (page 234)
4 eggs
½ cup sugar
½ cup flour
1 tablespoon vanilla
1 cup white Karo syrup
1 cup dark Karo syrup
2 cups pecans

Make the pastry and use half the recipe to line a 9-inch pie plate. Freeze unused pastry.

Preheat oven to 375°.

Beat the eggs and sugar thoroughly. Add the flour and vanilla. Add the syrups and pecans. Mix well, pour into crust, and bake 45 minutes. Cool before serving.

With an intricate lattice top, this mincemeat tart is especially beautiful.

Coconut Cream Pie
ONE 9-INCH PIE

This pie is best if you happen to have freshly grated coconut, but flaked coconut will do nicely.

1 recipe Perfect Plain Tart
  and Tartlet Crust (page 236)

FILLING
½ cup granulated sugar
4 tablespoons cornstarch
¼ teaspoon salt
2½ cups scalded milk
4 egg yolks
1 tablespoon vanilla
1½ cups flaked coconut
1 tablespoon butter
1 cup heavy cream
2 tablespoons confectioners'
  sugar

Prepare pastry recipe. Divide in half and bake one bottom crust in 9-inch pie plate. Refrigerate or freeze remaining pastry for future use.

To make filling, in top of a double boiler mix sugar, cornstarch, and salt. Stir in milk until smooth. Cook directly over medium heat until mixture thickens.

Beat egg yolks. Add 4 tablespoons of the hot milk mixture, whisking until well blended. Then stir egg mixture into remaining milk mixture. Cook and stir over hot water until custard is smooth and thickened. Remove from heat.

Stir in vanilla, 1 cup coconut, and the butter. Pour into pie shell; refrigerate until cold.

Whip cream with confectioners' sugar; stir in remaining ½ cup coconut. Spread or pipe over filling. Chill until serving time.

Sour cream raisin pie and coconut cream pie look luscious in an old-fashioned double-pie basket.

Pear Almond Tart
ONE 10-INCH TART

The crust for this tart is redolent of cloves and lemons. It goes especially well with the delicate flavor of the almonds and pears.

PASTRY
- 1½ cups unbleached flour
- 2 tablespoons sugar
- Pinch salt
- Pinch ground cloves
- ½ teaspoon grated lemon peel
- ¼ pound (1 stick) cold unsalted butter
- 1 egg yolk
- 5 tablespoons ice water
- Softened butter

GLAZE
- ½ cup apricot preserves
- 2 tablespoons dark rum

FILLING
- ½ cup finely ground almonds
- ½ cup sugar
- 1 tablespoon flour
- 9 firm, ripe pears (preferably Anjou), peeled, halved lengthwise, and cored

To make pastry, put dry ingredients and lemon peel in bowl of food processor fitted with metal chopping blade; process just to mix. Add butter and cut into small pieces; process just until mixture resembles coarse meal. Add egg yolk; process just until blended. With processor running, quickly add ice water. Process several seconds until pastry forms ball. Stop at once to avoid overmixing. Wrap ball in plastic wrap; chill at least 1 hour.

Butter a 10-inch quiche pan with a removable bottom. Roll pastry out slightly larger than pan. Carefully lift pastry to pan and gently press against bottom and sides. Trim edges; prick bottom and sides with fork. Chill for ½ hour.

Line pastry-filled pan with a circle

of foil, pressing it gently against pastry. Fill liner with uncooked rice or dried beans to weight. Bake in preheated 375° oven 15 minutes. Lift out liner with rice or beans (save for future pastry baking). Bake crust 5 minutes longer; cool on rack.

To make glaze, heat preserves and rum over low heat, stirring. Strain, brush tart shell with 2 tablespoons glaze. Reserve remainder.

To make filling, stir together almonds, sugar, and flour; sprinkle over glazed shell. Slice 12 pear halves crosswise. Place sliced halves in circle over almond mixture in shell. Chop remaining pear halves; use to fill spaces between sliced pears.

Bake in preheated 375° oven 40 minutes. Remove from oven; brush with remaining warm glaze.

Serve at room temperature.

Peach Cranberry Tart
ONE 10-INCH TART

Best in late summer when the local peaches are ripe. Use large, firm, unblemished yellow peaches. The tart cranberry glaze and the crunch of slivered almonds are a pleasing contrast to the delicate sweet peaches.

- 1 recipe Perfect Plain Tart and Tartlet Crust (page 236)
- 5 tablespoons sugar
- 8 peaches
- 2 tablespoons butter, in small pieces

GLAZE AND TOPPING
- 1 cup cranberries, fresh or frozen
- ¼ cup sugar
- 1 envelope gelatin softened in ¼ cup water
- ½ cup slivered almonds

Make one 10-inch tart shell according to directions. Sprinkle the bottom with 3 tablespoons sugar.

Arrange peeled peach halves on the pastry, cut side down. Sprinkle with remaining sugar. Dot with butter.

Bake in preheated 350° oven for 20 to 25 minutes, or until peaches are tender and juicy.

To prepare glaze, cook the cranberries with sugar for 25 minutes over low heat. Remove from heat, stir in the gelatin, and strain. Pour over the peaches, brushing to coat evenly. Sprinkle with almonds. Chill until serving time.

Old-Fashioned Double-Crust Apple Pie
ONE 9-INCH PIE

Cortland or McIntosh apples, Granny Smiths or Macouns—the most important thing to remember when baking this pie is to use tart, crisp, fresh apples and lots of them. The crust should be flaky and golden brown, and, depending on the number of apples used, can stand up very high.

- 1 recipe Perfect Pie Crust (page 234)

FILLING
- 8 to 9 tart apples, peeled, cored, and sliced
  Grated peel of 1 lemon
  Juice of 1 lemon
- ½ cup sugar
- 1 teaspoon cinnamon
- 3 tablespoons butter, in small pieces

Prepare pastry according to master recipe. Fit bottom pastry into 9-inch pie plate. Roll out circle for top.

Preheat oven to 350°.

Fill pie shell with sliced apples. Mound them up high. Sprinkle with lemon peel and juice, sugar, and cinnamon. Dot with butter. Cover with pastry top, making vents, sealing and crimping rim.

Bake 45 minutes, or until crust is brown. Cool before serving.

Black Bottom Pie
ONE 10-INCH PIE

My mother made this pie for special Sunday dinners. It was my father's favorite pie. (I like to eat it hours after dinner, when it can be enjoyed on an empty stomach.)

- 1 recipe Perfect Plain Tart and Tartlet Crust (page 236)
- 1½ squares semisweet chocolate
- 1 envelope gelatin
- ¼ cup cold water
- 1 cup sugar
- 4 teaspoons cornstarch
- ½ cup cold milk
- 1½ cups scalded milk
- 4 egg yolks
- 2 teaspoons vanilla
- 4 egg whites
- ¼ teaspoon salt
- ¼ teaspoon cream of tartar
- 1 tablespoon dark rum
- 1 cup whipping cream
- ¼ cup chocolate shavings

Make and bake the 10-inch pie shell.

Melt the chocolate in the top of a double boiler, over simmering water; soften the gelatin in the cold water.

In top of double boiler, dissolve ½ cup of sugar and the cornstarch in the cold milk. Add the scalded milk and boil over direct heat for 3 minutes, stirring constantly.

Beat the egg yolks and stir in 3 tablespoons of the cornstarch mixture. Add the yolk mixture to the milk mixture in the top of the double boiler. Cook over simmering water for 3 to 4 minutes, stirring constantly. When the mixture thickens, remove from the heat. Measure out 1 cup of the custard, add the melted chocolate and vanilla to it, cool completely, and spread in the bottom of the pie crust.

Add the gelatin to the remaining custard. Cool until just beginning to set.

Beat the egg whites with the salt and cream of tartar until stiff. Still beating, gradually add the remaining ½ cup sugar. Fold into the custard and add the rum. Pour over the chocolate layer. Chill until firm.

Whip the cream until stiff. Spread over the custard or pipe on top with a pastry bag fitted with a star tip. Sprinkle chocolate shavings on top. Chill until ready to serve.

Sour Cream Raisin Pie
ONE 8-INCH PIE

- 1 recipe Perfect Pie Crust (page 234)
- 1½ cups muscat raisins
- ⅔ cup sugar
- 1 tablespoon flour
- ¼ teaspoon each nutmeg, cloves, cinnamon
  Grated rind and juice of 1 lemon
- 2 eggs, beaten
- 1 cup sour cream

Prepare pastry according to master recipe. Use half to line an 8-inch pie pan; reserve other half for lattice top.

Preheat oven to 450°.

Over low flame, cook raisins in just enough water to cover, until plump and tender. Add sugar, flour, spices, rind, and juice. Cook until mixture is thickened. Cool.

Beat eggs with the sour cream. Add the raisin mixture and mix well. Pour into pie crust. Use pastry strips for a decorative lattice top. Bake for 10 minutes. Reduce heat to 350° and bake 20 to 25 minutes longer, until custard is set.

Pumpkin Molasses Pie
SEE RECIPE, PAGE 196

Desserts for Forty: Soirée Dansante

*O*NE WAY TO CAPITALIZE ON THE inherent elegance of a dessert party is to extend it: multiply your desserts into extravagance—enough for everyone and then several extras for show; add champagne; add ballgowns and black tie; pull up the rugs in the living room and hall and add dance music. Such an evening could be 1933, lyrics by Cole Porter.

In fact, just such a period piece evolved out of a dessert party last year. The month was January, ordinarily such a barren time for socializing that guests responded to the event with unusual zeal. The numbers were larger—two hundred people filled an expansive home in Connecticut, and consumed 30 desserts and 114 bottles of champagne—but the elements were the same. The dress was formal. In a gallery with a hard oak floor, we set up eight 24-inch café tables with gilt ballroom chairs and installed a five-piece dance band, which played nonstop until early in the morning. In the library, champagne was served, and to stave off hunger until the formal presentation of the dessert table, two girls made crêpes with fanciful fillings of praline, whipped cream, apples, Grand Marnier, or strawberries and cream. Behind closed doors in the dining room, we arrayed a series of three tables with an extravaganza of desserts that ran the gamut from plain baba au rhum to a clementine tart to an eight-foot-long chocolate roulade, filled with whipped cream and blueberries, which we called a "bûche d'été," to distinguish it from a bûche de noël. For the nonsweet tooth (a rara avis), on a fourth table we arranged cheese and French bread, and here and there little bunches of grapes and strawberries.

At ten o'clock, the fun began. With mock ceremony, the doors to the dining room were opened, and guests marched in to view our exhibition. They walked around the tables, and then around again, and again; no one touched, as if it were a purely visual display. One gentleman continued to circle for twenty minutes. Another inquired after the most sinful dessert. Then, as the guests sorted out their priorities, they closed in on the confections. Not a single person abstained, claiming diet or temperance. Predictably, the chocolate mousse disappeared first, then the Roberta hearts, then the cheesecake. At two o'clock, when music stopped, thirty platters were bare. We found a lone strawberry, the only trace of an eight-quart centerpiece, under the dining-room table.

Our large-scale event can be easily and successfully adapted to a more manageable group of forty. Where thirty desserts were necessary, eight to ten will be ample. Choose according to your fancy, striving too for a balance between fluffy and dense, creamy and

Cheesecake with a ground-almond "crust" and glacéed berries.

tart, pastry and soufflé. Plan, as we did, to provide a cheese and fruit alternative, as well as an urn of strong demitasse coffee served with twists of lemon peel. This fare should be displayed in a different corner of your home from the dance floor and champagne, to keep the party fluid and uncongested. If your party is formal, you might borrow or rent a silver samovar. As an alternative to a band, consider a good disk jockey, a rented jukebox, or a spectacular selection of records, augmented with borrowed music if needed. Invite your guests for 9:00 P.M., greet them with champagne, and introduce the desserts at ten o'clock, with a touch of ceremony.

As the table of desserts will be a showplace, plan its visual dynamics carefully. Collect flowers, ferns, leaves, fruit, vegetables, and any other decorative objects the morning of the party. Look for trays, platters, and bowls that will complement the various desserts, and have a dress rehearsal with your table to judge its effect. Also collect plenty of serving pieces, considering how each dessert is best served—the dense chocolate cake with a sharp dinner knife, the chocolate mousse with two small berry spoons, the crème Anglaise with a ladle. Because guests will want more than one dessert, count on at least two seven- or eight-inch plates per person, with adequate spoons and forks, and cocktail napkins. Make sure to have plenty of soda water and ice water on hand, too, for sweets tend to make guests thirsty.

❧ MENU ❧

Choose eight to ten.

Crème Caramel   Roberta Heart   Palmiers

Clementine Tart   Cheesecake with Glacéed Berries

Glacéed Oranges   Oeufs à la Neige   Baba au Rhum

Madeleines   Chocolate Mousse

Lemon Curd Tartlets   Poached Pears

Double Diablo

Ladyfingers   Charlotte au Chocolate   Crème Anglaise

Kiwi Tartlets   Meringue Kisses

Almond Torte   Grape Tart in Nut Crust   Bûche d'Eté

Pound Cake with Cherries and Raisins

Sable Cookies   Coconut Cake

Cheese Tray   French Bread   Grapes   Strawberries

Champagne, Café Filtre, Tea

Above: *Two dense chocolate Roberta hearts, piped with sweetened whipped cream and displayed on lemon leaves.*

Left: *Crème caramel garnished with candied orange peel.*

Crème Caramel

SEE RECIPE, PAGE 179

Roberta Heart

SERVES 10 TO 14

This is an extremely rich, moist dessert. Decorated with whipped cream, it is a spectacular addition to the dessert table. Served alone, the luscious heart will disappear as guests request seconds and even thirds.

I call the dessert "Roberta" because she made 38 of them in one day. You will need a large heart-shaped pan, 2 inches deep, or a 10-

inch round cake pan, 2 inches deep, buttered and lined with waxed paper.

21 ounces semisweet chocolate
3 ounces unsweetened chocolate
1½ tablespoons instant espresso coffee
6 tablespoons hot water
6 tablespoons dark rum
9 large eggs
¾ cup granulated sugar
1½ cups heavy cream
1 tablespoon confectioners' sugar
1 tablespoon vanilla

GARNISH:
1 cup heavy cream whipped with 1 tablespoon confectioners' sugar

Preheat oven to 350°. Put a pan (larger than the cake pan) in the oven and add boiling water to fill halfway.

Melt the chocolate with the coffee, water, and rum over barely simmering water. Stir until smooth.

Beat the eggs and granulated sugar in a double boiler over simmering water for 10 to 15 minutes, until thick and fluffy like whipped cream and almost tripled in volume.

Whip the cream in a chilled bowl until it forms soft peaks. Add the confectioners' sugar and vanilla.

Fold the smooth melted chocolate into the egg mixture. Fold the whipped cream into the mixture as gently as possible. Pour the batter into the prepared pan and set immediately in the pan of hot water in the oven. Bake for 35 to 40 minutes, or until a toothpick inserted in the center comes out clean.

Remove from oven and let cool in the water bath. When cool, cover the dessert and refrigerate.

To serve, warm the pan slightly in an inch of warm water. Invert onto a serving tray. Pipe the sweetened whipped cream onto the dessert with a decorative tip.

Palmiers

APPROXIMATELY THIRTY-
SIX 4-INCH PASTRIES

These crispy, caramelized pastries are made from buttery puff pastry. For a special variation, praline powder can be substituted for the granulated sugar.

1 pound Perfect Puff Pastry (page 237)
Granulated sugar

Roll pastry into a rectangle 8 inches wide and ⅛ inch thick. Cut edges so they are even. Sprinkle top of pastry with a light coating of sugar. Roll each long end to center of pastry rectangle, making sure pastry is tight and even. Cut crosswise into ⅜-inch slices.

Place palmiers 3 inches apart on water-sprayed baking sheets. Cover and chill at least 1 hour.

Preheat oven to 450°.

Bake palmiers 6 to 7 minutes, until bottoms begin to caramelize. Remove from oven and quickly turn palmiers over, sprinkle with addi-

tional sugar, and return to oven. Bake 4 to 5 minutes more, until tops are evenly caramelized but not burned.

Cool on racks. Palmiers can be stored in airtight container 2 to 3 days, or frozen.

VARIATION: To make praline powder, melt 1 cup sugar with 3 tablespoons water and cook over medium heat until caramel-colored. Stir in ½ cup chopped pecans, and turn onto lightly oiled baking sheet to cool and harden. When hardened, pulverize into a fine powder in blender or food processor. Sprinkle onto puff pastry before rolling and cutting.

Clementine Tart

ONE 10-INCH TART

Clementines are a variety of tangerines—small and highly flavored. Small navel oranges can be substituted.

1 recipe Perfect Sweet Tart and Tartlet Crust (page 237)

A heart-shaped copper tray piled with caramelized palmiers.

GLAZED CLEMENTINE SLICES
1 cup orange juice
½ cup lemon juice
1½ cups sugar
10 to 12 clementines (or 8 to 10 navel oranges)

NUT FILLING
2 eggs
2 egg yolks
1 cup sugar
¼ pound (1 stick) unsalted butter, very soft
1 cup ground almonds or pecans
½ cup Cointreau or other orange liqueur

Make and bake 10-inch pastry shell according to master recipe.

While pastry is resting, prepare the glazed clementine slices. Combine the juices and sugar in a wide enamel or stainless steel pan. Bring to a boil and simmer 15 to 20 minutes.

Peel the clementines and slice into ⅛-inch slices, removing any seeds. Add the slices to the syrup and simmer gently until the slices are almost translucent. Remove carefully from the syrup and drain on racks. When cold, cut each slice into 4 wedges. Reserve the syrup, boiling it down to thicken if it seems too thin to use as a glaze.

For the nut filling, beat the eggs and yolks with the sugar until light. Beat in the butter, then the ground nuts, and finally the Cointreau.

Pour the filling into the baked shell and bake until set (8 to 10 minutes) in a 375° oven. Set on a rack to cool. Brush with the glaze and arrange the clementine wedges in a decorative pattern on the tart filling. Glaze with any remaining syrup. (Heated and strained apricot jam can be substituted for the syrup as a glaze.)

Cheesecake with Glacéed Berries

SERVES 10

This is the very richest, smoothest cheesecake. The finely ground almonds which dust the pan are a pleasing contrast to the silkiness of the cake. Use a straight-sided pan 8 inches wide and 3 inches deep.

 1   tablespoon unsalted butter, at room temperature
¼   pound finely ground blanched almonds
 4   8-ounce packages cream cheese
½   cup heavy cream
1½ cups sugar
 4   eggs, lightly beaten
     Grated rind of 1 lemon
     Grated rind of 1 orange
 1   teaspoon vanilla

GARNISH
     1 pint Glacéed Strawberries (page 217)

Preheat oven to 325°. Butter pan and dust with ground almonds.

In electric mixer, beat cream cheese, cream, and sugar until smooth. Add eggs and beat again. Mix in rinds and vanilla.

Pour into prepared pan and place this pan in a slightly larger pan. Pour boiling water into larger pan to come ⅔ up side of cake pan.

Bake until firm, approximately 2 hours, adding more boiling water when necessary. Turn off oven, open door, and let cake sit until cooled.

Invert onto a platter. Garnish with strawberries.

An antique glass pedestal holds a mound of sweet glacéed oranges topped with candied orange peel.

Glacéed Oranges

12 seedless navel oranges of
   good color
4 cups granulated sugar
1½ cups water

With an orange peel stripper, strip
20 or so pieces of peel from the oranges. Immerse the peel in boiling
water for 5 minutes, then drain and
cool. Peel the rest of the oranges,
using a very sharp knife. Remove
all rind and membrane.

Heat the sugar and water together
in a heavy saucepan. Do not stir.
When sugar is dissolved, cover pan
and boil for 5 minutes. Remove
cover. Syrup should be clear. Continue cooking to the hard ball stage
(250°).

Lower heat and, working quickly,
dip each orange in the syrup, using
sharp pronged forks. Stack oranges
in a serving dish.

When all the oranges have been
dipped, add the peel to the syrup
and cook over low heat 3 minutes.
Remove the peel to an oiled surface
to cool. Keep pieces separate and
use to decorate the glazed oranges.

Oeufs à la Neige
(Floating Islands)
SERVES 10 TO 12

*Light-as-air egg whites are poached
in milk and served floating in a
light custard. Swirls of caramel
decorate the mounds of meringue. On
a recent trip to Paris, every
restaurant I visited served this
dessert, and from the number of
people consuming it, its popularity
was obvious.*

1 quart milk
¾ cup sugar
1 vanilla bean, split

8 egg whites
  Pinch salt
1⅓ cups sugar
8 egg yolks
¾ cup sugar
¼ cup sugar
2 tablespoons water

Heat the milk, sugar, and vanilla
bean to boiling. Remove from heat
and let sit for at least 15 minutes.
Remove bean.

To make meringues, beat the egg
whites with salt until they stand in
peaks. Gradually beat in the 1⅓
cups sugar, until whites are stiff,
glossy, and smooth.

Heat the milk to 170°. Spoon the
meringues into the hot milk. (I use
a large stainless steel spoon to form
the meringues.) Poach for 2 minutes on each side, turning carefully
with a slotted spoon. Lift the meringues onto a paper-towel-lined
tray. Cool. Reserve poaching milk.

To prepare the custard, beat the
egg yolks until they are smooth.
Add the ¾ cup sugar and beat until
pale and creamy, about 10 minutes. Strain the poaching milk and
pour gradually into the egg yolks,
beating constantly. Pour into a
heavy saucepan. Stir constantly
over low heat. The temperature
should never exceed 165° or yolks

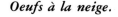

Oeufs à la neige.

will curdle. Custard is done when it
coats a spoon evenly. Remove from
heat, stir briefly over a bowl of ice
to stop further cooking, and then
strain to remove any lumps.

To serve, arrange cool meringues
on top of custard sauce. Mix ¼ cup
sugar with 2 tablespoons water and
cook over high heat until it cara-
melizes. Let the caramel cool for 2
to 3 minutes, then dribble the caramel over the oeufs with a fork.

Do not refrigerate, but keep this
dessert in a cool place until ready to
serve.

Baba au rhum with glacéed green and red cherries.

Pale golden madeleines dusted with powdered sugar.

Baba au Rhum
SERVES 8 TO 10

This ring cake is soaked with a rum-flavored sugar syrup, glazed with apricot jelly, and decorated with glacéed fruits. It should be served at room temperature with softly whipped cream.

1 package dry yeast
2 tablespoons sugar
  Pinch salt
2 large eggs
4 tablespoons unsalted butter, melted and cooled
2 cups all-purpose flour

RUM SYRUP
2 cups water
¾ cup sugar
⅔ cup dark rum

APRICOT GLAZE
1 cup apricot jam
2 tablespoons rum

GARNISH
  Red and green glacéed cherries

To make the baba, mix yeast, sugar, salt, and eggs together. Add the flour and cooled butter. (The dough will be very sticky.) Stir vigorously with a large wooden spoon or hands until dough becomes smooth and elastic. Place in a large, buttered bowl. Cut a deep "X" into the top of dough and sprinkle with a bit of extra flour. Cover and let rise in a warm place until doubled in bulk, about 1 hour.

Butter a 9-inch ring mold. Punch down dough and knead until smooth on a lightly floured board. Form into a ring large enough to fit in the pan. Let dough rise in pan, uncovered, until it has reached top of the mold. Do not let rise too much or it will collapse during baking.

Preheat oven to 375°.

Bake baba about 30 minutes, or until golden in color and shrinking from sides of pan. Remove from oven, cool for 5 minutes in pan, then turn out onto rack and cool just until baba is warm before soaking.

To make the rum syrup, boil sugar

and water until dissolved. Add rum and cool to tepid.

To soak baba pierce the puffed top all over with fork. Place puffed side down in shallow dish and baste entire cake with rum syrup. The baba should be moist but not soggy. Pour off excess syrup.

To make glaze, strain jam and melt with rum. Brush top of baba with mixture, and decorate with glacéed cherries.

Madeleines
SEE RECIPE, PAGE 168

Chocolate Mousse
SEE RECIPE, PAGE 93

Lemon curd tartlets with whipped cream and candied lilacs.

Lemon Curd Tartlets

SEE RECIPE, PAGE 92

Poached Pears

SERVES 8

These slightly pink pears, poached in red wine and flavorings, make a wonderful addition to the dessert party. The pears are poached until just tender, and when chilled are served with flavored whipped cream. Allow 1 pear per person if you are serving them as a dessert for a dinner party.

- 8   Bosc pears
- 1   to 2 cups red wine
- 2   tablespoons lemon juice
- 1   cup sugar
- 1   stick cinnamon
      Zest of 1 lemon
- 1   vanilla bean
- ½   pint heavy cream, softly whipped with 2 tablespoons cognac or rum, or 8 candied violets (optional)

Peel the pears without removing the stems. Put them in a deep saucepan.

In another saucepan bring the wine, lemon juice, sugar, cinnamon, lemon zest, vanilla bean, and enough water to cover the pears to a boil. Pour the liquid over the pears and simmer very slowly until just tender, 10 to 20 minutes.

Remove the pears carefully to a serving dish. Rapidly boil down the liquid to about 1 cup. Pour over the pears.

Serve cool or cold.

Tiny crystallized violets add a whimsical touch to this cut-glass dish of wine-poached Bosc pears.

Double Diabolo
ONE 12-INCH CAKE

This is one of the richest, most irresistible chocolate confections you will ever make. I like to bake it in a 12-inch cake pan. Leftovers stay fresh for weeks in the refrigerator. Bake the cake at least 1 day before serving. If more convenient, it may be made days ahead, wrapped and refrigerated until ready to use, and iced the day of the party.

½ cup raisins
½ cup Scotch whisky
14 ounces semisweet chocolate
¼ cup water
½ pound (2 sticks) unsalted butter
6 eggs, separated
1⅓ cups sugar
9 tablespoons cake flour
1⅓ cups finely ground blanched almonds
   Pinch salt

ICING

8 ounces semisweet chocolate
1 cup heavy cream

Soak raisins overnight in the whisky. Preheat oven to 350°. Butter a 12-inch cake pan, line bottom with waxed paper, and butter and flour paper.

In the top of a double boiler, melt the chocolate with the water. Stir in the butter bit by bit until mixture is smooth.

Beat the egg yolks with the sugar until thick and creamy. Stir into the chocolate. Add the flour and almonds, then the raisins and whisky. Mix together gently.

Beat the egg whites with salt until stiff but not dry. Fold by thirds into the chocolate mixture, taking care to deflate the mixture as little as possible. Pour the batter into the

A wreath of astroemeria lilies encircles a chocolate-glazed double diablo cake.

prepared pan, smooth the top, and bake for approximately 25 minutes. The cake should be moist in the center, but just beginning to shrink from the sides of the pan. Let the cake rest in the pan for 10 minutes before turning out onto a rack to cool.

To make the icing, melt the chocolate in the cream, whisking until smooth. If too thin, cool slightly over ice. Pour over cake, smoothing with a spatula.

Ladyfingers

APPROXIMATELY 36
LADYFINGERS

3   eggs, separated
½ cup granulated sugar
1   teaspoon vanilla
1   tablespoon sugar
     Pinch salt
⅔ cup sifted cake flour
     Confectioners' sugar

Preheat oven to 300°. Butter 2 large baking sheets. Dust lightly with flour. Fit a pastry bag with a ½-inch plain tip.

Beat the egg yolks with the sugar and vanilla until mixture is thick and pale yellow and forms a ribbon.

In a separate bowl beat the egg whites with 1 tablespoon sugar and the salt until stiff but not dry.

Fold the egg whites into the yolk mixture alternately with the flour. Do not overmix or deflate the whites. The batter must remain light and fluffy.

Spoon batter into the pastry bag and squeeze onto the baking sheets

Light and tender ladyfingers.

into finger shapes, 4 inches long and 1½ inches wide. Sprinkle heavily with confectioners' sugar. Turn pan upside down and with a few quick, hard taps dislodge excess sugar. If done carefully and quickly, the batter will not fall off.

Bake for about 20 minutes. Ladyfingers are done when slightly beige in color, crusty and dry, but tender. Cool on racks before storing in airtight container.

Charlotte au Chocolat

SERVES 10

It is imperative that you use homemade ladyfingers for this dessert.

     Approximately 22
     Ladyfingers
¼ cup orange liqueur mixed
     with ¼ cup water
CHOCOLATE CREAM
½ pound (2 sticks) unsalted
     butter, softened
¾ cup sugar
¼ cup orange liqueur
¼ teaspoon almond extract
1   cup pulverized blanched
     almonds
4   ounces semisweet chocolate,
     melted with ¼ cup espresso
     coffee
2   cups whipping cream

Charlotte au chocolat.

GARNISH
     Softly whipped cream, or
     Crème Anglaise (below)

To make chocolate filling, cream butter with sugar until light and fluffy. Add liqueur and almond extract, beating until very smooth. Add almonds and melted chocolate, mixing well. Cool completely.

Whip cream until almost stiff. Fold into chocolate mixture.

To assemble the charlotte, line the bottom of a 2-quart charlotte mold (with a 7-inch diameter) with a round of waxed paper. Cut ladyfingers into wedges and fit in bottom of mold, curved side down. Arrange whole ladyfingers around the sides of mold, curved sides facing outwards. Sprinkle ladyfingers with a bit of the liqueur mixture.

Pour chocolate cream into lined mold, and arrange leftover ladyfingers (lightly soaked with liqueur/water mixture) on top. Refrigerate, covered, at least six hours.

To serve, unmold charlotte onto serving plate. Remove waxed paper. Serve with softly whipped cream or crème Anglaise.

Crème Anglaise

APPROXIMATELY 3 CUPS

Every dessert table should have a bowl of this thin, delicate, lightly flavored sauce.

2½ cups milk
1   vanilla bean or 1½
      teaspoons vanilla extract
¾   cup granulated sugar
6   egg yolks
1   teaspoon cornstarch
2   tablespoons cognac

Boil milk with vanilla bean (do not add vanilla extract here).

Beat the sugar into the egg yolks until thick and fluffy. Beat in cornstarch. Add boiled milk in dribbles while beating at low speed.

Transfer the mixture to a heavy-bottomed enamel saucepan. Set over low heat and, stirring constantly, cook until the sauce thickens into a light, creamy mixture. Do not simmer or the egg yolks will curdle. (Maximum temperature before curdling is 165°.)

Remove sauce from heat, add cognac (and vanilla extract if bean was not used), whisk for a moment, and strain through a fine sieve. After cooling, refrigerate, covered.

Kiwi Tartlets

TWELVE 3-INCH TARTLETS

Kiwi fruits are fuzzy-brown, oval, mysterious looking fruits from New Zealand. Once peeled and cut, they reveal a bright green interior and an unusual tart-sweet taste. They are especially delicious atop a very light crème pâtissière in tarts.

1 recipe Perfect Plain Tart and Tartlet Crust (page 236)
5 to 6 ripe kiwi fruits, peeled and cut crosswise

CRÈME PÂTISSIÈRE (PASTRY CREAM)

1 cup milk
½ vanilla bean
¼ cup plus 1 tablespoon sugar
3 egg yolks
1 tablespoon flour (preferably rice flour)
1 tablespoon cornstarch
1 teaspoon unsalted butter
1 cup heavy cream, softly whipped

APRICOT GLAZE

1 cup apricot preserves, strained
1 tablespoon cognac

Prepare pastry according to master recipe.

To make crème pâtissière, scald milk, vanilla bean, and ¼ cup sugar. In a separate bowl, beat egg yolks with remaining sugar until thick. Sprinkle flour and cornstarch into mixture and continue beating until well mixed.

Remove vanilla bean from milk. Beat half the hot milk into yolk mixture. Return to remaining hot milk and bring to a boil very quickly, whisking to prevent scorching. Remove from heat and pour into a bowl to cool. Rub top of crème with butter to prevent a skin from forming. Cover with plastic wrap and cool completely. Immediately before using, fold in softly whipped cream with a wooden spoon.

To make glaze, melt strained preserves with cognac.

To assemble tartlets, spoon crème pâtissière into tartlet shells. Arrange kiwi slices in concentric circles on top of crème and glaze tartlets.

Meringue Kisses

APPROXIMATELY 50 KISSES

Stiff, sweetened egg whites can be used for many different purposes— for simple cookies such as these kisses, for vacherin, dacquoise, and as the base of a wedding cake frosting.

6 egg whites
Pinch salt
¼ teaspoon cream of tartar
1 teaspoon vanilla
1½ cups sugar

Preheat oven to 225°. Line 2 large baking sheets with aluminum foil.

Beat the egg whites until foamy. Add the salt, cream of tartar, and vanilla and continue beating. Add the sugar 1 teaspoon at a time, beating about 1 minute between additions. When all the sugar has been added beat an additional 6 to 8 minutes. Egg whites should be very stiff, glossy, and extremely smooth.

Spoon the mixture into a large pastry bag fitted with a ½-inch star tip and pipe out "kisses," leaving 1-inch spaces. Reduce oven temperature to 200° and bake for 1½ to 2 hours, until the meringues are dry to the touch and can be lifted from the foil. Cool completely before storing in a cool dry place.

Luscious green kiwi tartlets.

VARIATIONS: Using the same mixture you can make meringue mushrooms. Use 2 pastry bags, fitted with a ½-inch round tip for the stems and a ⅝-inch tip for the caps.

Holding the tip close to a foil-lined sheet, press out round tops for the mushroom caps. Twist the bag to avoid a pointed cap. (Any unwanted points can be smoothed with a finger dipped in cold water.)

For the stems, use the smaller tip. Hold the pastry bag in one hand and a small sharp knife in the other. Press out the stem, allowing 1 to 1½ inches height, and then cut off the meringue with the knife. The stem will have a flat top and will adhere more easily to the cap. Lightly dust the stems with cocoa. Bake as for the meringue kisses. Cool.

To assemble, melt 6 ounces good semisweet chocolate and with a small spatula spread a thin layer on the underside of the cap. Dip the tip of the stem into the chocolate and affix to the cap. Turn upside down and dry. (Egg cartons turned upside down are excellent racks for this purpose.)

Almond Torte
ONE 9-INCH LAYER CAKE

Two layers of rich, light almond cake are filled and topped with what the Portuguese call ovos moles, *or soft eggs, a sugar and egg yolk concoction of unbelievable richness.*

5 large eggs, separated
12 tablespoons sugar
⅓ cup fine white bread crumbs
1 teaspoon baking powder
1¼ teaspoons almond extract
¼ teaspoon salt
⅛ teaspoon cream of tartar
1 cup finely ground blanched almonds

Almond torte with meringue kisses.

SOFT EGGS
1¼ cups sugar
½ cup water
8 egg yolks

GARNISH
Meringue Kisses (page 258)

Preheat oven to 350°. Butter two 9-inch cake pans, line with waxed paper, and butter the paper.

Beat the egg yolks with 10 tablespoons sugar until thick and light. Add the bread crumbs, baking powder, and almond extract and beat until smooth.

In another mixing bowl, beat the egg whites with the salt and cream of tartar until soft peaks are formed. Add the remaining 2 tablespoons sugar and continue beating until stiff. Fold the egg whites into the yolk mixture alternately with the ground almonds. Be careful not to deflate mixture.

Divide the mixture between the 2 pans, spreading it smoothly. Bake for 20 minutes, or until the layers are springy.

Cool 5 minutes in the pans; turn out onto wire racks, and peel off the waxed paper. Cool completely.

To make soft eggs, boil the sugar and water together for 5 minutes. Cool slightly. Beat the egg yolks with an electric mixer. Beating constantly, pour the syrup into the yolks. Pour the mixture back into the pan and cook over low heat (never more than 165°) until the mixture thickens, stirring constantly. Strain the mixture and cool until ready to use.

To assemble, put one layer of the torte on a serving dish and spread with the soft eggs, cover with the second layer, and frost the top. Allow some of the topping to drip down the sides. Decorate with meringue kisses.

Grape tart in a nut crust—halved red and green grapes are carefully arranged in a crust of ground almonds and topped with a shiny apricot glaze.

Grape Tart in Nut Crust
SEE VARIATION, PAGE 241

Bûche d'Eté
(Chocolate Roulade)
SERVES 12

Two or more roulades can be joined together, then coated with whipped cream to make an impressive, very long cake.

> 6 ounces semisweet chocolate
> 3 tablespoons cold espresso coffee
> 6 eggs, separated
> ¾ cup sugar
> Pinch salt
> 2 tablespoons cocoa
> 2 cups heavy cream

Preheat oven to 350°.

In top of double boiler, melt the chocolate in the coffee over simmering water. Stir until smooth.

Butter a 10 × 15-inch jelly-roll pan. Line with waxed paper. Butter paper.

Beat egg yolks until fluffy. Add sugar gradually and beat until very thick. Add chocolate mixture and salt.

Beat the egg whites until stiff. Carefully fold into the chocolate mixture. Spread evenly in lined pan.

Bake for 15 minutes. Cool cake in pan, set on a rack, for 1 hour. Keep covered with a damp cloth towel.

Sprinkle top of cake with cocoa. Cover with waxed paper. Place flat baking sheet on top of cake and invert. Carefully peel off paper on top.

Whip 1 cup of cream until stiff. Spread evenly over cake. Using the waxed paper under the cake as a guide, roll cake from long side like a jelly roll. Place seam side down on a serving tray. Chill.

Whip the remaining cream and coat the roll with ¾ of it. Decorate by piping the rest of the cream on the cake in swirls and rosettes.

Pound Cake with
Cherries and Raisins
1 LOAF

Known as le cake in France, this rich yellow cake is enhanced with glacéed green cherries, raisins, and a light flavoring of rum.

> 1½ sticks unsalted butter
> 1 cup unbleached all-purpose flour
> ¼ cup cake flour
> 1 teaspoon baking powder
> ¾ cup dark raisins or currants
> 2 eggs
> 2 egg yolks
> 1 cup sugar
> ⅓ cup dark rum
> ¾ cup glacéed green cherries, rinsed in hot water and dried

Preheat oven to 350°. Butter and flour a 6-cup loaf pan. Line the bottom with waxed paper and butter the paper.

Soften 1½ sticks butter over hot water to mayonnaise-like consistency.

Sift flours with baking powder. Sprinkle a bit over raisins to prevent them from sinking during baking.

Beat eggs and yolks with sugar until light and fluffy, about 6 to 8 minutes. Add rum and beat until mixed. Fold in sifted flour, bit by bit, until just blended. Add butter and gently fold in, taking care not to deflate mixture. Quickly fold in raisins.

Pour half the batter into pan. Spread cherries on top and add remaining batter. Smooth top of cake. Bake approximately 1 hour. Cake is done when toothpick inserted in center comes out clean and cake begins to shrink from sides of pan.

Cool in pan for 10 minutes, then turn onto rack.

Slices of rum-flavored pound cake with raisins and glacéed green cherries.

Sable Cookies
SEE RECIPE, PAGE 98

A long silver tray holds perfect rows of buttery, golden sables.

Coconut cake looks spectacular sprinkled with toasted coconut.

Coconut Cake

This is an old-fashioned kind of cake, perfect for those who don't like exotic desserts. It is best made with fresh coconut and coconut milk.

1 cup coconut milk or 1 cup milk plus ½ cup shredded coconut
1 cup freshly grated coconut or 1 cup shredded coconut
¾ cup (1½ sticks) unsalted butter
1¼ cups sugar
1 teaspoon vanilla
3 cups sifted cake flour
4 teaspoons baking powder
¾ teaspoon salt
4 egg whites

SEVEN-MINUTE
BOILED ICING

3 egg whites
1¾ cups sugar
5 tablespoons cold water
¼ teaspoon cream of tartar
1 teaspoon vanilla
½ cup toasted shredded coconut

Preheat oven to 350°. Butter and flour two 9-inch square pans. Scald the coconut milk and pour over the coconut. Strain and cool the liquid, reserving the coconut.

Cream the butter and sugar until smooth. Add the vanilla. Sift the flour with the baking powder and salt. Beat into the butter mixture alternately with the cooled milk. Mix in the coconut.

Beat the egg whites until stiff but not dry. Fold gently into the cake mixture. Divide the batter between the 2 cake pans. Bake for 25 to 35 minutes, or until a cake tester comes out clean.

Cool 10 minutes in the pans, turn out onto racks, and cool thoroughly before icing.

To make the icing, place egg whites, sugar, water, and cream of tartar in the top of a double boiler over rapidly boiling water. Beat with an electric hand mixer or whisk for 7 minutes. Remove from heat, add vanilla, and continue beating until fluffy and glossy. Spread icing between layers and over exterior with a spatula. Just before icing hardens, sprinkle top and sides with shredded coconut lightly toasted in a 300° oven.

CHAPTER TEN

The At-Home Wedding

LAST WEEK A COUPLE WAS married under a waterfall in upstate Connecticut. Another couple took their vows on horseback and then received guests in a cavernous Yankee barn. Andy and I were married in the Columbia University chapel and lunched at a small hotel reception; my sister Laura was married two years ago, wearing Victorian batiste, in the Victorian parlor of our farmhouse; and my brother George was married last August in a formal ceremony followed by a country luncheon in our peach orchard. As indicated by the current diversity in weddings, by antique and avant-garde wedding apparel, by personalized

The wedding reception—sparkling crystal, summer flowers, delicious food, and a smiling bridal party contribute to a perfect afternoon celebration.

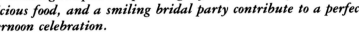

263

vows and hyphenated surnames, today the rules for this event are as liberated as they are for other forms of entertaining. What counts is not fussy etiquette, or the number of bridesmaids, or the social prominence of the reception site, but something as simple and incalculable as a special feeling.

One of the most obvious ways to individualize a wedding is to have it at home. In recent times, more and more young people seem to like this situation, because it is personal, because it is comfortable, and also because there is a poignant drama in the act of sending a child off into a new life from the lap of his childhood. This seems to hold true even if the home isn't literally the childhood home, but a sister's or aunt's or a friend's. A classic scenario would include several acres of rolling grass carpet, a rose garden, where the groom's mother talks with the bride's aunts, a great pink-and-white striped tent ballooning in a perfect breeze, an old sycamore tree, where the bride and groom will be photographed, white jackets and silk on the terrace, F. Scott Fitzgerald style. However, I've catered so many home weddings of such different character that I know there is no stereotype. Charming weddings have taken place in small apartments (gently cramped is convivial), in dark parlors (made fanciful and light with many baskets of baby's breath), in modest backyards (where a heated tent doubles house space), as well as on beaches (with bushels of fresh clams and champagne), on tennis courts, and in pine groves. One Sunday morning in Manhattan, I accommodated fifty people in the space provided by a large living room and office, and watched the ceremony, the brunch of omelettes, fruit, and champagne, and the cake cutting take place quickly and efficiently. On the other hand, several years ago when Jacques Pepin, Pierre Fessaguet, and Pierre Franey fêted the marriage of a compatriot's daughter, they took over an endless stretch of beach on Shelter Island and leisurely cooked up an amazing array of food over the course of many hours.

Planning

WHATEVER ITS NATURE, A wedding and reception take planning, and that planning, even if simple, can be time-consuming, given the heroic status of the day. If you have a year to prepare the event, you will probably need a year, for planning, like a ground cover, always seems to claim whatever space is available. Four or five months, however, is the usual, and the ideal time frame, especially for a wedding that will occur in the busy months of spring and summer. A month's time can suffice, too, provided the event is small and you are prepared to be flexible about some specifics, like rented chairs, tables, linens, and tents, and inventive with invitations.

Ultimately, planning is coordinating, a fact upon which wedding coordinators have founded a valuable profession. If you are engaging a coordinator, my advice is meant to provide ideas and perspective; if you are masterminding the day yourself, it is meant to aid and abet your efforts in the realms of aesthetics and menu. In either case, begin with basics: a bride's magazine for an overview; a notebook to which you commit every bit of minutiae; and a list of the broad questions:

DATE, LOCATION, TIME
SIZE (NUMBER OF GUESTS? ROOM CAPACITY?
    YARD CAPACITY? TENTS?)
STYLE (INFORMAL OR FORMAL? COUNTRY OR CHIC?
    CONTEMPORARY OR OLD-FASHIONED?)
MUSIC (BACKGROUND—STROLLING MUSICIANS, OR POP GROUP?
    DANCE BAND—COUNTRY, ROCK, BALLROOM?)
BUDGET

The answers will determine the shape of your event.

Once the time, place, and size are determined, you can address yourself to the aesthetics of your setting, and to the refreshment that will be served within that setting. The hour alone will suggest a general menu. The place, size, budget, and your personal taste will narrow down its specifics. Decisions build up, pyramid style—the broad ones at the base, the particulars later—until all elements are in place and in shape. Deciding upon a buffet lunch means at a higher level finding a caterer and/or a specific menu, renting tables and chairs, linens, dishes, and hiring bartenders, waiters, and waitresses.

Rental equipment has become more refined with the times. Tents, once uniformly striped, now come in misty solids—pink, sand, blue—in many sizes, and can be heated as well, for fickle fall and spring days. Linens, too, are more adventuresome than institutional, plain-bordered white. A range of choices exists in chairs (gilded ballroom, white wooden, school-auditorium metal), tables (many sizes of round, square, oblong), glassware, silverware, and dishes.

Aesthetics

SIMPLE AESTHETICS SHOULD prevail at home. A house or apartment or backyard has its own aura, from having been lived in, which can be set off, or even transformed, with just flowers—with masses

🍂

The Romantic Bouquet

Any flowers with a lasting quality that won't wilt within a matter of hours can be used in a bridal bouquet. The romantic bouquet pictured here is made with tulips, freisias, roses, lilacs, stars of Bethlehem, and delphinium blossoms. The only other types of flowers to avoid are those that are too fragile or that have too pungent an aroma. Seasonal garden flowers add a perfect personal touch and combined with a few more exotic blossoms purchased from a local florist make a bouquet of unique beauty.

The romantic bouquet and an antique heart cushioning the wedding rings.

Birdi Kins demonstrates how to create a romantic bouquet. Milliner's wire is wrapped around each blossom stem.

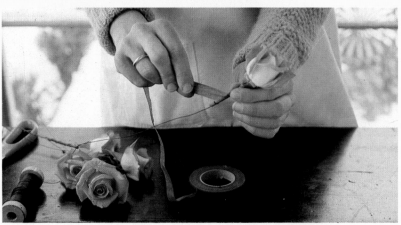

Florist's tape covers the wire-strengthened stem of large or limp blossoms.

A rose is the center of the bouquet, and other blossoms are wired around the rose.

Continue building in an even pattern, taping as needed to hold the flowers together.

Lilacs are added to soften and fill out the tight center bouquet.

The taped stems are wound tightly with satin ribbon.

Lace and tulle are attached to the bouquet with wire.

The underside of the bouquet.

Stephanotis blossoms are strung on satin ribbon streamers to affix to the bouquet.

of painted daisies, baby's breath, or giant peonies crowded into mushroom baskets, wicker baskets, or even bushel baskets spray-painted to match the decor. Most brides like to coordinate decoration, at least in spirit, with the bridesmaid's dresses. I like to be seasonal, too—gourds, pumpkins, and leaves in autumn, the most extravagant garden cuttings in summer, pine boughs and candles in winter—yet I have seen very dramatic statements made with the unseasonal choice. Spring blooms—irises, grape hyacinths, and lily of the valley, for example—seem all the more delicate and romantic in the dead of winter. And these days, it is possible to defy nature and special-order desert flowers, orchids, or tulips at odd times; months in advance, a florist will discuss possibilities and availability. If you have your own garden or meadow, open up to all its possibilities, for nature can extend your imagination and inspire fresh new ideas. Lovely decorations can be made using simple stalks of wheat, Queen Anne's lace, black-eyed Susans, branches of apple blossoms or flowering quince, bachelor buttons or ranunculus.

The bridal bouquet is an opportunity to be as expressive, romantic, and original as the bride wishes. Twenty-one years ago, I carried a big bunch of white daisies, because they seemed so fresh and pretty. My sister Kathy picked field wheat from a Texas roadside and combined it with lavender from my father's garden to create a very beautiful handful of nature. The guiding aesthetic is strictly what you feel like—a traditional bouquet, a Victorian nosegay, just roses, just gardenias. Several years ago, a young designer friend named Leslie Liebman, who doesn't like contrived-looking, formal arrangements of any kind, showed me how easy it is to make your own bridal bouquet, even if you've never worked with flowers before. It involves five or six simple steps: assembling your favorite flowers; adding a bit of whimsy, like a piece of antique lace that makes a bouquet even more special; wiring; taping; and then wrapping it all in satin ribbon.

Menu

WITH FOOD, AS WITH FLOWers, a wedding is a time to indulge in favorites and fantasies. Banish the notion of white bread canapés and chafing dishes, for wedding menus can be as varied as any buffet. Crudités, spring lamb and wild rice, poached fish, stuffed chicken breasts, pasta salads—I myself will go to great lengths to avoid a chafing dish; if there is going to be a heating device present, I would much prefer it to be a grill offering tiny skewered yakitoris, or scallops en brochette. Wedding food should be particularly pretty—light, elegant, a delicate contrast of color, texture, and shape—for, like the other elements of the day, it is addressed to romance. However, think too of your guest list, and if you know it to be dominated by hearty, elderly, or unadventuresome appetites, plan accordingly. I recently finalized plans for a colossal Arab-Italian pageant, and the hostess and I agreed that to serve anything other than a gargantuan banquet would be a profound disappointment to the guests, who, like Oblomov, would come to life on the third helping.

After the hour, budget will necessarily define your menu, for food, beverage, and service generally constitute the largest single expense of a wedding. With beverages, it is wise to plan far ahead to give yourself the opportunity to taste different champagnes and perhaps to even stumble upon a sale. The choice of open bar and/or champagne depends also on the proclivities of your guests—a wine bar is as ill-suited to a John O'Hara gathering as martinis to young environmentalists—and especially on the bride's desires. I know a young girl who had first tasted Dom Perignon as an impressionable adolescent, and had gone to sleep that night and many subsequent nights dreaming of the occasion of her wedding, when she would serve an inexhaustible fountain of this

The wedding cake—variegated ivy, lilac blossoms, delphinium, and rosebuds capture the day's romantic mood.

bubbling mystery to all her friends. Her father, confronted with the reality of Dom Perignon at $70 a bottle, quietly rationalized the once-in-a-lifetime extravagance for his daughter by not having an open bar.

With food, although there is a substantial cost difference between a tea-sandwich-and-cake reception and a sit-down dinner, one is not categorically superior to the other. Recently, the afternoon tea-sandwich reception, served post-lunch and precocktail, has fallen out of favor. Yet, although it is not appropriate when guests have traveled long, hunger-provoking distances to the wedding, it is a perfect solution for a small city wedding (a church ceremony followed by an apartment reception, for example) or a country wedding composed mainly of townspeople. I am planning just such a reception now, for a young couple who both work at the Cooper-Hewitt Museum and will be married in its aboretum and then receive in the nearby apartment of its director. Elegant food and unusual touches indeed can make this afternoon affair as memorable as a Rabelaisian bash. Tea sandwiches are tea sandwiches, but they do not have to be soggy or insipid; the Scandinavians have taught us that. Fancy chicken salad, made with pecans, on zucchini bread; Brie, prosciutto, and watercress sandwiched between thin slices of homemade French bread; smoked salmon on herb-buttered dark bread; even the prosaic cucumber and watercress rounds--this sort of fare recalls the often-forgotten joys of high tea. When the ingredients are fresh, and garnished with herb butters or homemade mayonnaise flavored with fresh dill or chervil, these are delectable miniatures, perfectly suited to that leisurely afternoon mealtime. A more literal high tea might be spelled out with sausage rolls, small smoked turkey sandwiches, glacéed berries and grapes, assorted pastries. Then a finale, the wedding cake.

To me, the wedding cake is the real and representational high point of a reception, the one part of a long tradition that should always be there. The serving of the cake marks the climax of festivities, signals the leave-taking, and provides an excuse for stagy, childish fun. As the tradition has endured, and the ornate shape of the cake remained, the flavors have changed, making a cosmetic joy a truly edible joy too. A wedding cake should be a special treat. Thank goodness the traditional, but insipid, white wedding cake has now been replaced by a succulent carrot cake, or a moist spice cake, or the densest, most devilish chocolate cake. My personal favorite is a combination of layers of chocolate almond and orange almond cake, coated with Grand Marnier Italian meringue buttercream. For decoration, the crowning bride and groom statuette has given way to antique figures, or Kewpie dolls, or other personal whims. One bride I know wanted gnomes; another, who collected frogs, found a chef extraordinaire to create a pair of sugar amphibians dressed in lace and top hat. I personally am drawn to flowers and fruit; I have festooned a cake with boxwood leaves and queen quinces, with delphinium blossoms, with pink artemisia, or, at Christmastime, with holly leaves and red candied cherry berries.

I think it is important to remember that a wedding reception is not a ritual, or a show, but a very special sort of party. It is necessarily more complicated than other forms of entertainment, but in a sense it is easier because the pageantry, the common interest, and the emotion at its heart will sustain it, even if the chairs don't match, rain falls, and the salmon mousse melts. What makes this occasion memorable is not always the obvious or predictable. When I look back on different weddings, I remember different things, such as the unusual tomato-red bridesmaids' dresses and bright yellow and red bouquets at a fall wedding in a pine grove in rural Maryland; elegantly dressed guests dancing for hours to Cole Porter tunes at another wedding; a huge colorful display of shiny vegetables at a pasta and salad supper for a young vegetarian couple. These things made the day memorable, not an expensive wedding gown or elaborate menu.

Afternoon Cocktail Reception for Fifty

MY SISTER LAURA WANTED A small personal wedding with old-fashioned, at-home charms. Because the date chosen was only a month away, and her finances very limited, circumstances suggested that her family and friends join in the staging of the event, which proved not only fun and economical, but in fact guaranteed a wonderful, original homemade quali-

271

ty. A friend hand-lettered the invitation on antique stippled paper, which, for time's sake, was reproduced in quantity by a printer. I offered our nineteenth-century farmhouse for the site, and my head and hands for the elaboration of the menu and wedding cake. Friend Leslie Liebman volunteered to do the bride's bouquet and the flowers, informal gatherings of flowering quince branches, with tulips and smilax, which she arranged in glass containers slipped inside Oriental baskets and an antique silver urn. My brother George selected and ordered champagne and wine, arranged for the rental of little tables, chairs, silver cake plates, and champagne flutes, and hired serving help—two bartenders (friends of the bride), two maids, and a teenager to clean up.

Two weeks before the day, we had worked Laura's favorite food into a simple but elegant menu of finger food. Laura combed the countryside for a Victorian dress and petticoat, while I rummaged through my collection of antique linens for table coverings, and borrowed heirloom silver serving trays from friends and relatives. I baked and froze the four tiers of wedding cake, and as the wedding day drew near, I embarked on food preparations.

Outside, the driveway was lined with brown paper bags holding candles in sand, to show the way. Inside, the house was dimly lit with dozens of votive candles. At 5:00 P.M. on this snowy New Year's Eve, Laura and Kim Herbert were married in our front hall,

to the accompaniment of recorded baroque music. The dining-room table was laid with a cold cocktail buffet, while hot hors d'oeuvres were passed from room to room. In the kitchen, champagne and white wine flowed—I had unearthed two antique cut-glass goblets for the bride and groom—and the cake sat majestically until cutting. In their toasts, Laura and Kim celebrated each other, each of us, and the heroic esprit de corps. We celebrated the lovely memory already fixed in place.

From top: **steak tartare in cherry tomatoes, poppy seed straws, crispy cooked asparagus, snow peas, enok mushrooms with anchovy mayonnaise, and shrimp vinaigrette wrapped in snow peas.**

❧ MENU ❧

Almond-Stuffed Dates with Bacon
Deviled Eggs with Red Caviar
Phyllo Triangles Filled with Curried Walnut Chicken
Shrimp Vinaigrette Wrapped in Snow Peas
Duck Rillettes
Sevruga Caviar with Homemade Melba Toast
Poppy Seed Straws   Crudités with Anchovy Mayonnaise
Smoked Scottish Salmon with Dill on Pumpernickel
Steak Tartare in Cherry Tomatoes
Crab-Filled Tartlets   Tiny Hothouse Lamb Chops
Smoked Trout Chevrons with Horseradish Cream
Chocolate Almond–Orange Almond Wedding Cake
Champagne, Sparkling White Wine, Still White Wine

Almond-Stuffed Dates with Bacon

DOUBLE RECIPE, PAGE 46

Wedding hors d'oeuvres should be simple, elegant, and delicious finger foods. **Below:** *Deviled eggs topped with salmon roe caviar.*

Deviled Eggs with Red Caviar

80 HORS D'OEUVRES

40 hard-boiled eggs
¾ cup homemade Mayonnaise (page 156)
¼ pound (1 stick) butter, melted
Salt and pepper
¼ cup finely chopped dill
7 ounces large salmon roe caviar

GARNISH
Dill

Peel the eggs and cut in half lengthwise. Put yolks in food processor and chop fine. Add the mayonnaise, butter, salt and pepper, and chopped dill. Blend until smooth. Taste for seasoning.

Put mixture in a pastry bag fitted with a large star tip and fill each half egg. Cover loosely with plastic wrap and refrigerate, up to 3 hours.

To serve, top each half egg with a few grains of red caviar. Arrange on a thick bed of dill to keep the eggs from sliding, unless you have old-fashioned deviled egg dishes, which are very decorative.

Phyllo Triangles Filled with Curried Walnut Chicken

SEE RECIPE, PAGE 52

Shrimp Vinaigrette Wrapped in Snow Peas

DOUBLE RECIPE, PAGE 42

Rillettes with French bread.

Duck Rillettes

2½ POUNDS

1 6-pound duck
⅓ bottle dry white wine
1 onion, sliced
1 bay leaf
1 clove garlic, peeled
Sprigs of fresh thyme
Salt and freshly ground pepper
Clarified Butter (page 84)

Quarter the duck. Brown in a heavy roasting pan in a 400° oven until the fat begins to melt, about 30 minutes. Turn the pieces to brown evenly.

Remove from the oven, add the remaining ingredients, and cover. Cook slowly on top of stove for 3½ hours.

Strain the juices and fat from the pan. Shred the meat into small pieces and finely chop the skin. Discard the bones. Add the meat and skin to the strained fatty liquid. Beat well with a wooden spoon. Taste for seasonings. Pepper improves the flavor immensely. Chill in the refrigerator, stirring with the wooden spoon every 30 minutes, until the rillettes are very

stiff. Pack into earthenware crocks and seal with clarified butter. This helps preserve the rillettes. Cover tightly. Keep refrigerated until 1 hour before serving.

To serve, scrape off the butter, put crock on a tray, and surround it with thinly sliced French bread, toasted if you wish. Provide a wooden spreader or silver butter knife.

Homemade Melba Toast

APPROXIMATELY 50 HORS D'OEUVRES

Melba toast is so easy to make, and the homemade variety is vastly superior to store-bought

2 pounds extra-thin white bread

Preheat oven to 300°.

Cut off bread crusts and cut each slice into 4 triangles. Place the triangles in one layer on baking sheets. Bake until dry but not browned. Cool on racks. Store in airtight containers.

NOTE: If you have homemade *pain de mie* on hand, slice it ⅛ inch thick, cut off crusts, cut slices into 4 triangles, and bake as above.

Poppy Seed Straws

APPROXIMATELY 12 DOZEN 10-INCH STRAWS

I started making these long ago, when I first mastered puff pastry. I love to munch on these lighter-than-air delicacies during cocktail time. They are especially good with champagne.

1 pound Perfect Puff Pastry (page 237)
½ cup poppy seeds (or white sesame seeds or a very light sprinkling of cayenne pepper)

Divide pastry into 3 parts. Cover and refrigerate the pastry you are not using. Roll 1 portion of dough into a rectangle ⅛ inch thick and 10 inches wide. Sprinkle on seeds and roll firmly, pressing seeds into surface.

With a pastry wheel (zigzag edges are nice) cut into strips ½ inch wide. Put strips carefully on a water-sprayed baking sheet and refrigerate until all the pastry is used up. Preheat oven to 400°. Bake strips until puffed and lightly golden, about 8 to 10 minutes.

Poppy seed straws.

Crudités with Anchovy Mayonnaise

SEE RECIPE, PAGE 70

Crunchy crudités—snow peas, Brussels sprouts, asparagus— surround a red cabbage bowl of anchovy mayonnaise.

Smoked salmon.

Smoked Scottish Salmon with Dill on Pumpernickel

SEE RECIPE, PAGE 96

Steak Tartare in Cherry Tomatoes

80 HORS D'OEUVRES

80 cherry tomatoes (about 2 pints)
1 pound freshly ground sirloin
½ cup tiny capers
1 clove garlic, pressed
¼ cup finely chopped parsley
1 egg, beaten
4 green scallions, finely minced
   Salt and pepper to taste

GARNISH
   Parsley

Carefully cut off the tops of the cherry tomatoes and scoop out the seeds. A small melon ball or grapefruit scoop does this well. Drain upside down on a rack.

Mix the beef and the rest of the in-gredients together. Fill each tomato with the tartare and garnish with a tiny sprig of parsley. Serve the tomatoes set on a parsley-covered tray to keep them from rolling.

Crab-Filled Tartlets

60 TARTLETS, 2½ INCHES
IN DIAMETER

2 recipes Perfect Plain Tart and Tartlet Crust (page 236)
2 6-ounce packages frozen snow crabmeat, thawed
½ red pepper, finely diced
½ green pepper, finely diced
1 stalk celery, finely diced
½ cup (approximately) mayonnaise
   Chopped dill
   Salt and pepper

GARNISH
   Dill sprigs

Make and bake tartlet shells according to master recipe

Combine crab, vegetables, and enough mayonnaise to make a moist but not soggy mixture. Add chopped dill and salt and pepper to taste. Refrigerate.

A few minutes before serving, put a teaspoonful of crab filling in each tartlet shell and garnish with dill.

Tiny Hothouse Lamb Chops

50 PIECES

This is a once-in-a-lifetime extravagance, as baby lamb chops (1-inch rib) command a premium price.

50 baby lamb chops with long rib bones, no fat
   Salt and pepper
   Rosemary

Season lamb chops. Place on broiler tray. Broil under high heat until just brown outside, pink in the middle, turning once (about 3 to 4 minutes each side). Decorate ribs with paper frills. Serve immediately.

Smoked Trout Chevrons with Horseradish Cream

SEE RECIPE, PAGE 51

Bright pink dogwood blossoms add color to a bowl of horseradish cream and smoked trout chevrons.

Wedding Cake

SERVES 50 TO 65

The layers alternate between chocolate almond and orange almond. There are four layers—two chocolate and two orange. You will need the following equipment:

Four cake pans, 2 inches deep, with the following diameters: 4 inches, 7 inches, 10 inches, 12 inches.

Wooden chopsticks to be cut into appropriate lengths to separate the layers.

Cardboard rounds to put under each cake layer. These can be purchased or cut by hand.

CHOCOLATE ALMOND CAKE

16 ounces semisweet chocolate
1 pound (4 sticks) unsalted butter, at room temperature
2¾ cups sugar
12 eggs, separated
Pinch salt
3 cups sifted cake flour
1 teaspoon almond extract
1½ cups very finely ground blanched almonds

Preheat oven to 350°.

Butter the 12-inch and 7-inch pans, line with waxed paper, then butter and flour.

Melt the chocolate in a stainless steel bowl in a 250° oven.

Cream the butter and 2½ cups sugar until fluffy. Add the egg yolks, 1 at a time, beating well after each addition. Continue to beat until mixture is very thick and pale yellow. Add the melted chocolate, beating just enough to incorporate the chocolate. Add the flour, almond extract, and almonds, again beating only enough to mix the ingredients.

In a separate mixing bowl, beat the egg whites until stiff but not dry. Add the salt and remaining ¼ cup sugar.

Fold the egg whites gently into the chocolate mixture.

Pour the batter into the prepared pans, filling the pans ⅔ to ¾ full. Bake for approximately 25 minutes. This cake should be slightly underdone in the center, but baked so that the edges are set. If center is overcooked, this cake is more like a conventional chocolate cake. If underdone, the rich, moist, creamy chocolate almond taste is achieved.

Cool cakes on racks. Wrap in plastic wrap and refrigerate or freeze until ready to frost. Cake should be refrigerated no longer than 2 days.

ORANGE ALMOND CAKE

½ pound (2 sticks) unsalted butter
1 cup plus 3 tablespoons sugar
6 eggs, separated
Grated rind of 2 oranges
⅔ cup strained orange juice
½ teaspoon almond extract
1½ cups finely ground blanched almonds
1½ cups sifted cake flour
Pinch salt

Preheat oven to 350°.

Melt the butter and let it cool.

Beat 2 cups sugar into the egg yolks until mixture is fluffy and pale yellow. Add the rind, orange juice, and almond extract, beating well. Quickly beat in the ground almonds, then the flour.

Beat the egg whites in a separate bowl until soft peaks are formed. Add the salt and 3 tablespoons sugar and beat until stiff but not dry.

Fold the melted butter little by little into the egg yolk batter. Delicately fold the egg whites into the batter, taking care not to deflate the whites.

Immediately pour batter into pre-pared 10-inch and 4-inch cake pans. Bake in the preheated oven for 35 minutes, or until tester comes out clean. Cool layers on racks. Wrap in plastic wrap for storage in refrigerator (2 days) or in freezer.

BUTTERCREAM FROSTING

This frosting cannot be doubled or made ahead of time; once made, it should be used immediately. Two batches will frost and decorate the 5 layers.

2 cups sugar
⅔ cup water
6 egg whites
Pinch salt
¼ teaspoon cream of tartar
1¼ pounds (5 sticks) unsalted butter, at room temperature
¼ cup Grand Marnier or 1 tablespoon vanilla extract

Dissolve the sugar in the water in a heavy enamel saucepan. Bring to a boil without stirring. Cover and let boil for 2 to 3 minutes, until there are no sugar crystals left. Uncover and continue boiling until syrup reaches soft-ball stage, 240° on a candy thermometer.

While sugar syrup is cooking, beat egg whites and cream of tartar in a mixer, using the wire whip, until very stiff peaks are formed.

At the moment 240° is reached, pour ¼ cup of the syrup into the stiffly beaten egg whites, drop by drop, beating at high speed. Gradually add the rest of the syrup in a fine stream and beat until cool (7 to 10 minutes).

In separate bowl, cream butter until fluffy.

When the meringue mixture is cool, add the softened butter, 3 tablespoons at a time. Beat well. Frosting should get thick and creamy with the addition of the buter. (If the meringue was too warm, the frosting may remain too thin, in which case stir over ice until it begins to thicken.) Beat in the Grand Marnier.

Frosting is ready to use. *Do not refrigerate frosting.* Keep it cool over a bowl of iced water.

Coat each layer of cake with frosting and refrigerate them at once.

To decorate the cake, make second batch of frosting and use pastry bag and tips to achieve desired design.

To assemble, put a cardboard circle under each layer. Cut the wooden chopsticks ½ inch taller than each layer. Cut 5 or 6 pieces for each layer. Set layers on top of one another. The wooden pieces provide a space between each layer and make the cutting of the cake much easier. (Always cut the cake from the bottom layer up.) Refrigerate cake until 1 hour before serving.

For additional decoration, greenery, flowers, strawberries, raspberries, glacéed fruits, etc. can be used.

Smooth the buttercream base before piping on frosting.

Using Ateco tip #48, pipe stripes of frosting on top of each layer.

Ateco tip #8 makes vertical stripes on sides of cake for basketweave; use Ateco tip #48 to simulate alternating basketweave strips.

Ateco tip #86 makes the shell edge on top and bottom of each layer.

The top of each layer is decorated with bows, French knots, and flowers using Ateco tip #2.

Insert chopsticks to support the layers in stacking the cake.

The decorated cake ready to be garnished with flowers.

Sit-Down Country Luncheon for One Hundred Seventy-five

FORTUNATELY FOR THE CAUSE of intimate detail, I have a younger brother, too, who planned another wedding, in another style and season. I offered my services as consultant and cook, and I offered our grounds and barn as reception hall, summer style. During the prenuptial preparations, I kept an informal diary, so that at some future date we would understand how, both methodically and miraculously, it all came together. I hoped it would also prove enlightening and instructional to others.

February: Surprise announcement of engagement. George and Rita make basic decisions. DATE AND TIME: August 8, twelve o'clock church ceremony and sit-down lunch. SIZE: One hundred fifty to two hundred guests. PLACE: Connecticut, lunch in Martha's garden, dancing in new barn, if George finishes constructing it. STYLE: Country elegant, formal dress (five bridesmaids, flower girls, morning coats). MUSIC: baroque quartet for lawn, country western for barn.

March: Reserve church. Further define reception: lunch under tent in lower grounds where garden will be backdrop, canopy to lead to barn. Give tea for bride. Minor troubles—families begin to argue about guest lists; bridesmaids disagree over dress choice and color (teal blue). Pastor has to change vacation plans.

A large white tent set in our field for George and Rita's reception.

April: Guest list disputes wax serious. Invitations planned and ordered anyway. Bride's mother chooses dress. Groom's mother's dress choice (big flowers) is rejected by daughters. George engages a maître d'; asks 20 of my best workers to reserve day. We define general shape of lunch menu—light and elegant: hors d'oeuvres, goblets of cold soup, grilled lobster, chocolate wedding cake. Reserve Big John grills. Reserve pink tents (one large, one service, one canopy) from Smith's in Greenwich. Reserve 200 white chairs, 20 round tables, 20 blue tablecloths, 200 white napkins, and enough dishes to avoid shortage from Taylor Rental. Hear of chintz tablecloth source—may change. Engage baroque quartet from Yale School of Music, Bill Lombardo (nephew of Guy) for country band. Best man runs limo service, and will provide limousines.

May: George works frantically on barn. Beehives moved from tent site in lower garden to secluded spot. Flower talk: as garden blooms, potential arrangements come to mind. George shops for champagne (as frequent maître d' and oenophile, he knows his way around). Quotes from local fisheries on lobster prices. Large fans rented to circulate air in tent. George's former employer offers vintage Rolls-Royce for wedding day; wife of former employer offers Nantucket house for honeymoon—both offers accepted. Reserve Griswold Inn for wedding night, and early morning ferry to Nantucket. I find perfect wedding gift at tag sale—an antique wicker picnic hamper complete with fittings. Will fill it with elaborate picnic fare. Alexis threads new loom with white linen to make napkins for basket. Weekend visits by bridesmaids for fittings and bride talk. Bride has weekly appointments for manicure and hairset; embarks on Scarsdale diet—she will be in perfect shape by August. After years of having to spell Kostyra for strangers, George decides he will take wife's surname—Christiansen.

June: Bridesmaid's fittings continue. Bride already radiant, regimen is working. Groom working so hard in his construction business, barn progresses slowly. New grass near reception site takes root. Vegetable garden blooming: promises plenty of tomatoes. Order 175 lobsters. Decide on the cold soup: vichyssoise with wild mushrooms, served in balloon goblets. I will make the wedding cake hexagonal—my first. Special order pans.

July: Changes cause temporary trauma: order *white* tents instead of pink—better for photographs; forsake blue tablecloths for chintz, with creamy background—perfect offset for August

flowers—with peach napkins. Reserve dance floor for center of tent because barn not done. Menu alterations: add fresh clam bar and cold shrimp with coriander-flavored guacamole to hors d'oeuvres (and two boys to shuck clams); cold lobsters instead of grilled, to combat heat; whole tomatoes stuffed with vermicelli and pesto, because of bountiful garden.

August: Begin prayers for good weather; it has not yet rained on a weekend, but will add canopies to join all tents if luck fails. In view of long walk to house from reception site, reserve two Port-O-Jons and 20' × 20' tent to camouflage them. Plan to add dressing table with old-fashioned pitcher and basin, flowers, soaps, perfumes to further disguise said utility. Engage Roma the hairdresser to spend wedding morning at house. Fix menu, once and for all:

❧ MENU ❧

Clam Bar   Phyllo Triangles with Feta and Spinach
Corn Muffins   Tiny French Rolls   Poppy Seed Straws
Mushroom Vichyssoise
Gingered Chicken Satés
Cold Poached Lobster with Sauce Verte
Coal-Roasted Eggplant and Peppers
Tomatoes Stuffed with Vermicelli Pesto
String Beans Vinaigrette
Cold Skewered Shrimp with Guacamole Dip
Mussels Vinaigrette   Cold Beef Salad
French Pound Cake with Grand Marnier Buttercream
Champagne, White Wine, Open Bar

With menu in place, I can make shopping lists, map out refrigerator space, and organize food countdown for wedding week. It seems ridiculously long, but makes me feel I'm in control. Everything is pinned down, even minutiae. Day-by-day preparations look like this:

Tuesday

BAKE AND FREEZE LAYERS OF WEDDING CAKE, ROLLS, PHYLLO, BROWNIES, POPPY SEED STRAWS

Wednesday

MAKE SOUP BASE

MAKE COCKTAIL SAUCE

ROAST PEPPERS

CHOP MIRAPOIX FOR
    BEEF SALAD

MAKE VINAIGRETTES

MAKE HERB BUTTER

MAKE PHYLLO FILLING

Thursday

BRAISE BEEF

MARINATE CHICKEN
    AND CHICKEN LIVERS

MAKE VICHYSSOISE

SLICE AND SALT
    EGGPLANT

COOK 100 LOBSTERS

MAKE SAUCE VERTE

TRIM 25 POUNDS
    STRING BEANS

SOAK WOODEN SKEWERS
    FOR SATÉS

Friday

SKEWER SATÉS

SAUTÉ EGGPLANT
    AND ADD TO PEPPERS

DEFROST CAKE

DEFROST AND ICE
    BROWNIES

COOK SHRIMP

STEAM MUSSELS AND
    PUT IN TOMATO
    VINAIGRETTE

SLICE AND MARINATE
    BEEF

DEFROST POPPY SEED STRAWS

COOK REMAINING
    100 LOBSTERS

MAKE FRUIT PUNCH,
    ICED TEA

COOK VERMICELLI

WRAP LEMONS IN
    CHEESECLOTH FOR
    CLAM BAR

MAKE PESTO

MAKE FROSTING AND
    ICE WEDDING CAKE

Saturday morning

STUFF TOMATOES

BAKE PHYLLO

SKEWER SHRIMP

MAKE GUACAMOLE

DECORATE WEDDING
    CAKE WITH FLOWERS
    AND KEEP COOL

ASSEMBLE AND
    DECORATE PLATTERS

During reception

FILL SOUP GOBLETS

HEAT FRENCH ROLLS

REHEAT PHYLLO

GRILL SATÉS

GRILL CLAMS

Our daughter Alexis standing in the receiving line. Her headpiece and bouquet were created from garden flowers and satin ribbons.

Above: *Inside the tent, large round tables were set with chintz cloths, peach napkins, and garden flowers.* **Left:** *The bridal flowers.*

Wedding week begins with attack of nerves. Unfolds as a party, a circus, an ordeal, or a trial, depending on moment. Lists posted everywhere. Refrigerators and freezers fill. Tents raised Wednesday (to keep ground dry until Saturday in case of rain). Thursday, truckload of seafood arrives. Begin to steam lobsters, four at a time. Neighborhood children come to make small bags of rice, from cheesecloth tied with ribbon. Friday, rentals arrive— linens, tables and chairs, dishes and silver, Port-O-Jons; my assistants help rental people set up. Take break to cut flowers from garden. Make centerpieces in antique jars and bottles. Make bouquets and refrigerate. Run off to rehearsal dinner at Hunt Club feeling edgy. Calm comes later as I walk through tents and grounds in cool dry evening. The scene is set: empty, lovely, expectant.

August 8, 12:00 P.M. As the skies outside drizzle, George Kostyra and Margaret (Rita) Christiansen are married in Darien, Connecticut, before one hundred seventy-four of two hundred invited friends and family. Rolls-Royce doesn't materialize, so George and Rita take limousine to farmhouse. Chamber music plays for hors d'oeuvres, making the gray day poignant, romantic. Rain stops, air is cool, better than muggy; food stays fresh, looks wonderful. Country music takes over, stepping up tempo. Lobsters take time to eat, which makes everyone leisurely and informal. By popular demand, band plays five hours instead of four. Children dance. Waiters and waitresses dance. Roosters crow continually.

An Evaluation

*T*O GIVE A WEDDING AT MY home was to be involved in the event as a hostess, caterer, sister, and guest, to be responsible, social, and emotional all at once. It was a major undertaking, even though I had more experience in the field than any other committed party would be likely to have. When you are having one hundred seventy-five guests at your home, many of them strangers, there is even more to worry about than the obvious preparations; inevitably, if you are as fussy as I am, the weedy garden, the torn wallpaper in the upstairs bath, and the state of the old sofa surface as potential imperfections in a day meant to be perfect. And yet, it is useful and possible to use the events on this scale to get things done. Somehow, miraculously, the driveway to the barn was finished, the porch no one would see was repaired, the garden manicured so that the flowers looked as if they were growing for the wedding alone. For all these chores, we accepted neighborly offers of assistance, we hired people, and because we didn't have anything approximating an unlimited budget, we did much ourselves.

For the next such event (all my brothers and sisters are happily married now, but I do have a daughter), I will remember:

1. the value of gathering advice from specialists like the tent man or the rental lady or even a landscape architect. It is difficult for anyone to envision how best to transform familiar home grounds into a gala setting for a reception, particularly a large one. A fresh and experienced eye can see space as an abstraction and help considerably in the complicated task of fitting ceremonies and dance floors and tents into spaces designed and used for other ends.

2. the importance of delegating a person to be in charge of each area of work—the flowers, rentals, etc.—and a person other than yourself to be in charge overall—a majordomo with a clear outside eye. One possibility is a professional wedding coordinator who will orchestrate all the different elements and keep things moving smoothly.

3. the necessity of demanding very professional service from your staff even if they are friends or relatives, for informal family affairs can easily become sloppy.

4. the effectiveness of good music at a big party in keeping everyone mobile and high-spirited. I didn't even know until I saw their gyrations that my family loved to dance so much.

The smiling bride and groom, Rita and George Christiansen, married August 8, 1981, in Darien, Connecticut.

My feelings about the joys of at-home weddings have been even further intensified, for I have seen again that home is the nicest, friendliest place to be. To have a wedding at home is to make a personal gesture, which results in a higher grade of elegance than usually possible at an outside site. The rewards are in the great sense of accomplishment and in the gratitude of the guests. Ultimately, I judged our event by general demeanor, which was happy, relaxed, and astonishingly appreciative. Everyone noticed a host of small details, the way one does in a home. When I was asked if I had grown the stand of sunflowers that feed our chickens in winter as a backdrop for the wedding, I knew it had been a nice day.

Phyllo Triangles with Feta and Spinach

APPROXIMATELY 50
TRIANGLES

FETA AND SPINACH
FILLING
⅓ cup olive oil
1 bunch scallions, chopped
2½ pounds spinach, washed and dried
1 bunch parsley
1 bunch dill
½ pound feta cheese, drained and crumbled
3 eggs, slightly beaten
Salt and pepper

1 pound phyllo pastry

To make the filling, heat the oil and sauté the scallions until soft. Add the spinach and cook until wilted, stirring frequently. Put the mixture in a colander over a bowl and press out liquid. Boil down the liquid until it measures 2 tablespoons. Mix the spinach, spinach liquid, and remaining ingredients until well blended. Cool completely. Taste for seasoning.

To prepare Phyllo Triangles, follow directions on page 52.

Phyllo triangles with feta cheese and spinach.

Tiny corn bread muffins.

Corn Bread Muffins

SEE RECIPE, PAGE 188

Tiny French Rolls

SEE RECIPE, PAGE 106

Poppy Seed Straws

SEE RECIPE, PAGE 274

Mushroom Vichyssoise

25 SERVINGS

2 cups diced leeks (white part only)
12 tablespoons butter
16 to 18 white potatoes, peeled and thinly sliced
1½ pounds fresh wild mushrooms or 3 ounces dried mushrooms soaked in 1½ cups warm water
1½ tablespoons salt
1 gallon (16 cups) rich chicken stock
3 pints half-and-half
Salt, pepper, and nutmeg
2 cups heavy cream

GARNISH
Chopped parsley

Sauté the leeks in butter for 10 minutes over low heat; do not brown. Add the potatoes, mushrooms, salt, and chicken stock and simmer until the potatoes are tender—about 30 minutes. Purée in the food processor. Strain to remove any lumps.

Add the half-and-half and season to taste with salt, pepper, and freshly grated nutmeg. Chill thoroughly.

To serve, stir in the cream, pour into goblets, and garnish with chopped parsley.

Gingered Chicken Satés

SEE VARIATION, PAGE 157

Cold Poached Lobster with Sauce Verte

There are myriad ways to cook lobster, but for a crowd we find this method quick and sure.

1 lobster per person (1 to 1¼ pounds)

Bring a very large kettle of water to a rolling boil. Plunge each lobster head first into the water and boil for 10 minutes. In a 10-gallon kettle cook no more than 8 lobsters at one time. There must be sufficient water so that the lobsters cook evenly.

Drain and cool the lobsters. If you are serving the lobsters whole, insert a bamboo skewer in the underside of the tail. This will keep the tail straight. If you are cutting the lobster in half lengthwise you need not use the skewer. Don't cut the lobster until it is thoroughly chilled.

Refrigerate the lobsters until just before serving. Crack the claws with a hammer or wooden mallet and serve with picks and metal lobster crackers.

Sauce Verte
1 QUART

This is a green sauce for cold lobster, poached fish, or crispy cooked cold vegetables.

  2 cups vegetable oil
  ½ cup tarragon vinegar
  ½ cup Dijon mustard
  1 bottle tiny capers, drained

  ½ cup finely chopped parsley
  ½ cup finely chopped basil
  ¼ cup finely chopped mint
  ½ pound fresh spinach, finely chopped
  2 cloves garlic, minced
     Salt and pepper to taste

Whisk the oil, vinegar, and mustard together until smooth and thick. Add the capers and other ingredients. Refrigerate until ready to use.

Right: *Cold lobsters en masse on the buffet table.* **Below:** *The wedding luncheon plate.*

Coal-Roasted Eggplant and Peppers
SERVES 25

This type of cooking is done a great deal in Tuscany, Italy. Use small tender eggplants and large yellow and red peppers, if you can find them. Serve at room temperature.

6 **small eggplants**
Salt
9 **peppers**
Excellent olive oil
Freshly ground black pepper

Cut each eggplant into 6 or 8 pieces lengthwise. Remove the stem end. Sprinkle with salt and let stand for 2 to 3 hours. Rinse with water, dry with towels, and grill over hot coals until charred and tender. Serve with best-quality olive oil and freshly ground black pepper.

Seed the peppers and cut into quarters. Place on the grill and cook until charred and soft. Cool slightly; rub off the blackened skin. Serve with olive oil and black pepper.

Arrange decoratively on large serving platters a mixture of the eggplants and peppers.

286

Above left: *Charcoal-roasted eggplant, peppers, and squash wedges.* **Above right:** *Platters of ripe red tomatoes filled with vermicelli pesto.*

Tomatoes Stuffed with Vermicelli Pesto
SERVES 25

These are a most colorful addition to a buffet. Serve at room temperature. Choose ripe, firm tomatoes all of one size. I use red and yellow tomatoes in summer for additional color.

25 **medium tomatoes,**
1½ **pounds vermicelli**
½ **cup Pesto (page 143)**
Basil leaves

Hollow out the tomatoes by cutting off the stem end with a sharp serrated knife and removing the seeds with a melon scoop. Turn the tomatoes upside down on a rack to drain before filling with pasta.

Cook the vermicelli in a large kettle of boiling salted water. Drain well. Mix in a bowl with the pesto. Cool to room temperature. Fill the tomatoes with the pasta and top each with 1 or 2 basil leaves.

Above: *Guacamole dip and skewered shrimp.*
Left: *A circle of red-onion slices contrasts with the green vegetables vinaigrette.*

String Beans Vinaigrette

SERVES 25

6 pounds green beans
2 cups French Vinaigrette (page 104)

GARNISH
Red onion slices

Blanche the beans in boiling water until just tender, 3 to 4 minutes. Drain and chill immediately.

Make vinaigrette according to directions.

Immediately before serving, toss beans in dressing and abundantly garnish with slices of red onions.

VARIATION: Thin asparagus, or a combination of the two vegetables, can also be used.

Cold Skewered Shrimp with Guacamole Dip

SEE VARIATION, PAGE 136

Mussels Vinaigrette

25 SERVINGS

This is one of my favorite summer dishes, probably because we live in view of Long Island Sound, which is where we go to pick fresh mussels whenever we have the craving for them.

6 quarts mussels
½ cup finely minced shallots
1 tablespoon oil
1 tablespoon butter
1 small bunch parsley
½ bay leaf
    Few sprigs thyme
½ cup dry white wine

VINAIGRETTE
½ cup Dijon mustard
1½ cups light olive oil
¼ cup wine vinegar
    Salt and pepper to taste
1 small bunch parsley, finely chopped

Scrub the mussels well, scraping away all barnacles, beards, and dirt. Soak in fresh water for an hour or 2.

In a large covered kettle, sauté the shallots in the oil and butter until soft. Add the mussels, herbs, and wine. Raise the heat to high, cover the kettle, and cook, shaking the pot every minute, for about 5 minutes. Do not overcook or the mussels will shrink. Cook only until the shells have opened. Drain in a colander and cool.

Whisk the vinaigrette ingredients into a thick sauce. Pour over the mussels and gently toss (with the hands if necessary) to coat the mussels completely. Sprinkle with the chopped parsley and serve cool.

Cold Beef Salad

SERVES 30 TO 40 AS PART OF A BUFFET

Rump of beef is braised on a mirepoix of vegetables in veal stock, chilled and sliced paper thin. It is then dressed with a lemony vinaigrette, garnished with capers and cornichons, and served from shallow platters. Made on a large scale, this is a delicious salad entree for a party and relatively inexpensive.

4 tablespoons oil
1 8-pound rump of beef, well trimmed of fat, tied with string to hold its shape during braising

MIREPOIX
3 onions, thinly sliced
3 carrots, peeled and diced
3 celery stalks, diced
3 cloves of garlic, crushed
2 bay leaves
    Fresh thyme and parsley

Salt and pepper
6 cups veal stock or beef broth, boiling

VINAIGRETTE
1 cup very good olive oil
⅓ cup freshly squeezed lemon juice
½ cup finely chopped herbs (parsley, tarragon, chives, chervil)
¼ cup tiny capers
1 clove garlic, finely minced
1 tablespoon Dijon mustard
    Salt and freshly ground pepper to taste
¼ cup sliced cornichons (tiny French sour pickles)

GARNISH
    Fresh herbs, boiled and sliced potatoes, cucumbers

To braise beef (this should be done 1 day ahead), heat the oil over high heat in a casserole large enough to hold meat. Brown the meat on all sides. Remove to a platter.

In the same pot, cook the onions, carrots, and celery for 10 minutes. Place the meat on top of the vegetables, add the garlic and herbs, season with salt and pepper, and pour in the boiling stock. Cover and put in a 325° oven. Cook for about 3 hours, or until tender. Regulate the oven temperature so that meat simmers, but does not boil. Cool meat in the casserole. Refrigerate overnight.

To make the dressing, shake all the ingredients together vigorously in a covered jar. Vinaigrette should be rich and creamy.

To serve, remove cold beef from broth. Remove strings and slice ¹⁄₁₆ inch thick. Arrange slices in an overlapping pattern in a large shallow platter. Pour dressing over sliced meat, and let marinate for an hour or 2 before serving. Garnish with herbs, skinned, sliced, boiled potatoes, or sliced cucumbers.

287

French Pound Cake with Grand Marnier Buttercream

APPROXIMATELY 20 SERVINGS

This traditional French pound cake makes a delicious wedding cake. It is firm enough to hold its shape, and withstands the rigors of stacking.

³⁄₄ **pound (3 sticks) unsalted butter**

6 **large eggs**

1³⁄₄ **cups sugar**

2½ **cups sifted cake flour**
Grated rind of 2 oranges
Grand Marnier Buttercream Frosting (page 277)

Preheat oven to 350°.

Prepare cake pans by buttering the pans, lining with wax paper, and buttering paper. Dust with flour.

Melt butter over simmering water until butter can be beaten into soft, mayonnaise-like consistency.

Beat eggs with sugar until well mixed. Increase speed of mixer and beat 5 to 6 minutes, until eggs have doubled in volume. Incorpo-

rate flour, adding in ½ cup amounts, into egg mixture, beating as little as possible. Do not deflate eggs. This entire step should take no longer than 20 seconds.

With a rubber spatula, fold butter into the batter by thirds, taking care not to deflate batter. Very gently fold in grated orange rind.

Spoon batter into prepared pans and smooth tops. Bake 30 to 40 minutes (depending on size of pan) until toothpick inserted comes out clean. Cool in pans about 10 minutes, then turn out on racks and cool completely before frosting or wrapping to freeze.

Prepare icing according to directions. Decorate as desired.

NOTE: This recipe was doubled to make the cake pictured. If you need to multiply the recipe more than 2 times, repeat the process. A large mixer is imperative if you are doubling the recipe.

The five-layer cake shown was made with special hexagonal cake pans with the following diameters: 5½ inches, 7 inches, 8 inches, 9 inches, and 10 inches. Made by Matfer of France, they are available by special order from the Bridge Company, 214 East 52nd Street, New York, NY 10022. Telephone number: (212) 688-4220.

A Catered Wedding Luncheon
for Two Hundred Seventy

WITHOUT THE BONDS OF FAM-
ily, my relationship to this wedding was simple: caterer. The last
of a long line of daughters who had been married outside the home

wanted to be married at home, in the big, sprawling suburban situation she loved, with simple and elegant food, free-flowing wine
and beer, speeches and dancing, unrepetitious traditional merri-

ment. The church ceremony was set for 12:30, a cocktail and sit-down luncheon buffet planned for 1:15 in a lovely green yard. I was to help articulate and elaborate the specifics of food, drink, and decoration.

This was a more typical situation than a do-it-yourself event, for most hostesses call upon outsiders to help with a production as demanding as a big wedding. In this case, the bride's mother had the experience of other weddings behind her; she knew the possibilities and she knew she could use a caterer's services without forsaking her individuality or taste.

She chose a caterer carefully, made thoughtful decisions, defined responsibilities clearly, and brought off an event that was deeply satisfying for both her family and for me and my staff. Her success was well deserved. Hiring a caterer is more than hiring a

Above: *Pre-wedding preparations include opening and chilling the wine and preparing trays of hors d'oeuvres.*
Right: *The sumptuous buffet table.*

servant, and using a caterer well means taking advantage of his or her specific skills, particular eye and experience, as well as her helping hands. Knowing how to choose the right caterer for you and how to establish a good working relationship is crucial to creating an occasion that has warmth, personality, and grace.

I often ask myself whom I would use if I were hiring a caterer, and because I am very critical, I find that a difficult question. But it is important to start your quest by being critical. Think of what sort of food and service you find not only acceptable, but impressive. Think of the good cocktail parties, dinners, and weddings you have attended, and find out who was responsible. If there is only one good caterer in your town, the choice is obvious. But in the last few years, caterers have proliferated so dramatically it is more common to have dozens of possible candidates. And it may be well worth your time to ferret out small, new catering firms, for they are more likely than large established institutions to be energetic and to offer more original food and menus, and fresh, imaginative presentations. Then make appointments with two or three (any more would be confusing) within one week's time (for the sake of clear comparison), and prepare yourself to ask good questions and take good notes.

In an interview, give a caterer as clear an idea as possible of your plans—the date, time, number of guests, location, style—and ask for appropriate menu suggestions. Don't ask for the printed list, which is likely to be standardized or outdated, but for the ideas in his head, what interests him at that moment. Ask too if he thinks your plans are good (sometimes they are not, and he will know from experience). Request approximate prices (exact prices come later, when a menu is fixed), and if you have a strict budget for food and service, inform the caterer, for if he is creative and wants the job, he will usually be able to work within that context. Rather than ask for samples or photographs of his work, inquire about parties of which he is particularly proud, and ask for references.

It is important to pose the same questions to all your candidates so that you can evaluate them fairly and soundly. It is also important that you should be enthusiastic and nice. The former quality is contagious and inspires a caterer, the latter essential for a decent working relationship. If you want creative results, then treat a caterer like the creative person he should be.

Once a choice is made, the caterer will prepare a formal menu for approval and a contract. Terms of payment usually require an initial deposit, perhaps one half the total, with the remainder paid upon completion. With a detailed menu in hand, a hostess can then proceed to confront the practical and aesthetic details related to food and drink and, in as few as one or two working consultations, set the event in motion.

At the first consultation, it is wise to include all the professionals who will be party to the production—the flower designer, the rental company, the tent company, and the caterer—for they can help one another with ideas and coordination. The rental people can expedite a caterer's decisions about the presentation of the food, a subject that involves a choice of trays, dishes, linens, and flatware. And a caterer may give the florist ideas for table or tent decoration that would complement his fare. I, for one, love to

work with flowers. I am also more deeply involved with my contribution to a wedding if I am included in the overall picture and made to feel like more than an impersonal takeout service.

As the hostess, it is essential to set forth your own ideas and desires very explicitly at the beginning, for only then can your staff be genuinely productive. If, for example, you want your tables to look tropical or Victorian, articulate this up front, for it affects both rental and decoration decisions. At this wedding, the bride's mother expressed her wish that the decoration complement the bride's dress, which was satin and ecru, and that the scene and the food be as festive and light as summer itself. Therefore, the dress colors were restated in a white tent, white tablecloths overlaid with lace, and white and orange pastel flowers. And I planned to create a merry garden party situation by setting up bars on a patio

Inside the tent, the musicians warm up before guests arrive.

and under inviting trees, and by having girls in summer dresses and organdy aprons pass many of the hors d'oeuvres. The food itself would be arranged without undue fuss or artifice to look fresh, cool, and colorful. And the cake would be festooned with fresh flowers.

The questions you initially ask a caterer are the ones that fix the details that make a reception work. How and where will the food and drinks be served (hors d'oeuvres, bars, dinner, cake)? What kind of help does he have? How many? What will they wear? Estimated hours of work? You must also determine what work spaces a caterer will need (kitchen? garage? basement? service tents?); what accommodations you must make for refrigerator space and clear counters; and what equipment will be necessary. You must discuss logistics: time of service, anticipated arrival at home; receiving-line arrangements (champagne passed or guests go to bar afterward?); hors d'oeuvres and buffet timetables; where and when the cake is to be cut. Slowly and surely, as decisions and details accumulate, the whole picture will come into focus.

Often I make a sketch of the physical setting, for the sake of clarity and coordination. I can then evaluate my own use of space, and also, when the time arrives to set up, effect that operation efficiently. In planning the placement of tents, bars, and buffet tables, consider how to use your natural landscape to best advantage, for setting a bar under a beautiful shade tree or beside a pool, using a rose garden or a stand of hollyhocks as a backdrop to an hors d'oeuvre table, will make a scene more personal. More pragmatic but equally important is to plan enough serving stations to avoid congestion, which can seriously dampen spirits, and to organize work space well out of general view. We allotted serving stations at each end of two long tables in a small tent joined to the central tent at the wedding, which kept buffet lines moving smoothly. Across the lawn in the garage, we prepared hors d'oeuvres and collected dirty dishes.

The Setup: In the case of a Saturday wedding like this one, the caterers should be on hand the previous afternoon to be certain that all rentals arrive in correct numbers and to begin to set any furniture in place. Using a reliable rental agency guarantees prompt delivery and pickup as well as immaculate materials. Be sure the caterer knows whether the agency expects its dishes returned washed, rinsed, or dirty, and that he plans accordingly.

We set tables and organized bars on Saturday morning, as the flower lady decorated tent poles and distributed centerpieces. By 10:00 A.M., we had begun our final food countdown. At noon the cocktail tables were filled with food, and at 12:30 the party began.

The Event: What was notable about this wedding was the gracious ease that ruled the day. It was September, the garden was still blooming, the light golden, the air warm. The guests ate and danced, ate more, danced all afternoon. Even to the organizers, like myself, and the family, who had every reason to be nervous, it seemed more like a glorious rollicking summertime spree than a military production, which big weddings in fact often are. Careful advance planning was instrumental in this feeling. The family was experienced and organized. The hostess made extra gestures like providing playpens and teenage baby-sitters for the infants present and stationing someone inside the house to replenish towels and

toiletries and direct people to the powder room or gift display. We left time to think of small niceties—passing the homemade breads in big country baskets, providing a fresh fruit punch for the children. Piece by piece it came together in the shape the bride had hoped for, and added up to an afternoon of enviable grace.

Following is the menu I served at this particular wedding. The recipe quantities have been reduced, however, for more workable home use.

❧ MENU ❧

Carpaccio on French Bread   Crudités
Tortellini with Broccoli and Pesto
Sliced Baked Ham   Sliced Smoked Turkey
Sliced Tomato Salad with Basil
Sliced Stuffed Chicken Breasts
Vegetable Frittatas
Tabbouleh Salad   Tricolor Pasta Salad with Black Olives
Salmon Mousse with Cucumber Sauce
Herb Butter   Strawberry Butter
Green Bean Salad with Walnut Dressing
Tea Breads: Zucchini, Carrot, Pumpkin, Banana
Orange Almond Wedding Cake
Strawberries
Champagne   Open Bar   Fresh Fruit Punch

A whole smoked turkey sliced and arranged for the buffet table.

Above left: *A country basket laden with carrots, golden pear tomatoes, asparagus, and green beans.*

Above right: *A cabbage filled with homemade mustard accompanies slices of baked country ham.*

Left: *Luscious garden tomatoes are sliced and dressed with a vinaigrette, red onions, and basil leaves for a simple, delicious summer salad.*

Carpaccio on French Bread

SEE RECIPE, PAGE 44

Crudités

SEE RECIPE, PAGE 68

Tortellini with Broccoli and Pesto

SEE VARIATION, PAGE 144

Sliced Baked Ham/ Sliced Smoked Turkey

Slice Baked Country Ham (page 57) into neat serving pieces and arrange on trays according to your fancy. I arrange circles of meat around a bowl of homemade mustard.

Smoked turkeys are a bit more complicated to slice. It is easier to skin the entire bird and then carve it as you would a roast turkey. The meat of smoked turkeys is very rich, so carve it into thin, small pieces.

Sliced Tomato Salad with Basil

I allow 1 large round tomato for 2 to 3 guests. Cut in even slices crosswise, and arranged in concentric circles or stripes on serving trays, the tomatoes are dressed with a French Vinaigrette (page 104) and decorated with fresh basil leaves. Do not bother making this type of salad unless the tomatoes are blemish-free vine-ripened garden tomatoes.

Stuffed Chicken Breasts
SERVES 24 AS PART OF
A BUFFET

This is probably the most popular buffet dish we make. Chicken breasts are boned and split, and the skin is left on. A rich savory filling is stuffed under the skin, the edges are tucked under, and the whole is baked for 30 minutes. These are delicious hot, warm, or cold, whole or sliced. They are relatively inexpensive to make, large quantities can be made easily, and they can be stuffed and baked the day ahead of an event.

2 medium onions, finely chopped

2 tablespoons butter

2 10-ounce packages frozen chopped spinach, thawed and drained

2 pounds whole-milk ricotta cheese

2 eggs, slightly beaten

½ cup coarsely chopped parsley

2 tablespoons fresh oregano, summer savory, chervil, etc.

Salt and freshly ground pepper
Nutmeg to taste

16 halves of chicken breast (order the chicken boned, split, with the skin on)

Sauté the onions in butter until soft. Combine with the other ingredients (except chicken) and mix well. Season highly.

Place each breast skin side up on a board. Trim away excess fat. Loosen skin from 1 side of breast and stuff approximately ⅓ cup of the filling under the skin. Tuck the skin and meat under the breast, forming an even, round, dome shape. Put the stuffed breasts in a buttered Pyrex or metal baking dish.

Fifteen minutes before baking, preheat oven to 350°. Bake breasts until golden brown, about 30 to 35 minutes. Don't overcook or chicken will be dry. Cool slightly before serving, and cool to room temperature if you are going to slice into smaller serving pieces. Arrange on platters and decorate with fresh herbs.

With skin side up, loosen skin from one side of chicken breast.

Spoon approximately ⅓ cup of filling into "pocket" under skin.

Tuck skin and meat neatly under the breast, covering filling completely.

Form breast into a neat, even round.

Place breasts in buttered baking pans and season with salt and pepper. Bake until golden brown. Many breasts can be prepared this way in advance.

Baked breasts must be cooled to room temperature before slicing. Cut into smaller portions and arrange on trays with herbs and cherry tomatoes.

Vegetable Frittata
SERVES 6 TO 8

Frittatas (baked omelettes) are an excellent way to use up leftovers. Serve frittatas either hot from the oven, at room temperature, or even cold. If you have used potatoes in your frittata, do not keep it longer than 1 day, as the potatoes darken. Use an 8-inch-diameter pie plate or ovenproof ceramic quiche dish to make the frittata.

- 2 tablespoons olive oil
- 1 yellow onion, thinly sliced
- 2 small cooked potatoes, sliced
- 1 small zucchini, sliced
- 1 small red pepper, sliced
- 6 black olives, sliced
- ¼ cup grated Gruyère cheese
- 1 tablespoon chopped parsley
  Salt and pepper to taste
- 6 eggs, slightly beaten

Preheat oven to 450°.

Pour the olive oil in the baking dish and arrange onion slices in the bottom. Bake for 5 minutes, while preparing the other ingredients.

Remove baking dish from oven. The onion should be slightly cooked. Arrange the potatoes, zucchini, red pepper, and olives on top of the onion. Sprinkle with cheese and parsley. Season to taste with salt and pepper.

Reduce oven heat to 400°.

Pour eggs over the vegetables and cheese. Bake for approximately 10 minutes, until the eggs have puffed and the center of the omelette is set. Do not overcook. Serve in wedges.

VARIATIONS: Add chopped ham, sausage, asparagus, or artichoke hearts.

*A **wicker tray** holds two vegetable frittatas.*

Tabbouleh

SERVES 10 AS PART OF
A BUFFET

Bulgur wheat is often considered just "health food," but mixed with chopped vegetables and flavored with fresh mint, it makes a light, pleasant salad for the buffet.

1 cup bulgur wheat
1 cup finely chopped parsley
1 cup finely chopped green onions
½ cup finely chopped fresh mint
3 medium tomatoes, peeled, seeded, and chopped
⅓ cup freshly squeezed lemon juice
⅓ cup olive oil
Salt and pepper to taste

GARNISH
2 seedless cucumbers, cubed
Sprigs of fresh mint

Soak the bulgur in water for 10 minutes to plump the grains. Drain well and add all the other ingredients, tossing well. Season and decorate with cubed cucumber and mint.

Fresh mint leaves and chopped cucumber are cool and refreshing additions to a warm-weather tabbouleh salad.

Tricolor Pasta Salad with Black Olives

SERVES 25 AS PART OF
A BUFFET

I use lumache, a pasta made in three colors—egg, tomato, and spinach. Cooked al dente and lightly dressed with a creamy mayonnaise, it is tossed with black olive slices, cherry tomatoes, and fresh chopped herbs.

4½ pounds lumache or other pasta noodles, cooked and cooled
3 cups mayonnaise, thinned with olive oil
1½ cups pitted black olives, sliced crosswise
1½ cups sliced cherry tomatoes
¾ cup chopped fresh herbs— parsley, marjoram, basil
Salt and pepper to taste

Toss the pasta with the other ingredients. Season and serve as part of the buffet.

Salmon Mousse with Cucumber Sauce

SERVES 12

COURT BOUILLON
4 cups water
¼ cup vermouth
Piece lemon
1 small onion
1 bay leaf
1 teaspoon salt
3 peppercorns

MOUSSE
2 pounds fresh salmon
2 tablespoons gelatin
¼ cup lemon juice
⅓ cup mayonnaise
½ cup sour cream
½ teaspoon freshly grated nutmeg
1 teaspoon salt
¼ teaspoon freshly ground pepper
¾ cup heavy cream

CUCUMBER SAUCE
2 large cucumbers, peeled and seeded
1 cup homemade mayonnaise
1 cup sour cream
1 tablespoon Dijon mustard
1 tablespoon lemon juice
½ teaspoon coarse salt
¼ teaspoon pepper
½ cup snipped fresh dill
¼ cup finely chopped fresh chives

GARNISH
Fresh dill, lemon wedges

In a large pot, combine all court bouillon ingredients and simmer 10 minutes.

Place salmon in court bouillon.

Bring to a gentle boil, reduce heat, and simmer, covered, for 10 to 15 minutes, or until salmon flakes easily with fork. Remove from heat and cool salmon in liquid.

Strain poaching liquid and set aside.

When salmon has cooled, remove skin and all bones carefully. Break fish into small pieces with fingers and add ½ cup reserved stock.

In a small bowl, soften gelatin in lemon juice.

In a saucepan, bring 1 cup reserved stock to boil. Add gelatin mixture and stir until dissolved. Set aside to cool.

In a large bowl, combine salmon, gelatin mixture, mayonnaise, sour cream, nutmeg, salt, and pepper. Mix together gently but thoroughly.

Beat cream until stiff. Fold into salmon mixture.

Oil a ring mold or loaf pan with 6-cup capacity. Carefully spoon mousse into mold. Cover and refrigerate to set.

To prepare cucumber sauce, grate cucumbers into bowl. Add remaining ingredients and mix well. Refrigerate until serving time.

To serve, invert salmon mousse on serving tray until it unmolds, and garnish with dill and lemon wedges wrapped in cheesecloth. Serve with cucumber sauce.

NOTE: Salmon can also be poached in Fish Stock (page 115).

Add gelatin mixture to salmon. For this catered reception, we used 18 pounds of salmon.

Mayonnaise, sour cream, and seasonings are combined with salmon mixture.

Whipped heavy cream is folded in.

Carefully fill the oiled molds to the top with mousse mixture (*above*), set on trays, and cover with plastic wrap before chilling (*below*).

297

Hollow squashes hold strawberry and herb butters.

Slices of dense spicy carrot bread arranged in a basket.

Herb Butter

SEE RECIPE, PAGE 92

Strawberry Butter

2 CUPS

I serve this sweetened butter with brioches, croissants, and freshly baked biscuits or scones.

1 pound (4 sticks) unsalted butter, at room temperature
1 cup strawberry jam

Using an electric mixer or food processor, mix butter with jam until well blended.

VARIATIONS: Substitute damson plum, blueberry, or raspberry jam or orange marmalade for the strawberry jam.

Green Bean Salad with Walnut Dressing

SERVES 25

6 pounds green beans

WALNUT DRESSING (2 CUPS)

20 walnut halves
8 tablespoons walnut oil
1 cup vegetable oil
8 tablespoons red wine vinegar
2 cloves garlic
Salt and pepper to taste

Blanche beans in boiling water until just tender, 3 to 4 minutes. Drain and chill immediately.

To make dressing, toast walnuts 15 minutes in 350° oven. Remove from oven, cool, and chop.

Mix all dressing ingredients and let stand 1 hour.

Immediately before serving, toss beans in dressing and remove garlic cloves.

Zucchini Bread

4 LARGE OR 8 SMALL LOAVES

This tea bread is a favorite on summer buffet tables. We serve it with cheese, with herb butter, and as a base for chicken salad hors d'oeuvres. The flavor is enhanced by

the addition of walnuts and walnut oil. Zucchini bread freezes very well.

6 eggs
3½ cups sugar
1¾ cups light vegetable oil
5 cups unpeeled grated zucchini
5 teaspoons vanilla
6 cups unbleached flour
2 teaspoons salt
2 teaspoons baking soda
½ teaspoon baking powder
6 teaspoons cinnamon
2 cups chopped walnuts
¼ cup walnut oil

Preheat oven to 350°. Butter or spray with vegetable oil 4 large loaf pans (9 × 5 inches) or 8 small (7¼ × 3¾ inches).

Beat the eggs until light. Add the sugar, mixing well. Add the oil, zucchini, and vanilla and mix thoroughly.

Sift the dry ingredients. Add by the cupful to the egg mixture. Stir until well blended. Add the nuts and walnut oil.

Spoon into the pans and bake for approximately 1 hour. Cool on racks.

Carrot Bread

SEE RECIPE, PAGE 60

Pumpkin Bread

6 LARGE LOAVES OR 9 SMALL LOAVES

2¼ cups (4½ sticks) butter
½ cup plus 1 tablespoon molasses
6 cups sugar
12 eggs
2 cups orange juice or water
6 cups pumpkin or squash purée
10 cups flour
1½ teaspoons baking powder
2 tablespoons baking soda
1½ tablespoons salt
1 tablespoon cinnamon
1 tablespoon ground cloves
3 cups raisins or currants

Cream butter, molasses, and sugar until light and fluffy. Beat in eggs, 1 at a time. Beat until light and lemon-colored. Add orange juice and pumpkin purée and mix well.

Sift dry ingredients together into a

large bowl, and add pumpkin mixture, stirring well with a wooden spoon to thoroughly combine all elements. Stir in raisins.

Spoon into buttered loaf pans. Bake at 350° for 1 hour, or until toothpick inserted comes out clean. Cool in pans for 10 minutes; then turn out onto racks to cool.

NOTE: Tea breads freeze extremeiy well.

Banana Bread

1 LARGE LOAF OR 4
SMALL LOAVES

½ cup butter, at room temperature
1 cup sugar
2 eggs
1½ cups unbleached flour
1 teaspoon baking soda
1 teaspoon salt
1 cup mashed very ripe bananas
½ cup sour cream
1 teaspoon vanilla
½ cup chopped walnuts or pecans

Preheat oven to 350°.

Cream butter, sugar, and eggs.

Sift the dry ingredients and combine with the butter mixture. Blend well. Add the bananas, sour cream, and vanilla; stir well. Stir in the nuts and pour into a well-buttered 9 × 5 × 3-inch loaf pan or several smaller pans.

Bake 1 hour. Turn out onto a rack to cool.

Orange Almond Wedding Cake

SEE RECIPE, PAGE 276

The orange almond wedding cake decorated with pink hyacinth blossoms and smilax.

Index

Photo Credits